Contents

Mediated Discourse as Social Interaction

LANGUAGE IN SOCIAL LIFE SERIES

Series Editor: Professor Christopher N. Candlin

Language and power
Norman Fairclough

Discourse and the translator
Basil Hatim and Ian Mason

Planning language, planning inequality
James W. Tollefson

Language and ideology in children's fiction
John Stephens

Linguistics and aphasia
Ruth Lesser and Lesley Milroy

Language and the law
John Gibbons

Literacy practices: investigating literacy in social contexts
Mike Baynham

The cultural politics of English as an international language
Alastair Pennycook

Fictions at work: language and social practice in fiction
Mary Talbot

Critical discourse analysis: the critical study of language
Norman Fairclough

Knowledge machines: language and information in a technological society
Denise E. Murray

Achieving understanding: discourse in intercultural encounters
Katharina Bremer, Celia Roberts, Marie-Thérèse Vasseur, Margaret Simonot and Peter Broeder

The construction of professional discourse
Britt-Louise Gunnarsson, Per Linell and Bengt Nordberg

Mediated Discourse as Social Interaction
Ron Scollon

Mediated Discourse as Social Interaction
A Study of News Discourse

Ron Scollon

LONGMAN
London and New York

Addison Wesley Longman Limited
Edinburgh Gate
Harlow, Essex CM20 2JE
England

and Associated Companies throughout the world

*Published in the United States of America
by Addison Wesley Longman Inc., New York*

First published 1998

ISBN 0 582 32725-3 Paper
ISBN 0 582 32726-1 Cased

British Library Cataloguing-in-Publication Data

A catalogue record for this book is
available from the British Library

Library of Congress Cataloging-in-Publication Data

Scollon, Ronald, 1939–
    Mediated discourse as social interaction: a study of news
discourse / Ron Scollon.
        p.   cm.
    Includes bibliographical references (p.) and index.
    ISBN 0-582-32726-1. — ISBN 0-582-32725-3 (pbk.)
    1. Mass media.   2. Social interaction.   3. Journalism.   4. Mass
media—Audiences.   5. Discourse analysis.   I. Title.
P91.S365   1998
302.23—dc21   97–34576
         .   CIP

Set by 35 in 10/12pt Palatino
Produced by Longman Singapore Publishers (Pte) Ltd.
Printed in Singapore

Author's Preface

This book is an attempt to bridge the gap between media studies and social interactionist discursive research. Media studies and studies of interactional sociolinguistics have until now not been viewed as mutually relevant fields of study. There is a serious gap, however, now recognized in media studies between analyses of texts and their production and studies of audience reception and behaviour. While a number of media analysts have taken up an interest in ethnographic study of audience behaviour, they are coming to this study with relatively little background in, or awareness of, the very extensive body of research in face-to-face social interaction. Interactional sociolinguistics from conversational analysis to ethnomethodology, on the other hand, while producing important insights into the nature of discursive behaviour in face-to-face interaction, has been methodologically and theoretically uninterested in coming to grips with mediated discourse. There have been virtually no studies of the social practices by which the discourses of the media are appropriated in common face-to-face interactions. On the one hand, media studies needs interactional sociolinguistics to open up to more reflective studies of media audiences. At the same time, interactional sociolinguistics needs media studies to enrich its understanding of the ever-increasing place of the texts of the media in daily social interactions. This book engages these two separate disciplinary discourses and produces an analytical and methodological framework which not only bridges this gap, but which refocuses attention on to the social practices by which mediated discourse forms a primary site within which contemporary social identities are constructed.

The thesis of this book is that mediated discourse is best understood as a kind of social interaction. The problem with taking this view is that such forms of discourse as news discourse (newspaper and television) are most often seen through a false analogy of the sender–receiver or writer–reader model. It is the goal of this book to argue that a newspaper news story and a television news story function as social interactions on the same principles as business telephone calls and other more frequently studied face-to-face interactions such as conversations. Whether it is a business call or a printed news story, the participants show the same concern with first establishing channel, then relationship, and finally topics. The theoretical framework I put forward argues that whereas in telephone calls the conversational interaction between caller and answerer is primary, the primary social interaction in such mediated forms of discourse as newspapers and television news shows is among journalists and such subsidiary personnel as producers, directors, or printers as the performers who produce a spectacle or posed and scripted display. At the same time I argue that the primary social interactions which involve reading/watching are among readers and viewers who, as observers of this posed spectacle, make a variety of uses of it, ranging from disattention as background or 'wallpaper' to other more focal social activities such as watching or reading and making commentaries. In any event, I argue that the primary social interaction is not between the producers of the spectacles (journalists) and the observers (readers/watchers).

In the framework developed in this book, the social interactions we see in mediated discourse are enacted among performers (journalists in this case, but I would also include academic lecturers and writers, football players, film actors and production crews, or any other producers of mediated discourse) as displays or spectacles for the appropriation of observers. Thus the evening news broadcast, the day's newspaper, a football game, a lecture, or a book, can be analysed as social interactions among the key players (journalists, editors, publishers/owners) and that so-called 'reading' is a kind of spectator social activity, not a primary social interaction between the players and the viewers, or writers and readers. For the 'reader' of such spectacles, the primary social interactions are among those co-present as watchers of the spectacle, not with the writer, news reader, lecturer, or player.

The analytical issue this book uses as its focal point is the social construction of the person in discourse. In business telephone calls, for example, I argue that the crucial distinction between client and colleague must be established as a prerequisite to the introduction of topics. In television and newspaper discourse, producers and editors are constructed as framers of communicative events, the stories themselves. Presenters and sub-editors are constructed as those with the power to delegate authorship and principalship rights to reporting journalists on specific topics; to put it negatively, reporting journalists are not constructed as equal participants in the discourse with the rights to free introduction of topics. Further, reporters, while they are given identity through bylining and other identifications, are not given voice; that is, they do not speak normally as first persons in news discourse. Newsmakers are constructed with only a limited voice as delegated by reporter, and no authorship rights. On the other hand, they are frequently handed full responsibility or principalship for the words crafted by journalists as their own.

While journalists can be said to have identity and little voice, newsmakers have voice but carefully controlled identity, readers are constructed within this public discourse as little more than the aggregates of social or demographic characteristics of the 'audience'. In the primary social interactions among journalists, the reader or viewer is nearly invisible. On the other hand, this book argues that the reader uses his or her reading as one of many means by which he or she strategizes social presence and social interaction. While journalists carry on their social interaction as a spectacle for the consumption of the reader or viewer, those readers and viewers are using the spectacle as an active component of the construction of their own social environments and social interactions.

Several kinds of research materials are used in this study. The book begins with a close study of business telephone calls to develop the framework from the point of view of more commonly studied two-person social interactions as studied in conversational analysis. The analysis of news discourse which follows is based upon a five-year ethnographic and critical discourse analysis encompassing both local social practices in a specific speech community, Hong Kong, and international journalistic practices. In addition to the ethnographic work in Hong Kong, comparative fieldwork on reading and watching was also conducted in several sites in the US, UK, Australia, Japan, Finland and China. An essential aspect of the argument is that the bridging of social interactional and media studies frameworks requires high levels of methodological interdiscursivity. This book seeks to both use and display that methodological strategy.

The book relies upon close analysis of numerous television news broadcasts and newspaper stories. The initial text corpus had as its core 28 local and foreign newspapers collected on a single day in Hong Kong in English and Chinese. Television stories were added and were collected as matched sets of both English and Chinese broadcasts as well as the same day's newspapers. In addition to these two matched sets of data, the news text corpus covers 200 newspapers in English, Chinese and several European languages and about 50 television news broadcasts in English, Chinese, Finnish and Brazilian Portuguese, as well as magazines and other periodically published news materials collected over a five-year research period. Most recently, a full documentation of two weeks' news in print and broadcast media, covering the range from newspapers through to infotainment shows, was collected and cross-checked with a readership survey as a way of establishing pathways or networks between the production of the texts of the news and the appropriation of those texts by readers and watchers. This data includes not only Hong Kong-based news sources but also China, Taiwan, BBC, CNN and CBS.

The ethnographic data collected as part of this same research project include interviews, photographs, maps, videotapes and, of course, field notebook entries with a focus on the contexts of the reception of print and televised news discourse in Hong Kong and the other overseas sites. Also included in this ethnographic data are historical, demographic and media consumption data collected through normal library, consumer survey and observational methods.

While the analysis presented here is meant to be applicable throughout contemporary international news discourse, the analysis in this book has been constructed in the cross-cultural and highly interdiscursive environment of Hong Kong for two reasons: to avoid falling into universalist generalizations on the one hand, and, on the other, because Hong Kong is one of the world's most active theatres of news discourse. That a population of just over six million people produces for itself to read over 2.5 million daily local newspapers (as well as importing thousands of foreign papers) indicates an ethnographically rich, diverse, complex and problematical public discourse. These various newspapers break out into approximately 50 dailies, 38 in Chinese and 12 in English with more than 600 other periodicals, mostly in Chinese (Howlett 1997).[1] In addition, newspapers from around the world are sold daily on news-stands.

Positioned as it is in one of the world's most active communicative zones internationally, Hong Kong is particularly well suited to highlight theoretically problematical counter-examples. This book relies on the cross-checking of English and Chinese, local and foreign news sources as a methodological guard against the problem of single-language or single-community analyses of mediated discourse.

The research has been supported in part by research grants from City University of Hong Kong and by the Public Discourse Research Group of its Department of English. Specifically, these grants include 'Discourse Identities in Hong Kong Public Discourse', 'Changing Patterns of Genres and Identity in Hong Kong Public Discourse', and 'Two Types of Journalistic Objectivity'. I would also like to thank members of the Lan Kwai Fong, the Interactional Sociolinguistics, and the Public Discourse discussion groups, all at the Department of English of City University of Hong Kong, for ongoing and stimulating discussion of the ideas presented here. David Li Chor Shing has been especially helpful in collecting and preparing the business telephone calls. In addition I would like to thank Vijay Bhatia, Paul Bruthiaux and Vicki Yung for ongoing discussions, for reading drafts, and for their comments. Janice Ho Wing Yan and Ivy Wong Kwok Ngan, my primary research assistants, were also helpful in both data collection and analysis. Discussions with Chris Candlin have been most useful both while developing the framework presented here and, more specifically, in the process of editing the book for publication. Suzanne Scollon has contributed substantially in providing a continuing critical reflection on this work both at the stage of the construction of the data and in this analysis. While my analysis owes much to the support of these grants and people, none of them is responsible for the problems which remain.

NOTE

1. Exact figures are difficult to obtain. Howlett (1997) is produced by the Hong Kong government Information Services Department. On a single page it gives the figures as '58 daily newspapers, 625 periodicals' and a paragraph later as '38 Chinese-language dailies and 12 English-language dailies' (p. 321). The same book refers the reader to 'http://www.info.gov.hk' which under media gives a graphic which on 8 June 1997 says '50 newspapers' and '659 periodicals' with a line saying 'Click here for a larger image'. A click produces a larger image and a slightly larger number: '51 newspapers' and 645 periodicals'. As for

circulations, one of the Hong Kong newspapers is, as of writing, under investigation by the Independent Commission Against Corruption for allegedly printing 'up to 23,000 extra copies a day and then selling them directly as waste paper' (*South China Morning Post*, 5 June, 1997, p. 1).

Publisher's Acknowledgements

We have unfortunately been able to trace the copyright holders of the articles by Fanny Wong and Scott McKenzie in *South China Morning Post* 25.2.94 and would appreciate any information which would enable us to do so.

List of Notations Used

(0.5) The number in parentheses indicates a gap in tenths of a second

: A colon indicates drawn out sound; the more colons, the more drawn out

– A dash indicates that the speaker stops in mid-utterance

[ ] Comments in brackets are for clarification; not recorded speech

(xxx) Words in parentheses are the transcriber's best guess at doubtful speech

( ) A blank in parentheses represents indecipherable speech

, A comma indicates self-interrupted speech or a micro-pause

N___ A capital letter followed by a blank underline indicates a person's name

< > Angled brackets indicates the content of the story

{ } Brackets indicate the form of identification

IDCE 'Identified; characters in English'

IDNO 'Identified; named by other'

IDNS 'Identified; named by self'

PART I:

THE PRIMACY OF SOCIAL
INTERACTION IN DISCOURSE

ONE

Mediated action as social practice

TEXT AND CONVERSATIONS, OBJECTS AND EVENTS

A newspaper story is a text. A conversation is an event. In many
ways that is the problem of this book. The common language in
which we talk about news discourse favours treating it as a body
of texts. The language we use to talk about a conversation posits it
as an event. Journalists, if asked what they have been doing all
afternoon are likely to say that they have been working on a story,
they have been working on tonight's broadcast, they have been
writing a feature article. In each case the focus is the end product,
the text which is ultimately printed or read. On the other hand, if
the same journalists had answered that they had been having a
conversation, we would most likely think of them as not doing the
work of journalism so much as passing the time among friends. The
focus is on the social participation, the social interaction. This is
how we see conversation. It is the analyst, the ethnomethodologist,
who sets about turning the conversation into a text for analysis, not
the conversationalists, though as conversation analysts and ethno-
methodologists have made abundantly clear, the conversationalists
themselves cannot move from utterance to utterance without engaging in a significantly interpretive analysis of the texts as jointly
and ongoingly co-constructed among the group of participants.

It is the goal of this book to try to accomplish two kinds of
suspension of our ordinary language about talk and text. On the
one hand, and in regards to the public discourse of the news, the
purpose is to reconstruct our language about it so that we can see
it as a process of social interaction in which participants use or
appropriate texts and produce texts as almost incidental (from our
point of view) tools by which they, journalists, owners of the media
and newsmakers alike, engage in the day-to-day social practices

within their communities of practice (Lave and Wenger 1991) and in doing which they construct for themselves various discursive identities. On the other hand, and from the point of view of the readers and viewers of those produced texts, the purpose is to reconstruct our language about that reading and watching so that we can come to see the role of those texts as tools by which the readers and watchers engage in the ordinary social practices of life in their communities of practice.

To bring about this reconstituted language it will be necessary to borrow back and forth interdiscursively from these otherwise separated discourses. We will need to come to speak of the newspaper or television broadcast not as texts alone, though we will need to do that as well. We will also need to speak of the social situations in which those texts work as tools for mediated actions (Wertsch 1991, 1994a, 1994b, 1995a, 1995b). When the television presenter passes the floor to the news reporter and in passing the floor limits topical relevance to a single topic, he or she is engaging in a social interaction that is analytically akin to the conversationalist who says, 'Come on, don't start in on that now'. This, in turn, is akin to what the sub-editor does when he or she places a journalist's story on the page for news of incidental value rather than the front page. In each case a participant in a community of practice has exercised his or her power to delegate voice to another participant in a way that not only specifically limits that voice but, in positioning it, imputes a particular social-discursive identity to the participant. In doing this kind of analysis we need to rely on a literature of interactional sociolinguistics cum conversational analysis cum ethnomethodology.[1]

At the same time, in speaking of what people are doing when they are watching television or reading a newspaper, we need to ask: What kind of social interaction is this? This book argues that both the social interactions in which the texts of news discourse are produced and the social interactions in which those texts are 'read' are primarily social interactions, not cognitive actions nor textual-interpretive actions. That is, when people sit together in the living room watching television (Ang 1996) the primary thing they are doing is sitting together and the television is just one of the mediational means (Wertsch 1991) by which they carry out that mediated action. I will argue further in Chapter 3 that even when they are, in fact, entirely alone watching television or reading a newspaper, that action can be usefully analysed as a social interaction in which readers and watchers claim rights to non-involvement and other forms of social positioning within their community of practice and in doing so also make serious claims of identity for themselves as participants. Mediated discourse is constructed in chained or linked mediated actions within communities of practice. As such, mediated discourse is properly studied within a social interactionist and ethnographic framework which elucidates the social practices by which journalists (both television and print), newsmakers, editors, and the owners of the media use texts to construct social relations within their own communities of practice. At the same time, this analytical framework deconstructs the acts of spectatorship of reading and watching as social interactions within communities of practice who appropriate the texts of the media within sites of engagement for their own purposes. A crucial aspect of the mediated actions within both journalistic and spectator communities of practice is the social construction of identity through the use of the texts of the media.

The analytical stance established in this chapter and which will be carried throughout the book is to challenge the sometimes explicit but nearly always implicit sender–receiver model of news discourse. I shall argue that the primary social interactive purposes of journalists are to write for other journalists, to position themselves among those journalists in relationship to the newsmakers on the one hand and the owners of the media on the other – these are the relevant communities of practice within which the texts of the media are constructed. In the same way, the primary social purposes of readers and watchers are better understood if the texts of the media are placed in an instrumental position. That is, I shall argue that readers/viewers exercise agency in appropriating the texts of the media in accomplishing mediated actions within their own communities of practice as significant means by which identity is socially constructed.

MEDIATED DISCOURSE

In what I have said so far I have sketched out the notion of how mediated discourse may be construed as social interaction but in doing so I have not yet clarified how I am using the term 'mediated discourse' except by implication. In current usage there are at least three common ways in which this term might be understood. In the first of these, one would mean the discourse of 'the media', that is, one would mean the discourse of newspapers, magazines and other periodicals, and perhaps most significantly television and possibly film. Another use of the term which is rapidly increasing is in the phrase 'computer-mediated discourse'. In this case the focus is on communications in which the computer – most often in the form of email or internet communications – is the primary medium of communication between two or more participants. The third common usage is the broadest and comes closest to the use I will make of mediated discourse in this book. In this third usage, the focus is on any mediation involved in carrying on common, everyday discourses. Thus, one would take into consideration written media such as letters, notes, memos, more technological media such as microphones, telephones and also computers, and even languages such as English or Chinese or perhaps modes of communication such as speaking, writing or sign languages.

As I shall use the term, mediated discourse includes virtually all discourse because the focus is upon finding a common basis in social interaction for analysing the ways in which mediational means from languages to microphones, literacy to computers, news stories to telephone calls are appropriated by participants in social scenes in undertaking mediated action. Thus I will want to include the 'media' and, indeed, much of the analysis is based on an analysis of the texts produced by the news media in the most common meaning of that phrase. At the same time, however, I want to argue that the products of those same news media are appropriated for mediated actions which often bear little resemblance to the commonly understood purposes of such texts as news stories. Further, in my analysis of telephone calls I will argue that any instance of communication, that is social interaction, entails the same fundamental concerns for establishing the basis for the social interaction (the channel), establishing the relationships and positioning among the participants, and that the ostensible topics of such social interactions are subsumed to these prior social conditions through the social practices of positioning of participants and framing of events.

TOWARDS A UNIFIED PERSPECTIVE ON PRACTICE

The language which we will need for this analysis includes at least four central phrases: mediated action, sites of engagement, communities of practice, and mediational means or texts. These phrases, taken together, form a minimal vocabulary for talking about mediated discourse as social interaction. An interactional sociolinguistic view of mediated discourse focuses on action as social practice and then looks to ask what media (mediational means or cultural tools) are used, how those mediational means support or undermine the purposes of the participants within their community of practice (Lave 1988; Lave and Wenger 1991), and how those media bring into the situation the historical, cultural or social practices of the larger society in which these mediated actions (Wertsch 1991, 1994a, 1994b, 1995a, 1995b) take place.

Critical discourse analysis (Fairclough 1989, 1992, 1995a, 1995b; Gee 1986, 1990), mediated action theory (Wertsch 1991, 1994a, 1994b, 1995a, 1995b) and situated learning (Lave 1988; Lave and Wenger 1991; Chaikin and Lave 1993) together form the primary analytical framework of this book. While these three analytical stances are largely practised independently of each other, they all co-articulate as a common perspective on a theory of social practice, especially as such a theory would be of use to us in analysing social practices in the production of news texts and in the appropriation of those texts by readers and watchers. All three of these research perspectives reference in part a common core of thought (Vygotsky 1978; Bakhtin 1981a; Vološinov 1986) which clearly originates in, but also departs from, Marxist sociopolitical analysis. More recently, Bourdieu's writings on social practice have significantly developed this framework (1977).

'Critical discourse analysis' is what Fairclough calls his version of this perspective, and his *Discourse and Social Change* (1992) and *Media Discourse* (1995b) are, for our purposes, the fullest and best treatments of it, though the collection of mostly earlier papers (in 1995a) offers important development. Gee uses 'critical literacy' or more often 'sociocultural literacy'. 'Mediated action' is what Wertsch calls his version. His *Voices of the Mind* (1991) is his most representative work in which he spells out the main points and the arguments in way of support. On the whole, Wertsch's perspective is spelled out in specific domains – largely ones having to do with public schooling in the US. 'Situated learning' is what Lave and Wenger call their version of this perspective in the book of the same title (1991).

All of these derive their work from a point in the Soviet Union – the 1920s – in which an attempt was made to develop a full-blown social/cultural/historical view of the relationship between society and the person and the role of language in this mediation. In the case of Fairclough, his primary focus is upon discourse and how it is constructive of, and constructed by, social practice. While Fairclough is careful to include discussion of the social construction of the person and gives much attention to identities and relations (1995b), his interest is primarily in the ways in which social practice is constituted by text and is constitutive of text. Of course his work has developed in tandem with Halliday's systemic–functional perspective (1978, 1985, 1989).

Wertsch's primary interest is in a theory of the person. As a psychologist his concern is largely to contest the hegemonic position of cognition, voluntarism, and individualism in American psychology. He is particularly concerned with overcoming the individualist–collectivist antinomy in the perennial argument between psychologists and sociologists. His solution is to select mediated action as the focus of study. Mediated action is the moment at which social practice is, in fact, practice (people doing things) and not an abstraction or a reification. In his view there is virtually no action which is not mediated, and the mediation is the means by which agents incorporate social practice (culture, history) into their activities. The focus is not on texts or social practice, but on how those are appropriated in action.

Lave is an anthropologist and her primary concern is with neither society on the whole nor with the individual in particular, but with the social groupings (communities of practice) which form the social matrix of practice within which what Wertsch calls mediated action takes place. Fairclough places texts within discursive practices and those in turn within social practices [social practice (discursive practice {text})]. Wertsch would have mediated action contextualized within social practices [social practice (mediated action)], in which Fairclough's 'texts' would be incorporated as the 'media' of the action. Lave would contextualize communities of practice within broader social groups and focus on participation as a form of learning [social groups (community of practice {participation/learning})]. In the reading of these three perspectives as I shall use them, the differences among them is largely in focus and attention. Fairclough uses text as the organizing principle, Wertsch uses the person, Lave uses the community of practice. The focus of this book shifts among persons, communities of practice, social practices, and the analysis of texts. Thus it relies on a co-articulation of the perspectives of critical discourse analysis, situated learning, and mediated action. As I read these, each of them has a means of incorporating the language of the other. Where Fairclough generally uses *intertextuality*[2] (from Kristeva 1986a, 1986b, who got it from Bakhtin 1981a and other texts), Wertsch and Lave use *dialogicality* (from Bahktin 1981a and other texts; they also sometimes use *heteroglossia* in various translations). None of these use or acknowledge Uspensky's (1973) *polyvocality* but it should be recalled that Goffman (1974) cites Uspensky as a major source (and therefore Bakhtin) in his formulation of *Frame Analysis* which is probably the first entry of *intertextuality, dialogicality, polyvocality* into American sociological usage. Fairclough does cite Goffman's *Frame Analysis*, however, as relating to his *intertextuality*, apparently without awareness of Goffman's citation of Uspensky.

Wertsch's 'cultural tools' ('mediational means') is roughly Fairclough's 'texts'. Lave seems quiet on the matter of the discursive aspects of communities of practice. I say 'roughly' because Fairclough's analysis is much more strongly focused on language than either Lave's or Wertsch's (actual instances of language – language as language in use such as genres or types of discourse rather than language as 'English', 'Chinese').

Of the three perspectives, Lave's says least about text or mediational means, most about learning, identity, and the idea of communities of practice. Identity is theorized as participation in communities of practice. These latter are constructed in a dialectic with identity. Learning is seen as inseparable from identity, both of which are integral aspects of participation. On this latter issue, all participation in communities of practice is understood as peripheral. That is, Lave is clear about not allowing the concept of communities of practice to become reified entities, but flexible constructs-in-situations. It is not entirely clear to what extent Lave's communities of practice should be understood as Fairclough's discursive formations (Foucault 1973a, 1973b, 1977) but certainly Lave's understanding of communities of practice is entirely consonant with Fairclough's concerns with *interdiscursivity*. That is, there is a tension and contestation both within and between such changing communities or discourses. Wertsch says relatively little about communities or discourses.

Each of these frameworks addresses issues which, for our purposes, are insufficiently treated in the available work of the others.

It seems that the areas least developed by all, but in no way incompatible with these frameworks, are the role of 'the media' (in this case I mean the broadcast and print mass communication media as social institutions), non-verbal communication, other non-linguistic semiotic codes, technologies of production and reception (cameras, word processors, television sets, pagers, prompters – these are often neglected as theory and observation keeps slipping upwards into metaphorized 'tools' and 'technologies' such as language, interviews, and the like). I shall argue, however, that taken together the key concepts of *mediated action, sites of engagement, communities of practice,* and *mediational means* or texts (taken in that sense) form a useful framework for understanding mediated discourse as social interaction.

The following, then, is an overview of the key issues upon which these concepts place the focus as well as areas in which it is crucial to problematize the concepts.

Mediated action

As proposed by Wertsch (1991), the concept of mediated action places the primary focus on actions, not on the reifications of actions such as texts on the one hand or 'acts' on the other. Wertsch's concern is with undercutting what he calls the individual-collectivist antinomy. Rather than entering into the argument about whether actions are primarily based in individual agency and cognition or social determination, Wertsch argues that mediated action is the point at which culture, society, or in our case the media enter into human action. Mediated action is the site in which social and discursive practice are instantiated as actions of humans; at the same time it is the site in which individual humans act upon society and its discursive practices. In Wertsch's view, virtually all human actions are mediated. As he points out, except for reflex responses, it would be hard to argue that any human actions do not call upon language and prior social learning as mediational means.

As useful as the concept of mediated action is to this analysis, it is crucial to be alert to ways in which the concept might be reinterpreted within a less productive reified framework, not unlike the way in which speech-act theory drifted over time from a focus on speech as action into a concern with classification of speech acts, a specification of their contexts, an analysis of potential felicity conditions and possible but indeterminate meanings (Mey 1993). While it is useful to ask what sort of mediated action is going on in any particular situation, it drifts towards reification to begin to ask how many mediated actions and of what kinds and in whose interpretation. The concept, to remain useful, must always remain problematized. It is crucial to test against participants' claims and contestations explicit and implicit about 'what's going on here?' As I shall use the concept here, mediated action as a unit of analysis is at best a point of view, however temporary, upon discourse as the social enactment of social practice.

Sites of engagement

While the concept of the site of engagement will not be taken up in any detail until Chapter 4, here it is useful, perhaps, to adumbrate that discussion. The concept was introduced elsewhere (R. Scollon 1997a) to focus attention to the windows within which texts are available for appropriation (reading, watching, interpretation) and use (writing, production, etc.) in undertaking mediated actions. Sites of engagement are the windows which are defined by a wide variety of social practices. A family may sit together eating dinner while the television is on. Social practices concerning who may introduce topics, for example, may make the television programme currently unavailable for comment or collaborative viewing much in the same way that a person at the table may be constrained from introducing a topic because of age, gender, or various other currently obtaining social practices. The concept of the site of engagement encourages the analyst to understand that in such a situation, the television broadcast is in effect 'wallpaper' – a present, perceptible aspect of situational contextual design, but not currently available for appropriation as a mediational tool within the ongoing situation. In this sense, the site of engagement is not just the neutral context, setting or scene within which mediated actions take place. The site of engagement is the window opened through the intersection of social practices in which participants may appropriate a text for mediated action.

While such sites of engagement may only be momentarily opened, much like topics in a conversation, the intervals between such sites of engagement may be brief or very long. In a conversation in which one participant brings up a topic and another responds, the site of engagement of that particular text and the time lapse between appropriation (as reception) and use (in mediated action) may be a matter of micro-seconds. On the other hand, the site of engagement within which I see (appropriate the text of) a film and the site of engagement in which I use it in another mediated action such as mentioning it to a friend in conversation may be separated by an interval of decades or more.

If the concept has value, it is to focus on real-time processes and practices and to avoid reification or the study of reified entities not otherwise available to participants. As I will argue in Chapter 4, a handbill passed out on a busy pedestrian thoroughfare is available for appropriation only for the few moments between when the person receives it and then decides to discard it in the nearest rubbish container. The programme on television is only available for appropriation during the moments when other conversationalists allow a topical window to open; the newspaper I am trying to read is only open to appropriation after I have selected my seat on the train, adjusted myself and my belongings, folded it into convenient size and shape, and satisfied myself that I am free from other social obligations such as conversation with the person sitting next to me.

While I will argue in Chapter 4 that the idea of the site of engagement is useful to the study of mediated discourse to focus our attention on just those moments when texts are actually in use, not just passively present in the environment, the idea must remain problematized by asking if there are any regularly occurring or universal social practices which govern sites of engagement. One imagines that the search for universal sets of social practices is doomed to overgeneralization and unuseful abstraction. On the other hand, if in any situation the social practices determining such sites of engagement are specific, concrete to that situation, and multiple, as I shall argue, then one must ask: How many social practices are the minimum to define a site of engagement? Or, must all participants be engaged in the same way? Finally, is there a critical difference between such sites of engagement and Candlin's (1987) 'moments of conflict' in which the contradictions between conflicting discourses present in a particular situation must be crucially resolved? Of course, I will argue that it is this discussion which is of value in coming to understand mediated discourse as social interaction. It is the negotiation of participants in a community of practice over the positioning of themselves and the other participants which is the key issue and the social practices governing sites of engagement are among the mediational means by which participants may undertake the mediated actions to position their own identities.

Communities of practice

As Lave and Wenger (1991) have defined communities of practice, the focus is on learning and identity. In their view, any learning by definition entails change of identity. At a minimum, one moves from claiming the identity of novice towards claiming the identity of expert within a community of practice, from newcomer to old-timer. In their view, participation in a community of practice entails learning as any actions fundamentally alter one's position in relation to others within the community. Thus, all participation is learning and entails change of identity. A key point in their analysis is that community of practice as an analytical concept must maintain a focus upon change, negotiation, differences in participation statuses, and claims, imputations, legitimations, and contestations of identity.

The idea of a community of practice as put forward by Lave and Wenger is broader than Goffman's 'with' (1963, 1971) which is understood to be keyed to the face-to-face social encounter. A community of practice is a group of people who over a period of time share in some set of social practices geared towards some common purpose. While each aspect might be problematical, there seems to be an understanding that such a group would largely be known to each other face-to-face (though telecommunications open up for analysis communities of practice with no face-to-face contact) through regular, patterned forms of social interaction, and that such a community of practice would develop a history over time of novices entering, moving through into expertise, and retirement from the community. In any event, it is crucial to note that a community of practice is not an abstract category such as a social group or social class.

While this idea is important in the analysis in the following chapters, problems remain. When the focus is on the concept of the community of practice, one can simplistically and for the sake of argument slip into thinking of communities of practice as totalizing entities. In fact, everyone is always multiply membered in various communities of practice. A journalist is a member of some practis-ing group of journalists, perhaps those who work for the same newspaper or television station. At the same time, this journalist may be a member of a family, a member of a fencing club, and a fiction writer who meets with other writing friends from time to time to talk about their work. A tailor's apprentice may be a novice within his employer's shop and at the same time may be the captain of their city league football team in which his employer is a player. Thus the two people may position themselves rather differently even within the same conversation depending on whether the topic is stitching or scoring goals.

Again, what is useful about this concept is not trying to establish who is a member of what community of practice at any particular moment; it is a matter of focusing attention on relationships among learning, participation, identity, and action as ongoing positionings carried through mediated actions in discourse.

Texts as mediational means

Texts are the stuff of discourse analysis, of course, as they are the stuff of media analysis as well. With the ever closer convergence of telephone, newspaper and television in the internet we seem to be coming nearer to Borges's Library of Babel with all of the possible texts in all of the possible languages.[3] Perhaps it is an occupational hazard for discourse analysts, media analysts and even interactional sociolinguists that analysis always returns to texts. I say occupational hazard because, while I will try to exemplify below that it is always essential to give close attention to the texts in the discourses we study, the hazard is that we will slip over into thinking that the analysis of the text is all the work there is to be done. From the point of view I am developing here, what is crucial is to see texts as mediational means – the tools by which people undertake mediated action. The purpose is not the production of the text but the production of the action which the text makes possible. While this may seem a fine distinction, it is a crucial one for my argument.

In a mediational view of action, texts are cultural tools or mediational means (Wertsch 1991). This is a perspective which derives, as I have suggested above, from the work of Vygotsky, Vološinov, Medvyedev and Bakhtin (1981a, 1981b, 1986, 1990, 1993). By taking this perspective on texts it is possible, on the one hand, to focus our attention to just those aspects of texts which are of relevance to the actions taken by participants in any particular situation. At the same time, it is possible to focus our attention not on the texts themselves, but on the actions being taken and to see how the texts become the means by which sociocultural practice is interpolated into human action.

Key issues concerning texts as mediational means revolve around the Bakhtinian notion that polyvocality is the nature of all human utterance. Communication in this sense must make use of the language, the texts, of others and because of that, those other voices provide both amplification and limitations of our own voices. A text which is appropriated for use in mediated action brings with it the conventionalizations of the social practices of its history of use. We say not only what we want to say but also what the text must inevitably say for us. At the same time, our use of texts in mediated actions changes those texts and in turn alters the discursive practices. A parent who takes up the jargon of his or her teenage son is almost certain to place that jargon into brackets for the son who then avoids using those same words.

The major problem we encounter here is that this polyvocality or dialogicality of all texts means that all texts are always intertextual and interdiscursive. That is, all texts borrow their language from other texts (intertextuality) and all genres borrow from other genres (interdiscursivity). To put it negatively, there are no 'pure' or 'original' texts or genres.

This produces a level of indeterminancy into any analysis of the texts of mediated action. While it is theoretically given that the utterer is not the original producer of a text, at the same time, to put it more broadly, it is always ultimately undeterminable who or what discourse is the original voice we are hearing. The crucial question is to ask how do participants in a community of practice use this indeterminacy in positioning themselves and others, to pull discursive practice into their actions to position selves and others.

NEWS PRESENTATION AND WATCHING
AS SOCIAL INTERACTION

Two fields of study, social interaction and media studies, have remained for some years at a considerable distance from each other. For example, studies of social interaction such as those of Goffman

(1959, 1961, 1963, 1967, 1971, 1974), while they made frequent use of materials collected from the press, for example, did not analyse them as instances of mediated communication as such, but only as examples of other social issues. Only with his *Gender Advertisements* (1979) and the article on Radio Talk (in 1981) did Goffman address issues of mediated communication directly. On the other side of the gulf, it is only relatively recently that media researchers have begun to look at the social interactions surrounding the use of media in society. A number of studies, for example, have argued that the people in the news are ideologically constructed through processes of naming, attribution and citation (Caldas-Coulthard 1993, 1994; Caldas-Coulthard and Coulthard 1996; R. Scollon in press). Such text-orientated studies have contributed to our understanding of the ways in which language may be used to reproduce the ideological structures of the society within which it is embedded (Fairclough 1989, 1995a, 1995b). There is a growing acknowledgement that whether the analysis is of printed or televised news, it must take into account the interpretive processes of the readers or consumers of news discourse (Morley 1980, 1990; Morley and Silverstone 1991; Moores 1993). These critiques have turned to a focus on the active work of consumers in producing the meanings of the texts encountered in print and on television.

At about the same time that Goffman was coming to take an interest in mediated communication, media researchers began to take an interest in the social constitution of media audiences. Many of them (Moores 1993) have come to analyse media audiences ethnographically in keeping with contemporary interpretive theories of media reception. While this shift in focus to the responses of consumers represents a considerable enrichment of our understanding of the processes by which news stories become meaningful in society, they do not resolve one crucial issue: What sort of social interaction is news discourse?

In this book I try to integrate work from both ends of this continuum of approaches to highlight areas of overlapping discourse in which one may observe processes of social interaction being conducted as displays for other observers in social interactions of higher complexity. Thus, I will argue that there is a class of social interactions which I call 'watches' in which one set of participants, the spectacle, takes on the obligation to display their behaviour in front of other participants, the watchers. Such 'watches' share many of the characteristics of what Goffman (1981) calls 'podium events';

that is, for example, between the spectacle and watchers there is a highly restrictive set of conventions prohibiting cross-over discourse between them. The audience may laugh, clap, shout, and in other ways show social and rhythmic entrainment with the activities of the spectacle, but may not directly join in the production of the spectacle. The spectacle may display appreciation of the crowd noises, but not directly respond to members of the audience. The questions I ask are: What is the social interaction here and how are social roles constructed in the forms of interaction present?

While the root metaphor of the sender–receiver conduit (Reddy 1979) in communication has perhaps weakened through more dialogic conceptions of language and communication (Bakhtin 1981a, 1981b, 1986, 1990, 1993), most studies of television discourse remain grounded in the notion that a news broadcast is a social interaction in which some sort of message is sent – 'constituted' would be a word more consistent with present usage – from the television set and received on the other end – here the preferred word might be 'interpreted'. That is, studies of television discourse seem still quite securely rooted in the notion that it is a social interaction between the producers of mass communication and the consumers. Analyses of newspaper discourse remain even more solidly rooted in the concept of the sender–receiver, however interpretive the activities of that reader are now conceived as being (Zhu et al. in press).

Much has been said to support the sender–receiver view, of course, but the research which I report here will argue that this view of mediated discourse may well disguise other significant aspects of the social interactions going on in the same situations. My interest is in the social construction of the identities we recognize as persons, in this case the persons we call journalists on the one hand, the reader/watchers on the other. Following upon Goffman's analysis, I argue that these persons are constructed in ongoing social interactions in which identities are claimed or projected upon others and, in turn, those identities are ratified by reciprocal claims and legitimations. While these claims, counter-claims, and ratifications are familiar enough to us in studies of face-to-face interaction, I believe it is important to see that they are also operative in such mediated forms of discourse as the ordinary television news broadcast and the daily newspaper.

In a study of ordinary phototaking (R. Scollon 1996a and Chapter 4), I have argued that there is a kind of social interaction which I call a 'watch' by analogy with Goffman's 'with' (1963, 1971), in which the two sides to the interaction polarize into two strictly constrained interacting sets, a spectacle and the watchers. The spectacle (the poser in the photograph, the lecturer, football players, and television news presenters) takes on the social obligations of adopting conventional poses, of restricting their direct attention to the matters of the pose (or the game, etc.), and give up social rights to symmetrical access to the watchers; that is, the spectacle gives up the right to call for feedback and accepts the obligation to perform in a state of *as-if* conventionalized poses.[4]

Watchers, on the other hand, take on the asymmetrical social rights to relatively unlimited observation including commentary without fear of recrimination, to movement, and to dropping in and out of observation. The primary social interactions among watchers become the 'withs' with which they are co-present and the watching social interaction becomes secondary in the same way that primary social interactions among the spectacle – ball players, for example – rarely are broken through by interactions with the watchers. In fact where they are, as in the case where a football player leaps into the stands or a fan leaps on to the field, these breaks in the conventional barrier to cross-over interaction are highly sanctioned.

THE ARGUMENT OF THE BOOK

While the central conceptual theme of the book is that mediated discourse is best understood as social interaction, an equally central issue is methodological. How does the analyst develop an approach to the news media or other forms of mediated discourse which is founded in ethnography on the one hand and which can link social practice and discourse theory to the social interactionist literature on the other? Thus this second methodological theme is taken up in the three chapters of Part II.

In Chapter 2 the central theme of the book is presented. This chapter argues that mediated discourse is most usefully analysed as linked mediated actions in which the texts of the media are appropriated within communities of practice. This analytical stance extends the scope of interactional sociolinguistic analysis from face-to-face interaction to interactions mediated by texts. In order to clarify the social practices by which events, participation structures and topics are jointly negotiated and constructed in direct social interaction, the book uses the example of business telephone calls. Telephone are intermediate between face-to-face interaction and the interactively distanced productions of television and print media. While there is a technological medium which intervenes between the primary participants, the social interaction calls upon the mutually co-constructive practices of face-to-face communication.

Using the telephone interaction as the representative anecdote (Burke 1945), the book is able to show that there is a nested set of social practices such that primary real-time attention is given to the establishment and ongoing maintenance of the broadest generic frame, what is often called the 'channel'. Within that constraint, attention is given over to establishing and maintaining a state of social interaction among the participants. Only within the technologically sustained channel and the mutually negotiated set of discourse identities do the participants turn to the establishment of the topic at hand for discussion. This chapter summarizes these social practices with three nested Maxims of Stance for social interaction:

1. Attend to the channel.
2. When the channel is established, attend to the relationships and identities.
3. When identities are established, attend to topics.

This analytical frame is then used in subsequent chapters to argue that mediated discourse works within the same social practices for the establishment of communicative events, the negotiations of identity, and, finally, the discussion of topics.

These Maxims of Stance, of course, parallel Fairclough's (1995b) concern with *representation, identities and relations*. Both my treatment here and that of Fairclough make the point that in any instance of discourse all of these elements are interacting as a means of producing identities and relations through representation in the text. Fairclough's primary focus, however, is upon 'how texts are designed' (p. 206) with a secondary focus on relations and identities, especially those *between* 'media personnel (journalists, presenters) and audiences/readerships', ' "others" (e.g. experts, politicians) and audiences/readerships', and 'media personnel and "others" ' (p. 203). This interest cuts across my primary focus on the relations and identities *among* media personnel in the production of text on the one hand and *among* media audiences/readerships on the other and my secondary focus on the construction of the channel, i.e., the sites of engagement within which texts are available for reading.

Having developed the social interactional framework for analysing communication in real time, Chapter 3 turns to the discursive practices for media reception as these practices are quite amenable to making a first approach to the ethnographic study of mediated actions. The chapter begins with an analysis of photo-taking as an event in which the ethnographer can elucidate the social practices by which participants in a social interaction mutually negotiate their separation into watching and spectacle roles. This provides the basis for arguing for a continuity in social practice from photographer to game spectator or television watcher to newspaper reader. Those watching roles, along with the social negotiations among watchers of a spectacle, are then taken up in turn; the discussion of the roles of the spectacle (person photographed, player of a game, news reader, or newsmaker) are deferred until Part III.

Chapter 4 then turns to the elucidation of the concept of the site of engagement. Taking a photograph, receiving a handbill on the street, buying a newspaper at a news-stand, turning on the television in a family while having dinner, or opening a book to read on the bus or mass transit railway are all instances of sometimes momentarily open windows of media reception. This chapter argues first that the news and other print and broadcast media are not always and openly available for interpretation, but, in fact, are tightly constrained within an interdiscursivity of social practice that makes them available as texts for appropriation only within the purposes, goals, and agency of members of communities of practice. Then it further argues that these sites of engagement – the places, times, moments in which the news media are appropriated – are at the same time sites for the discursive construction of the person. This analytical framework establishes a motivation for the mediated actions in which the media are appropriated by its 'audiences' as well as a methodology for the ethnographic study of media reception.

The three chapters of Part III are the heart of the book in that the social-interactionist perspective of the preceding chapters is developed in relation to the television and broadcast news media. The central argument is, first, that in the production of the texts of the news media, the primary social practices, and therefore the primary social interactions, are concerned with negotiations of power and identity within the communities of practice formed by journalists, newsmakers, owners and editors of the organizations. Secondly, in the communities of practice within which these texts are appropriated for use by readers and viewers, the primary social interactions are among viewers and readers, not between them and the producers of the texts. Chief among the issues within these two different kinds of community is the socially negotiated construction of discourse identities.

The primary interactive roles in television journalism are presenter and reporter and those, in turn, are nested within the broader frame of the television programming, often set by commercial breaks and programme identifications. Chapter 5 analyses several television broadcasts to argue that the Maxims of Stance first elucidated in Chapter 2 are the governing framing practices in television news broadcasts as well. Attention goes first to the channel frame. This is followed by producing the identities of presenters who, in turn, produce the identities of the reporters to whom they also delegate rights to the floor on whom they place topical relevance restrictions. Thus the power over the ongoing social interaction, the television broadcast, is framed and delegated in a series of controlled social and textual assignments. This chapter argues that not only does the television news broadcast analogously pattern like the business telephone call, it does so through the social practices and power distributions activated in that particular site of engagement.

Chapter 6 extends the argument developed in reference to television news broadcasting to practices of bylining and attribution in newspapers. Bylining of writers, attribution to news agencies, signatures of letters to the editor, and ownership identifications are analysed to argue that, like the business telephone call, the identification of journalists, editors, and owners constitute a negotiated social production of identity as the second of the nested maxims. The chapter argues that this identification (or its absence) is crucial to the production of textual topics – the news – and their interpretation.

The people who 'make' the news from politicians to victims of tragic accidents are argued in Chapter 7 to be secondary players in the negotiations over identity and voice which take place in the news media. The focus of this chapter is on the social practices by which newsmakers are given or denied voice in the processes of discourse representation used in these media. On-camera video clips, or actualities, in television parallel to some extent direct quotation in the print media, and by using the delegation (or not) of animation, authorship, and principalship, journalists exercise considerable power over the mediated construction of the identities of such newsmakers. Figures powerful within the sociopolitical world such as the American First Lady Hillary Clinton, Russia's Boris Yeltsin, and Hong Kong's last British Governor Chris Patten are positioned by journalists as either strong or weak and thus are argued to derive their power to a considerable extent as it is delegated to them discursively by journalists.

Part IV returns to the readers and viewers of the spectacles produced by newsmakers and journalists. Readers and viewers, of course, have the power to turn off the television set or to decide not to buy the newspaper. Chapter 8 argues that from the point of view of the communities of practice within which the news media are received, the negotiations of identity and the positioning of participants is in relationship to other members of the community of practice, not in relationship to journalists, newsmakers, or the owners of the media. Based on ethnographic studies of television viewing and print news readership practices, this chapter argues that the texts of the news media more often function as 'wallpaper', i.e., unobtrusive background decorative design than as focal sources of analytical attention. Thus the crucial questions for an analysis of media reception are less a matter of determining how readers and viewers are positioned within the texts themselves, although this is certainly not a matter to be dismissed as it is crucial within the community of journalists to have some concept of a readership/audience, but these questions are more a matter of coming to understand how and for what purposes these texts are appropriated by people in the conduct of their daily lives. A biting political commentary positioning the reader as ignorant and uninformed is nicely preempted when the paper is used to wrap fish.

This chapter closes with an analysis of the interdiscursivity among journalists and entertainers, and among them and ordinary readers and viewers as each of these often functions in one of the other positions. Journalists read the stories of other journalists; television viewers take to the stage in talk shows. While a book of this focused nature cannot take on directly the issues of how in any particular historical moment journalists and readers, broadcasters and viewers alike are engaged in the particular broader discourses of the stage on which they act, this chapter closes with a brief analysis of these forms of interdiscursivity, in an attempt to forestall any discrete-category analysis of journalists and readers, broadcasters and viewers, which could serve as a platform for the reintroduction of a linear sender–receiver model on the one hand or the equally unuseful separation of readers and viewers from broadcasters and writers on the broader stage of historical, social and cultural practice on the other.

Chapter 9 closes the book by first rounding up the key ideas and then by sketching in broad outline a programme for the ethnographic and interactional sociolinguistic study of mediated discourse. The methodological substance of the chapter is based on a series of such studies now being carried out by the author and his colleagues. Crucial aspects are a focus on (1) identifying key sites of engagement and their attendant communities of practice, and (2) strategies for data collection, especially where communities of practice are relatively closed, such as homes and private meetings on the one hand, or where behaviour is public but socially uninterruptible as when people are reading on buses and trains. This chapter argues that a degree of methodological interdiscursivity must be achieved which matches the kinds of interdiscursivity of practice being analysed. It argues, as the book seeks to exemplify, that a full analysis ultimately rests on the discursive study of texts, the ethnographic study of communities of practice and sites of engagement, theoretical interdisciplinarity, and the grounding of analysis in the social practices of the communities of practice under study.

NOTES

1. In most cases, while it will perhaps make participants in each of those named communities of practice uncomfortable that I move somewhat freely across their boundary peripheries, I would argue that they have in common the analytical practice of using the social interaction itself as the primary test of the validity of analytical constructs and that this is of primary significance to my analysis here.

2. *Intertextuality* in Fairclough's use should not be confused with *interdiscursivity*, also a significant concept in this book. The latter is a broader concept encompassing the multiple ways in which not texts, but whole genres interpenetrate each other. The advertisement may borrow the style of hard news reporting, for example. The distinction which Evans (1976) makes between 'bought' space and 'editorial' space in the newspaper is constantly being eroded by this interdiscursivity.

3. Though not so near as some of the information superhighway enthusiasts would like us to believe. At the moment what we have is more like an awful lot of the most predictable texts in the world's most clichéd language.

4. Bourdieu's (1900) study of photography as social practice suggests to what great extent the ordinary photographer and his or her subject are working to embody the practices of the community of photographers. As I will indicate below, the dominant community of practice whose practices ordinary weekend photographers emulate is fashion photography.

PART II:

SITES OF ENGAGEMENT

TWO

Maxims of Stance: social practices in the interactive construction of business telephone calls

BUSINESS TELEPHONE CALLS AND MEDIATED DISCOURSE: A SITE OF ENGAGEMENT

The purpose of this chapter is to begin constructing the discursive bridge between studies of social interaction on the one hand and studies of the news media on the other. A crucial concept for the study of both the production and reception of media is the site of engagement and so I will begin with that here.

We understand conversations to be largely conducted by people who are face-to-face and whose attention is focused in real time towards the other participants. In many ways conversations are our prototype of social interaction as the common concept implies that all of the participants will be co-present in the same physical as well as social space. By this latter notion I mean, as Goffman (1963, 1981) has pointed out, that while people may be together in the same physical space such as when they are standing waiting for a bus and while they may at the same time be talking, we would not consider it a conversation until we are fairly certain that they are in some way socially together and that their speaking is to each other. Our evidence for this is a wide range of 'tie-signs' (Goffman 1963, 1971) such as exchanging eye contact, attending to each other's gestures, ecological proximity – they position their bodies close to each other with the fronts oriented towards each other.[1]

In conversations, the dominant mediated action might be casually called 'having a chat'. This action is mediated by the appropriation of a number of cultural tools or mediational means (Wertsch 1991, 1995b). The first which comes to mind is usually the languages in which the participants are speaking. Here we mean not just named languages such as English or Chinese or French, but in the Bakhtinian sense (1981a) we mean to say the voices which are appropriated by the conversationalists. We mean the styles, registers, phrases – in fact, we mean the entire repertoire of ways of speaking (Gumperz and Hymes 1972) upon which the participants can call to sustain the social interaction.

Of course the conversationalists also appropriate other cultural tools which range from the spaces within which the participants have convened the social interaction to the manner of dressing and otherwise displaying themselves. A conversation on a crowded urban bus may be contextualized and interpreted quite differently from one held in an elegant café. In any case, these aspects of the scene, while not to be neglected, are not ordinarily the primary focus of our attention when we ask what are the cultural tools by which the participants undertake the mediated action of having a conversation.

Mediated social interactions such as telephone calls, but we might also want to include fax exchanges, email discussions, internet lists, and traditional letter correspondences, are somewhat intermediate between the face-to-face social interactions of conversations and the writing and reading of newspaper stories. While there is a give-and-take series of exchanges in which participants orientate towards each other and within which they draw conversational inferences (Gumperz 1977, 1982), based to some extent upon contextualization cues, the utterances of participants are carried on some technological medium of exchange. Thus the mediational means of the telephone, the computer, the fax, or letter and all of the largely unseen but highly crucial socioeconomic infrastructure of telephone lines, power grid, postal service and the like is called upon by the participants to mediate their actions. In such social interactions, the role of the mediational means can no longer be simply set aside as mere context.[2]

Finally, in the case of the news story, the line from newsmaker through journalists and editors through printers, distributors and news-stand agents to reader or through television presenters, camera operators, directors and producers to viewer, the chain of mediated actions becomes so long, tenuous and hidden that we rather easily come to accept the convenient fiction of the implied writer and the implied reader (Chatman 1978; R. Scollon 1996a). We come to analogize the writer and the reader as standing in the same relationship to each other as two face-to-face conversationalists with 'nothing but' the medium in between. We rather easily forget that the primary social interaction a journalist has is with other journalists in the news room, the primary social interaction the television presenter has is with the other presenter in the news desk and, together with the camera operator, the director, producer, lighting specialists and a host of other technicians, they engage in the mediated action of making the evening news broadcast. We tend to forget that the primary social interaction is among the people sitting together having a conversation while the evening news is playing or among a group of people having morning tea while one of them reads the newspaper.

In this sense then, the site of engagement begins in the real-time, live circumstances in which people undertake mediated actions together as a form of social interaction. From this point of view our focus on mediated action is a focus on sites of engagement such as the newsroom, the news interview, the purchase of the newspaper at a news-stand, the reading of a newspaper while having a cup of coffee, having a chat and noticing there is a story on the television news broadcast which you want to watch. Sites of engagement, however fleeting and momentary, are the windows within which mediated discourse is operationalized as an instance of actual communication. As I will argue in Chapter 3, a newspaper story is only a physical object, a piece of paper with print on it until I ask the person with me to wait a moment while I read a certain bit.

This latter point is crucial to my definition of a site of engagement, because it is not just the physical setting in which the participants are face to face with each other. The site of engagement is a window constituted in social practices which enable that particular instance of discourse. It would ultimately be impossible to determine all of the social practices out of which such windows are constructed, but as I will argue in Chapter 4, one would expect several would be a minimum. My reading of the newspaper relies on my ability to read the language in which it is written. This, of course, is grounded in a large number of social practices of socialization from formal education to the communities of practice within which I claim membership. Am I a *Guardian*, *Times*, or *USA Today* reader (Bell 1991)? But reading that article also calls upon the social practices of establishing the right to ignore others present at the same breakfast table. In Hong Kong that right is differentially distributed among men and women and thus reading that article articulates with social practices of gender stratification found broadly throughout the business community.

In the discussion which makes up the rest of this chapter, I will turn to an analysis of business telephone calls. Such calls have proven particularly useful in highlighting the social practices through which conversations are constituted since Schegloff's (1972) pioneering article adumbrated the broad outlines of a highly active field of conversational analysis. In my analysis here, business telephone calls are also useful in providing a bridge between face-to-face conversation and the extended chains of mediated actions we call news discourse. I will argue in later chapters that the primary social practices through which conversations, whether face-to-face or by telephone, are constructed are the same social practices by which power alignments are negotiated and distributed among newsmakers, journalists, and the owners of the news media. The broadest scope for the exercise of power is constituted in the power to frame communicative events, that is, to control the channel. Within that is the power to position participants in relationship to each other through delegating or withholding the delegation of topics. Finally, within that is the power to speak in one's own voice or to control the representation of the voices of others.

In the following discussion, which focuses on three business telephone calls, I will argue that not only are these three modes of power distributed differentially in society, as we shall see later on in regards to news production, but in the more mundane business of making a telephone call the establishment and control of the channel is taken on by all participants as their primary task, the *sine qua non* of further communication. Hierarchically subordinated to this concern is to establish and maintain the relative positioning of the participants and then, finally, only as the positioning remains out of focus to be taken for granted can the participants turn to the topic at hand – the purported reason for the discourse to take place at all. Thus I shall argue that in the business telephone call can be seen the interactions among social practices which underlie all forms of mediated discourse.

'LET'S GET TOGETHER FOR LUNCH':
COLLEAGUE OR CLIENT?

One would imagine that business calls would be about business. Calls emanating from and received in businesses during business working hours purport to be about the serious matters for which the business is constituted, and one might assume that other matters will be given the marked status of requiring that they be accounted for. Nevertheless, business practices reflect the social practices of the societies within which they operate, and business phone calls show themselves frequently to mix business with pleasure, or at least with interpersonal social relationships. This is not, in fact, treated as an accidental or unfortunate liability which distracts the participants from getting on with the business at hand. As we shall see, it is a crucial and central social task, even within business telephone calls, to reflect the social grounding of the participants.

Within the business world two broad classes of social identities are acknowledged to exist, clients and colleagues (which are often also referred to as contacts or friends). While this broad distinction is widely recognized, I do not mean to suggest that there is a firmly held boundary between these two categories which, once it is established, forms a definitional basis for all subsequent social interaction. On the contrary, through the analysis of three typical business telephone calls, I intend to show that it is a crucial aspect of business telephone calls to present for mutual ratification a current and jointly produced analysis of just how the participants position each other as colleagues or as clients. Indeed, it is my point that the establishment and ratification of the colleague or client role is a prior condition to the introduction of the main business at hand when a business telephone call is made.

Among people in business it is taken as essential to cultivate and maintain contacts. Success, power, influence, and efficiency of operation accrue to the person who can quickly locate an avenue of entrance or inside favours. The more widely a person's net of contacts is cast, the more likely he or she is to be able to call upon this network for information or action, and these favours can then be used for profit in transactions with clients.

The three telephone calls I study here were all made by the same person, a male native speaker of English, within 20 minutes of each other and in the sequence I will present them in the course of a morning's work at his desk in a bank in Hong Kong. The tape recording and transcript below record only the caller's speech. The answerer's speech and other aspects of the interaction, including the participants' relationships, like much else in communicative study, must be inferred. I will argue that these inferences indicate a pattern of behaviour that take his contacts among colleagues as a matter of primary concern to the business of this business caller.

Business and relationships

Crowded restaurants at lunchtime in business sectors of major cities attest to the significance of the lunch as a social practice for maintaining a network of contacts as much as to the appetites of their customers. This is so much so that the lunch itself has come to hold symbolic status in the discourse of business. 'Having lunch' has become a phrase which does the work of displaying a relationship which extends beyond the purely instrumental and utilitarian tasks of the business day. A passage from the *Memoirs* of Kingsley Amis will provide an instance as well as an entrance to this study.

> Our encounters were rare and fleeting but they always ended with the disgusting formula, 'We must have lunch some time.' Then, not particularly soon after one of these, he rang me up out of the blue. The year would have been 1979.
>
> 'You know that lunch we're always promising each other we're going to have? Well, this time let's really have it. Have you got a free day next week?'
>
> This ought to have put me on my guard at once. An old lunching hand like me should have seen clearly that the suggestion put in these circumstances must mean that James wanted something from me. But I said, 'Sure,' and we were on.
>
> (Amis 1991: 110)

Kingsley Amis calls our attention at first to three aspects of the lunch formula as a social practice:

1. It is a formula, i.e., it comes in a somewhat fixed or at least regular linguistic format.
2. It comes at the end of a social encounter, i.e., it is a way of bringing a conversation on some other topic to a close – neither participant is to understand it as the main topic of the current encounter.
3. Because it is a closing formula, while it is assumed that there is the potential of its being accepted as a legitimate proposal to have lunch, the proposed lunch is to be at some other time than the present.

Amis refers to this formula as 'disgusting', not, I presume, because he does not eat lunch; he characterizes himself as 'an old lunching hand'. One is led to believe that his disgust is the novelist's somewhat ironic disdain of the clichéd in normal human communication, especially where this communication is between two professional writers who, one might assume, are highly conscious of the forms and rhythms of day-to-day conversational regularity.

Amis's point, however, is not to give a social practice analysis of the 'Let's get together for lunch' formula; that is my task. Amis brings this up in his first paragraph as a preface to accounting for his colleague's topicalization of the formula in his phone call one day 'out of the blue'. In this reported telephone call, the caller's opening topic is not something else, but the formula itself. Forwarding the lunch formula to the opening topic of the phone conversation was, Amis tells us, his surest cue that something else was going to be asked of him. In this opening position, the lunch suggestion cannot be taken as to be deferred to some future indefinite time; it is to be dealt with in and for itself. It is in that way stripped of its formulaic nature and given literal pragmatic status. It is no longer a departure formula (in Goffman's 1967 characterization), it is the main topic of the encounter. Amis was to find out only later – at the agreed upon lunch, in fact – what his friend had in store for him as the deferred topic.

Linguists (Sapir 1921, 1929), sociologists (Garfinkel 1967; Goffman 1967, 1974, 1981; Schegloff 1972, 1986; Sachs 1984), anthropologists (Bateson 1972; Gumperz 1977, 1982, 1992), linguistic pragmatists (Brown and Levinson 1978 [1987]), sociolinguists (Tannen 1986, 1989a, 1989b, 1990), and critical discourse analysts (Fairclough 1989, 1992, 1995a, 1995b) have all pointed out that any social encounter, including any of those in which talk is exchanged, has as its logically first and interactionally ongoing highest priority to position the participants in the social encounter in relationship to each other. Whatever else we do in speaking to each other, we make claims about ourself as a person, we make claims about the person of our listeners, we claim how those persons are related to each other at the outset of the encounter, we project an ongoing monitoring of those multiple relationships, and as we close the encounter we make claims about what sort of relationships we expect will hold upon resuming our contacts in future social encounters.

Topics which are introduced into such social encounters must be seen to arise naturally from these relationships. Indeed, as in the case of the lunch formula, the topic may be seen to function as little more than a topical carrier wave on which is superimposed the central message about the relationship between or among the participants.

These claims about relationships and topics set a communicative stance from which the participants then enter into the communicative encounter. These claims might be lumped together into a preliminary and admittedly over-simplified set of what I might call *Maxims of Stance*:

1. Identify the self you are claiming for the current social encounter.
2. Identify the self you are willing to ratify for the other participant(s).
3. Identify the topic which will serve as the overt carrier of self you are claiming as well as the self (or selves) you are ratifying for the other participant(s) while claiming your right to speak on this topic.
4. Make your claim as to why you are addressing this topic to the other participant(s).

I recognize that there is more to these maxims than this quick list suggests; for example, the word 'self' does not immediately suggest that it will become significant to distinguish among such production roles (Goffman 1981) as author, principal, and animator. A personal secretary, for example, may, in a telephone call, pass on a message from his or her superior. It will be significant for this secretary to make his or her claim to being animator (the person who gives the message its actual spoken instantiation, but not author (the person who has formulated the wordings which are spoken) or principal (the person who takes responsibility for what is said) of this communication. Such a phrase such as 'Sandra has asked me to call and tell you that she is sending a Fax today to Singapore which says X Y Z' may do the work of separating animator from author and principal of the words in X Y Z.

And it is still not that simple: this personal secretary may have, in fact, been not only the animator, but the author of these words as well. It is common in business practice for a person to say, 'Contact Sydney and tell them our response', in which case it is understood that the person told to do so has been given licence to become author and animator on behalf of the principal. In such a case, however, this person would be expected to frame the wordings as coming from the principal *as author* as well as principal, 'Sandra says, X Y Z'.

The difficulties do not stop there. Again, it is common practice for a principal to ask a subordinate to author text which he or she will animate. This is the case when a subordinate or speech writer prepares a speech or remarks to be delivered by the principal as if they were his or her own remarks. These complexities of the production format lie behind the socially and communicatively simplified word 'self' I have used in the maxims above.

There are other complexities; those of footing (Goffman 1981) address the problem of what is being momentarily established as the person in communication. One might imagine a telephone opening such as the following:

> [ring]
> JANE: Hello.
> TOM: Hello [choking noises]. Excuse me, I just choked on my coffee. Hi Jane, how are you?
> JANE: Tom, just fine. Only now you're having your coffee?

We might call the footing on which this caller, Tom, begins that of the ordinary person making an ordinary friendly telephone call. This self is one who prepares for entry into a routine social encounter where he may be expected to present himself as ready to talk. Schegloff (1986) has pointed out that this preparation may be considerably more complex than either caller or answerer will claim and often includes highly ritualized productions of formulas for answering. A person is often clearly identifiable by his or her 'hello' which may be produced in a voice and style unlike anything else in that person's verbal repertoire. My father, for example, could be observed from anywhere in the house to be approaching the telephone to answer it by a very loud and ritual clearing of his throat. The phone would be answered with a long drawn out 'HA:::lo?' containing a vowel not otherwise in his phonological repertoire.

Tom's brief aside, 'Excuse me, I just choked on my coffee', is performed as a change in footing; it is a temporary departure from the person claimed – one who has prepared himself to make a telephone call. Tom's choking noises expose him as insufficiently prepared to claim the telephoning self and so he momentarily shifts his footing to account for this lapse. As Goffman (1981) has pointed out, this change of footing is, in fact, temporary; it does not undermine the established (or in this case proposed) footing of the ordinary participants in an ordinary telephone call. That this change in footing is temporary is attested by his resumption of the default footing with the identification sequence, 'Hi Jane . . .'

At this point, however, Tom has manifested two communicative selves through this change in footing: one is the person making a telephone call, the other is the person who, behind the scenes as it were, is having a cup of coffee. Jane, in her remarks, attends to both of these selves: the offical self which has entered into the 'howareyou' (Schegloff 1986) sequence and the unofficial self which is having a cup of coffee.

Production format (author, principal, and animator), the authenticity of these roles, and footing all provide complexities for the concept of the self which is being claimed by participants in enacting the Maxims of Stance. My goal is not to elaborate on these complexities here; the reader will find ample elaboration of such questions in Goffman (1974, 1981). My point is simply to alert the reader to the extent of the complexities masked by apparently straightforward and ritualistic exchanges such as the one we are considering here in the formulaic 'Let's get together for lunch'.

Opening frames in telephone calls

In a number of articles over two decades, Schegloff (e.g., 1972, 1986) has elaborated our understanding of the social constructive work done by the ritualized sequence of opening moves in telephone conversations. The three central tasks to be accomplished are first, to open up the channel of communication, secondly, to constitute or reconstitute the relationship between the participants, and thirdly, to establish what will be talked about. These will be realized, as Schegloff has indicated, with three sequences, the summons/ answer sequence, the identification sequence (which may, under some circumstances, include a *howareyou* sequence), and the first topic introduction sequence.

One is not to think of these sequences as entirely independent linguistic exchanges so much as the communicative jobs to be done upon opening a telephone conversation. As Schegloff's material amply illustrates, it is common in American non-business friendly conversational telephone calls for the summons/answer sequence and the identification sequence to be accomplished simultaneously through claims of voice recognition. A typical opening quoted by Schegloff is as follows:

[ring]
NANCY: H'llo:?
HYLA: Hi:,
NANCY: Hi::.
HYLA: Hwaryuhh=
NANCY: =Fi:ne how'r you,
(Schegloff 1986: 114 [with slight transcriptional modifications])

As Schegloff points out, among the assumptions made by both callers and answerers is that some people are more likely to be calling than others and that some people are more likely to be answering than others. A call made to a friend's home, for example, places the known residents of that home on the list of potential answerers so that one is in the position of needing to select only among those who are expected to answer.

Where business telephone calls are concerned, Schegloff points out that explicit self-identification is a convention of business or office form, voice recognition being restricted in American usage to what are considered personal phone calls. This observation of Schegloff's has been reconsidered, however, by Houtkoop-Steenstra (1991) who points out that in Dutch telephone calls of a personal nature explicit self-identification is also the norm, and voice recognition is restricted to calls among those with intimate relationships if it is used at all.

In summary, then, there are three kinds of social activity going on in any strip of social encounter which involves talk such as a telephone call. Before I can take these up, I first need to account for the somewhat opaque term 'strip' that I have just used. I cannot be certain whether or not Goffman coined this usage of the word 'strip', but he makes it clear (Goffman 1981) that he uses the word as a methodological strategy to avoid prejudicing his analysis in favour of a priori folk understandings of how social activity is organized. I have used the phrase 'any strip of social encounter which involves talk such as a telephone call' as a caution against forgetting that as the telephone calls I will study are being made there are other people present in the same office as the caller and there may be presumed to be people present in the office of the receiver of the calls. Furthermore, those co-present people may or may not be engaged socially with the maker of these calls even though they may not be socially ratified as primary participants in the communication.

As an example of this latter possibility, it is common practice in business for a person to make a telephone call and while the call is in progress to be exchanging papers, messages, glances, and other socially constructed communications with other people in the same social situation. These side-plays and by-plays (Goffman 1981) are not understood to be part of the main-play, the telephone call, but are, nevertheless, constituted in the ongoing social activities of the people who are co-present in the situation.

The use of the phrase 'strip of social encounter which involves talk' also is a strategy I have borrowed from Goffman for avoiding making an a priori decision about whether or not this social encounter is primarily constituted for the purpose of the talk. Talk itself may play either a central or a peripheral role in such social encounters. While I recognize that one can come to use such methodological cautions excessively, I believe that in this case it is important to keep alive the idea that such day-to-day activities as making and receiving business telephone calls are analytically quite problematical.

To return now to the three kinds of social activity which are going on in any strip of social encounter which involves talk such as a telephone call, one activity, the essential opening activity, is to establish the channel of communication. In telephone calls the opening of the channel is accomplished (partly mechanically) with the manipulation of the telephone by the caller and by the ringing of the telephone in the environment of the answerer. Bearing in mind that this activity is only one aspect of the ongoing social encounter, it is worth remembering that not only is the channel of communication opened up for a telephone call, other channels of communication are closed or at least temporarily suspended. A telephone caller might, for example, motion with his or her hand to signal to someone else in the same office that he or she cannot respond to something being said because someone is speaking on the other end of the line.

The second activity, the logically and sequentially fundamental one, is to constitute the relationship between the participants in the newly opened channel. This is done through various social practices for identification which may or may not include a *howareyou* sequence. The third activity is to get some topic established as the opening or first topic of the communication. And without considering this point in detail, it can be said that the right to introduce the first topic conventionally goes to the participant who has initiated the call (Schegloff 1972; Scollon and Scollon 1991, 1995a).

In respect to business telephone calls, however, it should be pointed out that common everyday understanding of these is that they are highly instrumental; that is, it is commonly understood that they are dominated by a utilitarian purpose which is reflected in their topics. Swales (1990), for example, separates personal telephone conversations from business telephone conversations on the basis of the salience of purpose in business calls. From this common assumption we might be led to expect that such topics will come on to the floor rather quickly in comparison with less utilitarian personal or friendly telephone calls. This assumption is strongly supported by skill-orientated textbooks on professional communication (Bateman and Sigband 1989; Jones and Alexander 1989a, 1989b, 1989c).

Three telephone calls

I will now turn to an analysis of a sequence of three business telephone calls. As I have indicated above, these calls were recorded as an uninterrupted sequence of calls made as part of an ordinary morning's business in the office of a senior native English-speaking officer of an international bank in Hong Kong. While the bank officer was aware that the recording was being made, there is no evidence that his behaviour was modified in these telephone calls because of awareness of the recording. The full transcript of the calls with further details of the circumstances of their recording follows.

This transcript represents a continuous recording made on 22 September 1992 in an office of an international bank located in Hong Kong. The principal participant, here designated by the initials BF is the head of his division of the bank and is organizationally placed near the top of the corporate structure. The recording was made by his secretary with his permission, and with the assurance that his confidentiality and that of his business would be guarded. The recording was made by placing a battery operated SONY Professional Walkman (WM D6C) cassette tape recorder with stereo microphone on the desk next to the person making these calls and by recording continuously for a period of over an hour. These calls took place about 20 minutes into the period of recording.

The transcript was made by the author in the few days following the recording. The transcript and the first draft of the analysis

.ve been read by the secretary who made the recording and her corrections and clarifications have been incorporated into the transcription and the analysis.

Names of the participants have been changed to protect their confidentiality, but in any event this has not affected the substance of the analysis. The following conventions have been used in presenting the transcription:

(0.5)	The number in parentheses indicates a gap in tenths of a second
:	A colon indicates drawn out sound; the more colons, the more drawn out
–	A dash indicates that the speaker stops in mid-utterance
[ ]	Comments in brackets are for clarification; not recorded speech
(xxx)	Words in parentheses are the transcriber's best guess at doubtful speech
( )	A blank in parentheses represents indecipherable speech
,	A comma indicates self-interrupted speech or a micro-pause
N_____	A capital letter followed by a blank underline indicates a person's name

Business Call One: 'Peter'

1 [single click of telephone touch key: dialling outside telephone line]

2

3 [seven clicks of telephone touch key: dialling local telephone number]

4

5 [shuffling papers]

6

7 BF: Peter N___, please.

8

9   ( ) N___, This is F_____?

10

11   Who, who – ( )(ech es noch lieber. Ech liebe noch.)

12

13   That's – [laughs] . . .

14

15   And em, yeah, no, things, things are much easier there since(0.3)and, and, and South Africa, not

16   all, not all the good news coming out for the moment –

17

18   Where's, where's the (fund rand) now?

19

20   At four?

21

22   And, ah, cause actually in fact that's why I'm calling you,
      just a minute. And commercial rate

23   about 2.72?

24

25   [low voice] to Hong Kong. [whisper] OK [Normal voice]
      One of my clients has called me.

26   He's going to visit South Africa.

27

28   I mean, you, you guys, well, none of the South African
      banks, you're, you're not selling any

29   traveller's cheques or rand traveller's cheques or any
          thing like that. What, what should he do?

30

31   Just take foreign currency?

32

33   Yeah, yeah, that's what I told him.

34

35   So what is the best currency to take to South Africa at the
      moment?

36

37   US dollar?

38

39   Well . . .

40

41   I mean w –, if, if he took Hong Kong dollars? They would,
      em

42

43   Mmm?

44

45   Probably US I would think, yeah, that's what I said to
      him.

46

47   OK, so there's no way he can buy any rand here or
      anything like that?

48

49   ( )

50

51   So probably US dollars?

52

53   And em, and rates and fees and things like that, will they, no there shouldn't be any fees, anyway.

54   They'll just –

55

56   Yeah.

57

58   Is it, do you think, do you think it's best to do it at the, at the airport, as opposed to

59

60   To go to a bank wherever?

61

62   Ah yeah, not to go to a hotel, yeah, but sort of any, any bank at the airport or any bank.

63

64   (3.5)

65

66   ( )

67

68   OK

69

70   ( ) yeah, yeah::

71

72   ( )

73

74   Yeah, yeah, yeah.

75

76   Then he go, yeah, then he goes in, the little ( ) says, 'Who you? [laughs] Gimme your passport,

77   mate. Sorry, you can't, you can't get your money,' yeah.

78

79   OK, otherwise that's the lot, is it? Life goes on.

80

81   Yeah, yeah.

82

83   OK, well, what about

84

85   ( )

86	
87	Next week I've got lots of lunches, but I was saying this week aren't(0.8)dudes from Paris, but I'm
88	looking at, I mean, em
89	
90	( )
91	
92	Alright, Gee, next week I really have(0.5)hah, I have f –, one lunch is probably going to be
93	cancelled, maybe it looks as i –, oh no, may –, well, I'm not sure, I, I have a lunch on Friday
94	the second that may be cancelled. I might know later today.
95	
96	Let me, let me give you a call in the next day or so, once I know about this one. This week seems
97	to be a busy lunch week. Hm.
98	
99	OK we'll, we'll organize something.
100	
101	Oh, the famous one, yeah, OK, Yeah.
102	
103	OK
104	
105	Yeah, maybe you're ( )
106	
107	Book under Frazeli or something, em, [laughs]
108	
109	OK, let me see, I need to sort out that one and if, if it's cancelled, I'll give you a call.
110	
111	Good. OK, Peter.
112	
113	Thanks.
114	
115	Bye.
116	
117	[hangs up phone.]
118	
119	**Business Call Two: 'M'**
120	

121   [click: automatic dialling]
122
123   [shuffling papers]
124
125   BF: M_____, B____ here
126
127   Yeah, no, the the South African banks have, they, they
            don't sell any(0.5)South African travellers'
128   cheques or anything like that. So, basically, it, it would
               be to take foreign currency there.
129   Em, but em, you know, he, it's, it's obviously better
               taking currency in than taking it out.
130
131   Em, so, you know, probably US dollars, or even Hong
            Kong dollars.
132
133   But then, yeah, you're gonna get, you're not gonna get on
            the right side. So I –
134
135   Probably US dollars, and then the best deals you're going
            to get ( ) when you're in the country,
136   don't go to the hotels, he'll just go to one of the local
               banks. Even at, at the airport, em, he
137   will immediately come across s – some banks there and
               just drop in and get some rand.
138
139   Yeah.
140
141   Em
142
143   They will probably only have currency at, at, at the
            airport. If
144
145   If he went to a, if he went into a bank, and said he wants
            to buy some rand travellers' cheques, that
146   would be no problem.
147
148   Where(0.5)is he, is he travelling around in South Africa?
149
150   OK ( )
151

152	Yeah, I know.
153	
154	( )
155	
156	Even from, even from him personally?
157	
158	Yeah, they're probably ah, something like that. That's why it's better to get it into travellers'
159	cheques, if anything does happen.
160	
161	But em, as a, as a tourist the places he'll be going to, sort of, you know, hotels and em tours and
162	things like that, it's, it's quite safe.
163	
164	But yeah, no, if, ah, rather lose your travellers' cheques than your bank notes. Yeah.
165	
166	When does he go?
167	
168	Oh. ( )
169	
170	Yeah, if he needs sort of any information or hotels or anything
171	
172	Ah, alright, so
173	
174	So, he's mainly ( )
175	
176	OK
177	
178	Oh, that's good!
179	
180	OK, if you need anything else, give me a shout.
181	
182	Do what I can, M_____.
183	
184	Thanks.
185	
186	Bye.
187	
188	[hangs up phone]

189	
190	[long pause]
191	
192	
191	**Business Call Three: 'Jean'**
194	
195	[dial tone: speaker telephone]
196	
197	[single touch tone: dialling outside telephone line]
198	
199	[second dial tone: outside telephone system]
200	
201	[seven touch tones: dialling local telephone number]
202	
203	J: A:llo.
204	
205	[click: telephone speaker turned off]
206	
207	BF: Hello.
208	
209	Jean! Bonjour, B____F____.
210	
211	Fine, and you?
212	
213	I haven't spoken to you for a long time.
214	
215	Good, yeah, good. Already forgotten about, but eh, no, it was very good, it was eh, a long trip, a
216	lot of travelling and that, but it was very good.
217	
218	Yeah.
219	
220	And you, did you, what d-, what did you do? Did you, your family all came here?
221	
222	Ah, good.
223	
224	So that the family came to, to Hong Kong?
225	
226	Oh, good.
227	

228	And ah, otherwise you still, living in Shanghai are you?
229	
230	Ah!
231	
232	Oh right. Well I caught you just in time. You issued a cheque in favour of Southeast Piece Goods,
233	for one thousand and forty.
234	
235	But, ah, you didn't sign the cheque.
236	
237	[loudly laughing]
238	
239	So, OK I w – I will pay it.
240	
241	And
242	
243	[laughs]
244	
245	No, I just wanted to make sure that you, it's, it's not a stolen cheque or anything like that. It's OK
246	
247	
248	No, that's all. I tell them today.
249	
250	OK And w – when are you back from this trip?
251	
252	Alright, OK Oh, so that's (xxx) OK
253	
254	Gimme –
255	
256	Give u – give us a call and, so when you're back and we'll try and get together.
257	
258	Good.
259	
260	OK
261	
262	All back at school and life goes on as normal. Yeah.
263	
264	Yeah.
265	

266	Anyway, I'll tell you about the US, but it w – it was good. It was a nice trip.
267	
268	Yeah. No. No.
269	
270	OK Jean. We – we'll speak to you then.
271	
272	OK
273	
274	Thanks.
275	
276	Bye.
277	
278	[hangs up]
279	
280	[period of soft, unintelligible speech away from microphone]

Business call one: 'Peter', a colleague call

The first transcript I will consider is of a telephone call made by BF to a person I will call Peter. The first task, establishing the channel of communication, proceeds as one might expect from the research literature. There is a single click of a telephone touch key, a pause, then seven clicks of telephone touch keys. In this office a single number connects the caller with an outside line and in Hong Kong local telephone numbers at the time of this call consisted of a sequence of seven numbers. There is a shuffling of papers which suggests that BF is waiting for an answer at the other end, and in line 7 his request to speak to Peter N_____ indicates that the answer has followed a predictable summons (or call)-answer opening sequence (Schegloff 1972).

Before moving on to line 9 where BF produces the identification sequence, I would like to make another digression into a common business practice concerning the establishment of the channel of communication. This opening move may be socially somewhat complex in many instances. Often a caller will ask someone else such as a secretary to place the call. In such a move he or she is delegating the opening sequence to another person. The role of caller is socially separated into two distinct roles, that of the person in whose name the call is being made, usually a 'boss', and that of the person who does the mechanical work of placing the call, often a secretary or other subordinate. In this case, the opening move was made by BF himself, but it seems likely that the answer was made by some such delegated answerer since BF asks to speak to Peter N____ (line 7).

In the quite common two-stage process, two secretaries, a call placer and a call answerer, do the work of establishing the channel of communication for two other principals. As part of the work of opening the channel these second-echelon callers and answerers will also do most of the work of identification, and, in fact, may often also do considerable preparatory work regarding the topic. For example, consider the following hypothetical business call exchange:

May I say who's calling?
It's Mr Hutchins regarding Mr Wong's appointment with
the director.

One understands that it is not, in fact, Mr Hutchins who is speaking, but rather a subaltern speaking on his behalf. In such a case the principals will engage each other directly at what Schegloff (1986) calls the 'anchor position'; that is, they will engage each other knowing that the channel of communication has been opened and verified, that the participants have been identified and their participation ratified (i.e., Mr Hutchins, if he is answered by Mr Wong, knows that Mr Wong is prepared to discuss the appointment and that Mr Wong knows that Mr Hutchins intends to introduce this topic). All of this interactional work will have been produced by other than the principal selves to this social interaction.

In this delegation of channel preparation and relationship positioning we can see a further negotiated positioning of the participants into primary and subaltern statuses. Thus the social practice of delegation of the first two stages constitutes a distribution of power which legitimates the stratified positions of primary and subaltern statuses. As I shall argue below in regards to news discourse, a significant form of discursive power is the power to delegate or to withhold delegation of discursive roles and topics to others.

A second issue to be seen at this point just in passing is that the second-echelon caller and answerer may choose to claim and ratify an unofficial conversational status in their own role as principals. For example, consider the following reconstructed fragment from my own secretarial past:

[ring]
(1) Bowles's AA: Mr Bowles' office.
(2) Caruso's A: Is he there?
(3) Bowles's AA: Yeah, is the bowling sheet done?
(4) Caruso's A: Just finished it.
(5) Bowles's AA: Mr Bowles, Joe Caruso on 3.
(6) Bowles himself: Joe, what's up?
(7) Caruso himself: (responds ...)

(1) is Mr Bowles's administrative assistant. In (2) 'he' refers to Mr Bowles. Bowles's AA knows by voice recognition that the caller is Joe Caruso's assistant, that 'he' conventionally refers to Mr Bowles the Plant Manager, and that, therefore, Joe Caruso's assistant is calling so that Joe, not his assistant, can speak to Mr Bowles. In other words, by the second turn it has been established that this is an instance of a second-echelon caller placing a call to a second-echelon answerer on behalf of two principals.

Nevertheless, at this stage Bowles's AA takes the opportunity to introduce a quick exchange of side-play regarding the bowling sheet. Mr Bowles's assistant is an avid bowler in the plant bowling league; Joe Caruso's assistant has the job of typing up the results. Both know this and the work of this side-play is conducted in a simple two-turn topic exchange which borrows on the channel opening sequence and the identification sequence of Mr Bowles and Joe Caruso's 'serious' business telephone conversation. Such side-plays are far from rare in day-to-day business communications. In business telephone conversations the roles of caller and answerer may be functionally delegated to different persons. While it might be placing too fine a point on matters to say that the second-echelon participants are momentarily seizing power from the delegating principal, this functional separation allows an opening for such incidental side-plays.

COLLEAGUE OR CLIENT?

We have now come to our main consideration. Business calls, at least as business textbooks might want us to think, are highly purposive forms of social interaction, the success of which purposes can be measured by utilitarian standards of how well the participants get down to the business at hand, the purpose of the call (Bateman and Sigband 1989; Jones and Alexander 1989a, 1989b,

1989c). I want to leave aside as a hopeless issue the question of whether or not we can believe BF when he says in line 22 'That's why I'm calling you'. While arguments could be made in this and other cases that we should not take at face value the statements made by participants in social interaction, it seems necessary to treat them as at least provisionally claiming that they be treated by participants as true.

One can imagine, if we had been able to hear Peter, that after line 22 he might have said, 'Are you kidding? I know you've really called just to bring up all that about South Africa. You're always doing that, and I'm getting annoyed with you for it.' Had he said that, however, it is almost impossible to imagine the conversation continuing as we see that it did. The conversation which follows in lines 22 through 30, where BF states quite explicitly his reasons for calling, shows no evidence that Peter (or BF for that matter) has any overtly expressible doubts that BF's topic is as he has stated it – to find out what his client should do about taking money to South Africa.

We have, then, a clearly stated topic which indicates a clear purpose for this call. Our problems to be resolved, then, are (1) why does BF not state his purpose in line 11 when he reaches the 'anchor position', and (2) why does he continue on after he has reached the end of his purpose? I will argue that this is because BF is concerned to establish in this phone call that he is claiming for himself the relationship of colleague (as opposed to client) and in doing so is simultaneously ratifying Peter's implied claim to the same status.

The first move is BF's. As has been widely observed since Schegloff (1972) first introduced the notion, the right and responsibility to introduce the first topic is given to the participant who initiates the telephone call. This is so whether that initiator has in one person taken on all of the opening moves or the first sequences are accomplished by a person delegated to this task. There is an apparent contradiction, then, between BF's right as caller to introduce the first topic in line 11 and his explicit statement beginning in line 22 that he is calling to find out what his client should do.

The first move BF makes is in line 11 with the introduction of a few sentences in Afrikaans. What BF has accomplished with this code-switch is to displace, at least temporarily, his responsibility to be explicit about his reasons for calling. He has taken his position as caller as an opportunity to introduce not the topic for which he will purport to be calling, but rather to step aside into a rather extended sequence of what Fred Erickson might want to call co-membership talk (Erickson and Shultz 1982).

In the interactional work of the first segment of this conversation, BF can be seen to be establishing at least three aspects of his co-membership with Peter: (1) they are both either South Africans or highly knowledgable about South Africa; (2) they are both members of a banking community of practice;[3] and (3) BF is in need of current financial information about South Africa.

BF accomplishes the first of these three aspects of co-membership by using what is apparently Afrikaans in line 11, though we cannot say from this transcript whether this momentary switch into this language was initiated by BF or Peter. The pause and unintelligible portion of line 11 suggests a moment or so of simultaneous speech.

In the second instance, BF brings their co-membership in this banking community of practice on to the table through presupposition in line 18. He presupposes that Peter will be able to answer quickly and easily the question of the current value of the rand, the South African unit of currency. The very quick answer implies that Peter not only knows this value (and therefore is a member of this community of practice), it implies as well that he is willing to ratify BF's claim to banking co-membership. As an aside I might comment that in this instance of mediated action, it is the foreign exchange values, of course along with the telephone, the English language, and Afrikaans which serve as the mediational means by which these identities are claimed and ratified.

BF introduces his need for current information under somewhat false pretences. What he actually says in line 22 in itself suggests at first that his purpose in calling is to discover the current exchange rate. One imagines, of course, that this information might be rather readily discovered within BF's own bank without occasioning an outside telephone call. In other words, the potential syntactic sequence is misleading: 'Where's the rand now, because that's why I'm calling?'

BF himself calls attention to this potential misreading by tagging on to the end of this sequence a change in footing. His 'just a minute' in line 22 indicates that he is temporarily stepping aside from his immediately preceding claim that he is now giving his reason for calling. He goes on to ask for the commercial rate (more banking discourse co-membership – and probably also unnecessary information) which he records in a distinctively low voice. He then terminates the change in footing with the whispered, 'OK' in line 25.

BF's resumption of the reason for his call is taken up with a shift to his normal voice on 'One of my clients . . .' in line 25. He completes his statement of his purpose in calling with the quite direct question, not about currency rates at all, 'What should he do?'

There is another bit of work being done in lines 25 and 26 which helps to resolve the question of why BF has engaged in this delay in taking up his prerogative as caller to initiate his topic. By making reference to 'one of my clients', BF implies that Peter is, in contrast, not a client of his, but a colleague. One is inevitably stuck with inferences, of course, but it seems quite likely that if BF were making a quite different claim, that is, if he had been making the claim that Peter was a client as well, he would have been more likely to have referred to this person as 'another client of mine', or some similar formulation.

Of course, this set of potential forms is large and includes as well such forms as 'somebody I know', 'a friend', 'my boss' and an actually indeterminately large set of possible selections. BF has chosen to indicate that this information is being gathered on behalf of a client. This can be taken in this instance to imply that he is speaking to someone who is not a client. At least it is someone for whom he is claiming some non-client status. BF in this conversational interaction is, among other things, seeking to project and have ratified a relationship which might be referred to as that of colleagues as opposed to one of clients. Thus, this lexical choice is a strategy for positioning himself within a community of practice with Peter but in a different community of practice in his client/server relationship with the client.

The question of lunch

Two further kinds of evidence might be sought to bear upon the hypothesis that BF is claiming a collegial relationship. One is internal to this conversation and lies in how it is terminated, the other lies elsewhere in seeing how this same BF talks with someone with whom he wishes to constitute or ratify an already existing client relationship. The latter case will be taken up below in looking at the second telephone conversation.

Once BF and Peter enter upon the topic, the purported reasons for the phone call, they go on at some length about how BF's client might best transport money to South Africa. This section comes to a conclusion with a little scenario staged by BF in which his client is posed as a hapless traveller unable to get his hands on his money for having carried it in an unconvertible form. As the conversation to this point has been carried on with a serious, all-business face, this slight shift in implied production format (that is, BF animating the hypothesized character lost in a foreign bank) introduces a non-business stance again while nevertheless ostensibly maintaining topical coherence. It might be taken as a signal that he is prepared to bring this portion of the conversation to a conclusion. It further suggests that the direction of the change he is seeking is towards reaffirmation of the friendly, even joking relationship first claimed in lines 11 through 16.

While we cannot determine what is said by Peter in line 80, BF's use of 'OK' (Owen 1981) and the summarizing statements 'that's the lot, is it? Life goes on' in line 79 indicate that BF is relinquishing his claim over topic control. Further, the tag question form he has proposed to Peter can be taken as an invitation for him to introduce a second topic if he should choose to do so.

Again, it is not possible to know what the content of Peter's turns was; nevertheless, it is clear from what follows that Peter has suggested that they take lunch together.

In the talk which follows, from line 85 to 111, it is clear that the participants undertake a somewhat serious consideration of just when they might arrange to have lunch together. What we cannot know, of course, is just how much either participant really wanted to have lunch with the other. Unfortunately, human intention remains opaque; what we have on which to draw inferences is only the forms of behaviour which come to our attention. In this case, what can be seen is that both participants invest a considerable amount of work in trying to establish a mutually convenient time to meet for lunch.

If we return to the formulaic nature of the lunch suggestion, one observation we can make is that with any formula we need to be alert to both possible functions of the formula, its literal function and its metacommunicative function. If the purpose of the lunch formula is to serve as a departure formula which ratifies the participants' friendly, collegial relationship as opposed to a more utilitarian and 'businesslike' client relationship, then one could argue that the more time spent working through the formula, the stronger this metacommunicative meaning is being emphasized.

It is clear that in line 109, BF is asking for permission to give up the attempt to find a suitable time to manifest the formula literally in a meeting for lunch. We are ultimately not able to discover in this strip of social interaction whether it was the literal job of finding a time or the metacommunicative job of communicating the relationship which was uppermost in the intentions of either participant.

Business call two: 'M', a client call

Looked at from the point of view of simple interpersonal relationships using, say, Brown and Levinson's (1978 [1987]) notions of face politeness, there is little to distinguish the language of the second telephone call from the first. The style is quite relaxed, informal, and yet 'business-like'. One might conclude that BF is speaking to someone with whom he has a relationship quite like that manifested in the language of the first call I considered. Nevertheless, there are striking differences between this call and the first one, particularly on the question of topics.

The channel is opened by automatic dialling in this case. There is a single click which activates a pre-set number followed by a period of shuffling papers before BF enters the identification sequence in line 125. This automatic dialling suggests that the client, M_____ is someone whom BF calls regularly. In both the first telephone call to Peter and the third telephone call to Jean, the telephone numbers are entered one number at a time by BF. This indicates that these two colleagues are not people whom he has placed on his roster of automatically dialled telephone numbers.

BF's first move, then, is a quick ratification of the identity sequence, after which he moves immediately to his topic, line 127. This phone call shows the direct introduction of the business at hand, a move which one might expect to see in ordinary business telephone calls. My point is that the proto-typical business call is, in fact, a call placed between participants who are positioning themselves in a client–service relationship, not one placed in a collegial relationship.

Before rushing into the client relationship, however, another possiblity needs to be considered. That consideration is that this is not an initial phone call but a call-back. As Schegloff (1986) has suggested, such a call-back may evidence a pre-emption of sequences which might be expected in a first call. Therefore, we need to consider that because this is a call-back, the extended collegial co-membership work we saw in the preceding transcript has already been accomplished in some preceding call.

The only evidence we have of the preceding call is what BF has said in the preceding transcript, that one of his clients needs this information. In that case we argued that, in fact, BF chose to characterize his relationship as that of service to a client.

In this telephone call there is little mention of anything but the business at hand, conveying information to BF's client about the best means of transporting money to South Africa. Little mention, however, is some mention and so it is worth a moment's examination of the section from lines 170 through 182. Goffman (1959) has pointed out that departures make claims about the current status of the relationship as well as projecting claims about the status of this relationship in the next encounter. The significance of the lunch formula in this view is that it makes a claim that the next encounter will be a purely social encounter, that the business transacted this time is either incidental to the relationship, or that in some other way the speaker wishes to foster the relationship over the business aspects of the interaction.

In light of the way the lunch formula was used in the first telephone call, it is the absence of the lunch formula or of anything comparable in this call which indicates the client status of the relationship. While this is a call-back, and while it is conceivable that some form of co-membership facework might have been accomplished in the preceding phone call, nevertheless, for this call to offer evidence of a collegial relationship, there would have to be some indication in the departure that this was the claim being made by the participants. There is nothing of the sort in this conversation.

Where BF does detour from the immediate topic at hand – of what form of money to take – it is a quite minor detour into other closely related matters such as hotel information for his client (actually, it is for his client's contact). He makes no attempt to set the interaction on a non-business basis more than to use quite informal language in saying, 'give me a shout'. While he communicates a close, informal relationship, it remains in the last analysis a non-collegial client relationship.

Business call three: 'Jean', colleague as client

The third telephone conversation I want to consider is much like the first in overall structure. There is an introductory bit of talk following on the anchor position which is not the purported reason for the call (lines 211 through 230) but which attends to matters of the relationship between BF and Jean. Following the business at hand (the cheque which Jean has neglected to sign) there is an extended bit of discussion again about the relationship, including in line 256 the assertion that the participants will 'try and get together'.

In form, the first and the third phone calls show the same 'sandwich' or buffered structure of *relationship talk + business talk + relationship talk* which I would like to argue is characteristic of collegial business telephone calls. There is a difference, however, which I believe is worth giving more attention. This is, in fact, a client call to a colleague. This interesting interdiscursivity serves to highlight the distinctions for which I am arguing.

The business at hand in this telephone call is not simply a matter of information which one colleague is passing on to another colleague as part of their mutual maintenance of networks of professional contacts. The business at hand has arisen because Jean is, in fact, a client of BF's bank. He has issued a cheque on BF's bank which he forgot to sign. This is, of course, a matter of potential difficulty in that it could be a stolen cheque.

The transcript opens with one indication of this potential difficulty. BF himself dials the number which initiates the call. We hear this process from both sides through the speakerphone BF has switched on. What follows then is a double identification sequence. In the first case, Jean answers in the format expected for non-business telephone calls by giving his name alone and BF responds in kind. At this point the speakerphone is switched off. We do not know, of course, to what telephone number this phone is addressed. It is, perhaps, addressed to the residence of Jean and, hence, the personal format for opening and identification.

In line 209 BF again uses the code-switching strategy of the first phone call by using a few words in the (assumed) language of the answerer, in this case French. In both of these moves it is clear that the prior issue with which BF is dealing is the constitution of this telephone call as a collegial call if not simply a personal call.

Line 213 brings us to the anchor point. This is where we should expect the first topic to be introduced if this is a client call or where we should expect some preparatory co-membership work if this is a collegial call. What we get is neither the topic at hand nor simple preparatory co-membership. What we get is actual topicalization of the relationship itself. The relationship is not presupposed or asserted indirectly as in the first phone call, 'Peter', nor is it backgrounded as in the client phone call, 'M'. In this case it is brought to the front for explicit consideration by saying, 'I haven't spoken to you for a long time'.

While BF has not gone so far as the friend of Kingsley Amis with which I began this analysis, by starting with the idea of lunch together, he has quite explicitly raised the issue of the lapse in their relationship. By topicalizing this relationship he makes it possible for Jean to then ask (apparently) into BF's trip. BF continues the sub-theme of the topicalized relationship and how long it has been in a state of lapse by suggesting that he has already forgotten about this trip. Having completed this sub-routine on BF's trip, BF then brings up the question of Jean's family visit. This is followed by the question about Jean's current residence in Shanghai. All of these exchanges stand apart from those of the first transcript in that it is the aspects of the personal relationship, the non-business relationship, which are brought into focus.

This considerable extra interactional work then sets a frame about the quite explicit client relationship which follows in lines 232 through 248. It is further significant that BF tries to close this frame rather quickly beginning in line 239, again in line 245 and again in 248. His insistence on closing this frame can be taken as an attempt to minimize this intrusion upon an otherwise collegial relationship. This minimization is further emphasized by his laughing loudly in line 237 and again in line 243.

On the other hand, the repeated (apparent) moves by Jean to keep the topic alive might be taken to be testing BF's intent to close out this topic. One can interpret them as the equivalent of asking, 'Are you sure this is only a trivial intrusion into our collegial relationship?' It is quite likely, finally, that BF's 'No. No.' in line 268 was in response to one further attempt by Jean to test the framing of this relationship.

This transcript opened by BF's topicalization of the relationship between him and Jean. It is symmetrically fitting, then, that he should be the one to suggest in line 256 that they get together. In contrast to the first call, however, there seems to be little extension of this invitation as a literal invitation to actually get together. Instead it is taken as a metacommunicative claim about the extension of the relationship into the next meeting. Notice that line 262 can be inferred to be in response to a question about BF's children, not an attempt to establish a luncheon date. In this, Jean parallels BF's opening strategy (line 220) of making direct reference to members of Jean's family.

Client calls and colleague calls

From the analysis of these three transcripts we may infer that there are two types of business telephone conversation: those between colleagues and those between business people and their clients. Nevertheless, in some cases it must happen that people who in one instance are colleagues become clients of each other in others. In such a case, the collegial relationship may be at risk if the inter-action takes, on the surface, forms of the business–client relationship. As this analysis indicates, one solution in such a case is to raise the focus on the collegial relationship through topicalization of that relationship in the opening frame of the social encounter. Such topicalization may be seen somewhat paradoxically as either a warning of a changed relationship to come or of the trivialization or temporary marginalization of the embedded business–client relationship. In either case, as in the passage quoted from Kingsley Amis, when a colleague begins with the topic of lunch, one is well advised to move on from there carefully.

'OK. THANKS. BYE.': THE CLOSING FRAME IN BUSINESS TELEPHONE CALLS

In Hong Kong's Kai Tak airport I saw a child of about two years of age, whose parents were otherwise occupied, pick up the receiver of a public telephone. He smiled and 'said' something, paused, began a long string of highly voluble, though still unintelligible, syllables, and then finally slammed the receiver down on the instrument and walked away looking somewhat smugly angry. We may infer with some confidence that this child has observed about telephone calls that they begin with an answer which consists of some speech (and perhaps a neutral or pleasant countenance), there are pauses in which there is no speech from the person one observes on this end, and that in some cases they end with a banging down of the receiver which is associated with an angry countenance.

My task in this section will show little more observational sophistication than that displayed by this two-year-old, and since I continue to restrict myself to the three business telephone calls already analysed in the first section, I will have only inferential explanations for his banging down of the receiver. My purpose is only to provide some evidence that in closing telephone calls there is a rather high degree of regularity, that this regularity arises from an underlying implicational logic governing the complex of social practices which we call a telephone call, and that departures from or breaches of these practices are themselves communicative.

The three business telephone calls we have been considering end as follows:

One	Two	Three
Good. OK, Peter	OK, if you need anything else, give me a shout.	OK, Jean. We – we'll speak to you then.
	Do what I can, N____.	OK
Thanks.	Thanks.	Thanks.
Bye.	Bye.	Bye.

The two-year-old in the airport, if he had been wanting to be more civil to the person on the other end might well have said, OK, Thanks, Bye. It certainly ranks as a relatively fixed formula if these three telephone calls are any evidence. One certainly sees little to take exception with in this formulaic closing sequence.

The question for my analysis is: Why does this speaker perform his closings with such apparent regularity? This could also be put as: Where did he learn to do this? One suspects that he did not consult one of the many textbooks on the market for students of business or professional communication. There are two reasons I believe this: BF is a native speaker of English and it is quite rare for native speakers, unless they are actually teachers or materials developers, to have any awareness of what is taught in such pedagogical sources. That is my first reason, but there is a more important reason for believing that he did not get his closing out of a textbook; textbooks are mysteriously taciturn on the subject of closings.

While openings of telephone calls are treated in some depth in most of the textbooks I have reviewed, closings are apparently left to the unexamined social practices of the callers. My purpose here is to see what can be drawn out of these three business calls about such social practices.

Early in my analysis of the three telephone calls I put forward a set of tentative Maxims of Stance, a set of principles which I suggested inevitably underlie the opening moves of such telephone calls. I then moved very quickly to suggest just how tentatively I regarded these maxims by elaborating on a number of problems we would have to face in clarifying the concept of the self or the person who is constructed as the caller and as the answerer. Nevertheless, what I hope to have established, following upon Schegloff (1972, 1986) and Schegloff and Sachs (1974), is that the interactional work of opening up a telephone conversation occurs in an implicational sequence. First, the caller and the answerer must be identified. They must also present a set of claims about themselves, such as who they are and what their relationship is, and these claims must be ratified before the participants can move on to taking up the purported main topic of the telephone call.

I argued above that where the relationship being claimed and presented for ratification is that of colleagues, an extended series of exchanges occurred following upon what Schegloff calls the anchor position, that is, the position immediately following the identification sequence. These sequences of exchanges which we might want to call facework, following Goffman's (1959, 1967, 1974, 1981) usage of the term, were again taken up following the conclusion of the purported main topic with the suggestions of getting together for lunch. In other words, in collegial telephone calls, the purpose of the call, that is, the informational transaction which justifies its being conceived of as a business call, can be seen to be embedded within the brackets or framework of interpersonal and collegial facework.

The client telephone call is a more directly utilitarian social task. While the language as considered within the Brown and Levinson (1978 [1987]) face politeness framework shows little difference in politeness strategies, it is clear that the self presented for mutual ratification in the second telephone call is sufficiently identified as falling within the domain of business–client relationships. While this is a call-back and we therefore cannot draw much inferential substance out of the initial identification sequence in line 125 ('M_____, B_____ here') other than that these two people speak to each other on a first-name basis, in the closing sequence BF volunteers nothing further than the possibility of further information on hotels 'or anything'. In this as in other cases of conversational inference, nothing (or the absence of something expected) may be of significance; BF does not suggest to M___ that they should make an attempt to get together. He in fact suggests nothing further than the possibility of another telephone call (line 180, 'give me a shout').

There is, then, an implicational priority of at least a logical type, if not a chronological sequence, between what we can call the relational work and the topical work of these telephone calls. The successful introduction of the purported reason for the call is treated by the participants as depending upon or subordinated to the successful presentation and ratification of their mutual relationship positionings.

It is the third telephone call which shows this implicational hierarchy most clearly. The purpose of this telephone call, because it is not simply a request for information, but rather a business–client transaction, risks the reconstitution of the collegial relationship between the caller and the answerer. To mitigate this risk, BF topicalizes the relationship itself as the first topic of the conversation in a move which presents their relationship at least initially as the purported reason for the call.

We might summarize this implicational hierarchy of social practices as a simplified sequence of two maxims as follows:

1. Attend to the relationship.
2. When the relationship can be safely presumed upon, attend to topic.

It should be remembered, however, that while the maxims might be stated sequentially, and while the initial opening of the conversation may, in fact, deal with these maxims sequentially, they remain a matter of implicational precedence. To put this another way, following upon Bateson (1972), the question of relationship may never be put aside as having been permanently dealt with; it is a matter of ongoing, even if backgrounded, concern for all of the participants.

Topics in discourse

I have sidestepped an issue long enough. In what I have written to this point, I have made reference to 'the topic', 'the main topic', and 'the purported purpose', relying upon the intuitions and good faith of my reader to let me remain rather vague about just how either the original participants in these telephone calls or we who are playing at this analysis actually know what they are talking about. Keenan and Schieffelin (1976) proposed the idea of the discourse topic to be clear about the distinction between the concept of topic in grammatical analysis and the considerably broader concept of what a discourse 'is about'. Their proposal has been extended in many ways, perhaps most usefully by Brown and Yule (1983) in their notion of the 'topical framework'.

In this case it seems that there is little difficulty in these three telephone calls in determining that there is such a topic (or primary purpose for the call) since it is relatively explicitly stated by the caller. In line 22, for example, BF says, 'that's why I'm calling you' and goes on to specify that it is to learn what his client should do about taking money to South Africa. The second telephone call does not have such a statement within the telephone call; it is stated, however, in the first call. If we can accept the well-warranted inference that M____ of the second telephone call is, in fact, the 'client' referred to in the first call, there is little difficulty in taking the opening lines (127–129) as the topic since this is the information passed on to him by the answerer of the first phone call. The third telephone call implies a purpose in line 232 when BF says 'I caught you just in time' and follows this 'catching' with the statement of his business.

In each case one is fairly confident in assigning to these segments of the discourse the importance of being the main thing talked about and, in fact, the reason for the call. Recall that within the framework analysed by Schegloff (1972, 1986), unless the right is pre-empted, the right to introduce the first topic goes to the person who is taken to have initiated the telephone call. What evidence do we have that this framework of interpretation is used by the participants in these calls?

In the first call, the right to the first topic is granted to BF. BF, nevertheless, defers taking action upon this right for the reasons given above; he is attending to the prior problem of re-constituting the collegial relationship. He does not, however, abdicate this right, nor does his answerer (apparently) make any attempt to pre-empt this right when it becomes clear that BF is not moving directly to his main topic, his reason for calling. That BF both retains the right to introduce first topic and that he is aware of his responsibility to

4

4
4

do so becomes clear in line 22. We can take 'actually' to begin signalling BF's dismissal of his introductory comments. As it might be understood without a context, 'actually' signals that the speaker intends to depart from some (possibly falsely) assumed understanding. Consider the following short question and answer sequence:

Are you going to lunch now?
Actually, I've just come back.

In such an exchange we would understand the first speaker to be assuming that it is now lunch time and that the second speaker might be about to go. With 'actually' the second speaker calls into question the presuppositions made by the first and then clarifies the meaning.

As a move in the first telephone call, 'actually' signals not that the preceding syntactic or semantic presuppositions are being called into question – BF is not to be taken literally as calling into question Peter's statement that the rand is 'at four' – what he is calling into question is the possibility that Peter will be taking him to be primarily concerned about the current value of the rand. The sentence said is in fact directly contradictory of its apparent meaning. What BF is saying is: 'Actually, that's NOT why I'm calling you' (i.e., to discover the value of the rand, but for another purpose). The 'actually' is directed towards the structure of the discourse. It is directed towards the assumption which appears to be violated in this case that the caller will introduce the first topic.

This suspended state of affairs which is called into topical prominence with 'actually' in line 22 is further manifested in BF's 'just a minute' later in the same line. This bit of footwork is rather adept. BF has used 'actually' to bring on to the conversational table his awareness that he has not yet fulfilled his obligation to account for having issued the summons or call. Then with 'just a minute' he establishes his intention to continue asking after the value of the rand as a kind of new footing (Goffman 1981). This new footing is sustained by a lowering of his voice, finally reaching a whisper in line 25.

Finally, at the end of line 25 BF takes up the reason for his call, which has been his right and obligation to introduce from the beginning and which he has foreshadowed with 'actually' in line 22. This moment of resolution is signalled in three ways: BF whispers 'OK', he resumes his normal voice, and presents a clear, syntactically declarative opening statement, 'One of my clients has called me'.

'OK, that's the lot': closing the topical frame

This moment at the close of the opening sequence in line 25 in the first telephone call brings to our attention BF's use of the form 'OK' as a bit of spoken punctuation. While barely whispered in this case, it is heard as signalling that BF has reached a point of conclusion. If we bear in mind that any discourse is mutually constructed among the participants, we can understand that 'OK' signals that BF intends to drop his current topic. Perhaps it would be better to say that he is ready to relinquish claims to his topical ownership or dominance.

The next instance of 'OK' (line 47) also shows this terminating or summarizing function, though in this case BF's answerer is currently holding the conversational floor. BF follows his 'OK' with a summary statement of what he has heard his answerer to have said. His preceding comment indicates that BF has reached a point of having his own information corroborated. In other words, we can infer that BF's 'OK' in line 47 indicates that at least from his point of view they have reached a concluding point.

The other speaker, Peter, continues, however. BF makes little attempt to divert him from his topical continuation; but his sequence of 'yeah' (line 56), 'OK' (line 68), and then 'yeah, yeah' and 'yeah, yeah, yeah' (lines 70 and 74), coupled with a diminishing audibility, all suggest that he in fact has little further interest in continuing this line of topic development.

Finally, BF makes an overt move to realign the topic away from the business at hand and ultimately move towards conclusion. The 'OK' in line 79 once more signals his sense of completion; and then he overtly claims an interest in moving elsewhere with 'otherwise' as a transition and his call for summary conclusion in 'that's the lot, is it?' 'Life goes on' is a not overly subtle suggestion that there are more interesting topics and activities than his client's trip to South Africa.

The conversation concludes with the negotiation over lunch which I have discussed above. For our purposes here it is interesting to note that BF makes at least two, perhaps three, attempts to put this new topic aside and to come to conclusion. In line 83 it is not at all clear how 'OK' is to be interpreted, though it seems most likely that BF's intent is to agree to the idea of trying to establish a lunch date. In other words, this instance of 'OK' does not seem a likely candidate for a terminating turn.

Line 99, on the other hand, is clearly a signal that BF has said all he has to say on the subject of lunch with Peter for the moment. 'OK' indicates his intention of ending, and 'we'll organize something' gives explicit agreement that lunch will ultimately be arranged. This is followed by 'OK, Yeah' (line 101), 'OK' (line 103) and then finally 'OK' plus a very specific promise to give Peter a call, even though this promise remains mitigated by the conditional 'if it's cancelled'.

'OK, Peter': closing the relationship frame

The first problem of conclusion for BF was to get his main topic off the floor once he had introduced it. As I have just noted, it took a sequence of two or three moves to bring this central portion of the conversation to a close. Having done so, and having relinquished the floor to Peter, BF then took another sequence of some four or five terminating signals to bring to a close the lunch topic.

I gave evidence above that there is an implicational hierarchy of tasks in opening up a conversation on the telephone. Those were summarized in two maxims:

1. Attend to the relationship.
2. When the relationship can be safely presumed upon, attend to topic.

The contingent nature of the second maxim carries with it the consequence that when the topic is no longer being dealt with, the focus will return overtly to the relationship. In other words, I can now introduce a provisional set of closing maxims:

3. Close the topic.
4. When the close of the topic has been negotiated, attend to relationship (because it will have remained an actively open issue).

BF attends to the relationship upon closing the topic in the succinct form of making a direct reference to the person he is speaking to by name, Peter. This reference by name neatly closes out the frame established in line 7 where BF uses Peter's family name, N_____.

In this one-sided recording of the conversation we can only make inferences about what is said by the other participant, Peter. What we can say, of course, is that he is likely to have said something in line 112. We can also make some guesses about the nature of what he would have said. If we remember that the structure of this call is an outcome of an ongoing negotiation between the two speakers, we need also to remember that BF is not free to close out topics unilaterally (as I have argued above) nor to assert the relationship without ratification. His closing move in line 111 must be interpreted as such a move before the conversation can be ratified as having closed by mutual agreement. We can assume that that was the nature of Peter's turn in line 112.

But that move too must be ratified as having been heard as a successful concluding move, and that ratification is given by BF in line 113, 'Thanks'. Again, we have only inferential access to what might have been said in lines 115 and 116. It seems probable that the thanking sequence ['thanks'/'you're welcome'] is what filled that slot.

'Bye': closing the channel

Much of the earliest study of telephone conversations dealt with an issue I have not yet mentioned, that of opening and maintaining the channel of communication (Schegloff 1972, 1986). The main points of that analysis can be quickly summarized. The matter of first concern is to establish that there is a potential set of speakers and hearers who are both able and willing to open up between them a state of communication.

I will not take up the question of the problems underlying the use of the words 'speakers' and 'hearers' more than to say that I mean to include the concept that each participant will be expected to accept and grant both roles reciprocally in a pattern of negotiated exchange, and that each role may be taken with varying degrees of what Goffman (1981) calls production format; that is, a person may only be mouthing words as 'animator' which are 'authored' by another, or only pretending to listen; a person may behave with greater or lesser degrees of sincerity or role commitment. Schegloff (1986) conveys this caution with the apt notion of a 'mouth and an ear ready to talk'.

In mechanical communications, that is, in communications in which a mechanical device such as the telephone intervenes between mouth and ear, routinized work needs to be done to establish the openness of the channel between mouth and ear. This is accomplished by the familiar, but increasingly complex, routines of placing a telephone call. There are mechanical and social complexities in the placing of a business telephone call. On the side of mechanical complexities are the 'smart' telephone and paging systems now found within most business environments in which calls may be routed to follow a potential answerer's movement throughout an office, city or, in fact, across the surface of the earth. Among the social complexities are the specialized roles of receptionists or other delegates of potential callers and answerers who undertake the preliminary stages of establishing the openness of communication channels on behalf of the principals of these communications.

Such issues of channel are now stimulating fresh discussion in the research literature in light of the very rapid changes of recent years in telephone/computer technology as hundreds of citations on a recent internet search attest. That is not my purpose here. My purpose is simply to call attention to the well-established point that the opening of the channel in the placing of a telephone call sets up a matter of ongoing communicative concern with channel. Channel is the concern of the first logical priority even though it may normally be discursively backgrounded. At any time it may override the secondary concern of identification, constitution, and ratification of social roles and relationships.

Examples of the ongoing concern with channel are not far to seek, even though our sample of three telephone calls did not produce any overt evidence of this concern beyond the initiation and termination of the calls. Schegloff (1986) brings into evidence the use of such forms as 'hello'. This form provides an initial multiple function of both opening the channel of communication and of producing a sample of the caller's speech for voice recognition. In initial position, the multiple roles of 'hello' are somewhat difficult to untangle. Nevertheless, the ongoing concern for channel surfaces whenever there is a temporary halt or lagging in the aural feedback from the hearer. The following fragment of telephone conversation is typical:

A: Our office will be in touch again within a few weeks once we've determined a supply source.
B: [silence]
A: Hello?
B: Yes, OK, that's fine.
A: Oh, I thought maybe there'd been a broken connection.
B: No, I was just making a note.

A expects a response, but when none is forthcoming he reverts to the use of 'hello' as a check on the channel. B then reconfirms his presence along with supplying the response expected by A. Then, having shown himself to have been in error over his assumption of a broken connection, A accounts for his attention to the channel. In such a fragment we can see that the channel is always present even though backgrounded as the most fundamental concern and must be confirmed to be continuing in an open condition throughout the conversation.

In mechanical communications which depend upon sound such as the telephone and radio, channel confirmation is accomplished through continuous talk or at least sound. Radio's abhorrence of 'dead air' is paralleled in telephone conversations by checks such as 'are you still there?' or 'hello?' at moments when more than very brief pauses are sustained. In other mechanical communications, such as television, which carry visual images as well as sound, somewhat longer periods of no sound may be tolerated, but rarely without visual images to sustain the openness of channel. In face-to-face communications, channels are mutually demonstrated to be maintained as open by a complex structure of eyegaze, head nods, backchannel responses such as 'uh huh' and other sub-syntactic vocalizations.

Channel must be mutually ratified as being sustained in an open condition by the participants. Even the most momentary failures to respond may be interpreted as potential failures of channel. Recently I received a telephone call, the opening of which can be reconstructed as follows:

RS: Hello.
GL: Hello, Ron?
RS: Yes.
GL: This is Geoffrey.
RS: Geoffrey, where are you?
GL: I'm in Seoul.
RS: Oh, it sounded like you were right here.

There are two issues of interest here. In the first place, Geoffrey was calling my office for the first time. It is evident that he expected an office-like identification sequence rather than the 'hello'. Although he believed he had recognized my voice, his 'Ron?' opened a second sub-routine, a confirmation sequence. For my part I had recognized the voice as familiar but had not identified it at first.

Schegloff (1986) has pointed out that neither callers nor answerers are an infinitely large list of potential participants. A call placed to a residence, for example, narrows the list to the set of people expected to be at that telephone. A red hot-line telephone has very specific potential callers as well as forms of talk. A person who is not normally a potential answerer may, nevertheless, answer the telephone, but in such a case, he or she is likely to account for this change in anticipated expectations. When John F. Kennedy was president of the US he made it his practice to walk around in government offices and answer telephones. His answer, 'Hello, this is the President', was known to elicit laughs and jokes at first but then full alarm when his distinctive New England accent was recognized. It is said that this practice put all of Washington on alert to the potential of presidential eavesdropping.

Place is also a question in establishing this potential list. My telephone is in Hong Kong; Geoffrey was calling from Seoul. Not having spoken to him by long-distance telephone before, he was not (yet) on the list of potential callers, and further, being new myself to that particular telephone, that list remained a relatively short list. That accounts for my failure to make an immediate identification of Geoffrey, a good friend, simply by voice recognition.

Beyond the issue of the identification sequence, however, is the question of channel. My expectation was that Geoffrey would be in Seoul. The connection was very clear and from that I apparently thought that perhaps Geoffrey was not, after all, calling long distance. Then having called attention to the channel, I made the closing move of accounting for why I had raised it to attention by saying, 'it sounded like you were right here'.

The two points I want to observe in this case support Schegloff's (1972, 1986) argument that (1) throughout a telephone call channel remains the matter of the most fundamental priority over relationship and topic in turn, and (2) where channel itself becomes topicalized, speakers feel it necessary to account for their attention to it.

IMPLICATIONALLY NESTED SOCIAL PRACTICES: CHANNEL, RELATIONSHIP, TOPIC

I have tried to give evidence and some argument for considering telephone conversations to take place within three enclosing frames:

channel on the outside, relationship within that, and topic as the innermost. These three frames form an implicational hierarchy so that at any particular time attention to the next higher bracket may pre-empt any ongoing activity, but in turn, that pre-emption must be accounted for in returning to the ongoing activity. In other words, while attention to these nesting frames of activities may be carried out sequentially in opening and closing telephone conversations, at any time all three frames must be understood as being sustained throughout the interaction.

One consequence of this hierarchy of frames is that any disruption at any higher level carries with it disruption at lower levels. When the channel breaks down, concerns with relationship and topic are put aside until the openness of the channel is restored. When the relationship breaks down, the current topic or topics are put aside until the relationship is restored. For example, Erickson and Shultz (1982) have shown that in conversations between college counsellors and their students, when the relationship breaks down, there is a corresponding breakdown in topical cohesion. This is reflected in repetitions, hesitations, stuttering, redeployment of physical stances, and abrupt topic shifts. Elsewhere (R. Scollon 1985) I have argued that any disruption in the flow of talk is ambiguous since it may be interpreted at any of the hierarchical levels of the structure of the discourse. To put this another way around, a continuation on the same topic or a smooth transition from one topic to another implies that both the relationship and the channel are being ratified as successfully constituted. At the next level of framing, even a hostile relationship with topic disruptions ratifies that the channel is still being sustained. A successfully opened and maintained channel is the a priori assumption for any communication. A successfully and mutually ratified relationship is the a priori assumption for topic agreement. It does not matter whether the relationship is friendly or hostile.

To return to the three business conversations I have studied here, there is no variation in the means by which BF closes the channel. He uses the single syllable word, 'bye', followed by the mechanical termination in hanging up the telephone. Taken together, then, the sequence found with minor variants in all three of these calls is 'OK. Thanks. Bye.' These form the closing three frames on topic, relationship and channel, respectively.

To see this as a closing formula, however, is to mistake two aspects of this communicative activity, if by formula one means an utterance given in a fixed sequence. The concept of a formula implies that the words thus sequenced form a unit which is (at least relatively) internally fused. What is missed by the concept of a closing formula is the fact that each of these three forms, 'OK', 'Thanks' and 'Bye', is addressed to a different level of the preceding discourse. The domain over which the topical close 'OK' stretches goes back, in the first telephone call, only to line 79 at the earliest; it goes back to the point where BF relinquishes his main topic and Peter brings up the topic of having lunch together. 'Thanks', however, extends back to cover a larger domain. It must be seen to encompass at least the favour asked regarding what BF should tell his client, and it may well be seen as extending to cover the entire encounter from the anchor position on. In other words, this 'Thanks' closes the relationship bracket or frame, not just the frame of the preceding topic. Finally, the 'Bye', in closing the channel, extends back to cover interaction initiated by BF in placing the call. Since these forms are addressed to closing different and hierarchical brackets, their closest logical connections are not with each other, as closely as they may be articulated together.

There is a second question, however, which is of probably even greater significance. These three forms – 'OK', 'Thanks', 'Bye' – are not spoken as a one-person sequence. In each case there is an intervening contribution (we assume) of the other conversational partner. We do not know, of course, what his contribution has been in this case. The evidence we have is only the pauses between these closes. Nevertheless, abundant evidence may be gleaned from almost any telephone call that each of these closes is offered as a move in a negotiation towards a close.

We have discussed 'OK' above. This final 'OK' is not the only occurrence in these telephone calls. In each case when 'OK' is used, except for the last, it can be seen quite clearly as being offered as BF's signal that he, at least, is ready to terminate. In some cases, this is what happens. In other cases, the other speaker maintains the topic through several more turns. In other words, 'OK' cannot be interpreted as a unilateral close of the topical frame; it is one speaker's move which must be reciprocated by the other speaker in order to form a closure. I would argue that 'Thanks' and 'Bye' form reciprocal pairs of closes as well. Each is offered as a move to close a bracket or frame, but the bracket is not closed until the closure is ratified by the other participant.

Pre-emptive closure

I am now in a position to offer an interpretation of the telephone behaviour of the two-year old whom I mentioned above. Moves in opening or closing the frames of topic, relationship and channel are reciprocated movements, not unilateral movements. A telephone conversation is a social interaction, that is, participants move together in constructing the openings of the nested frames. In that sense at no level does the interaction 'belong' unilaterally to one of the participants; he or she must signal his or her intention to open or close a frame and then wait until that intention is acknowledged and reciprocated before moving on. In such social interaction, unilateral moves become communications of disregard of or even hostility towards the other.

The child I observed showed his awareness of the opening social neutrality or even friendliness expected in normal telephone calls. He closed the interaction by showing his awareness of the extreme hostility which can be communicated by the pre-emptive closing of the channel without reciprocated closings of topic and relationship.

Further analysis of these three business telephone calls shows that the ends of telephone calls close out the frames opened up at the beginning. The hierarchy of matters to be dealt with at the beginning – that is, channel, relationship, and then topic – is symmetrically tied up in a reciprocated sequence of closes, first of topic, then of relationship, and finally of channel. Far from being a simple and fixed closing formula, the sequence 'OK. Thanks. Bye.' reflects reciprocated attention to the hierarchical structure of the telephone call as an instance of the social practices which mediate social interaction.

MAXIMS OF STANCE

Now I am in a position in which I can present a fuller statement and rephrasing of what I have called above the Maxims of Stance. In opening a discourse:

1. Attend to the channel. Attend to the social interaction, including any mechanical carriers such as the telephone connection.
2. When (or if) the channel may be taken for granted, attend to the relationship(s) among the participants. Produce claims of

identity, conventional or culturally given relationships, or undertake the constitution of relationships.

3. When (or if) the relationships may be taken for granted, attend to the introduction of the first topic. Once the relationships are mutually ratified, or if the relationships are conventionally given, e.g., taxi driver and passenger, the initiator may exercise his or her right (and responsibility) to produce the purported reason for having initiated the discourse.

A discourse is closed with a corresponding, though perhaps more simply stated, set of three maxims:

4. Close the topic frame.
5. Close the relationship frame.
6. Close the channel frame.

Taken as hierarchical frames these maxims may be schematically drawn as in Figure 2.1.

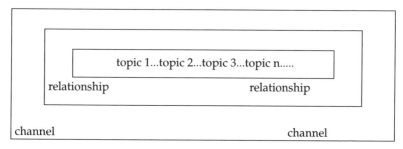

Figure 2.1: Maxims of Stance

Business telephone calls show evidence that topics are of a lower social-interactional priority than the positioning of speakers and hearers. They are hierarchically bracketed within social relationships as part of the larger social interaction. Similarly, the relationship-positioning frame in which the social interaction is constituted is bracketed within the larger frame of the constitution of the channel of communication.

As I will argue with regards to news discourse, these hierarchical frames are the basis in social practice by which participants in a community of practice construct the discursive power relations among themselves. The power to open or construct a channel preempts the lesser power of acting as a principle. That power in turn may be used to delegate topics and voice to other participants. Thus the Maxims of Stance, as I have called them, provide a framework in social practice for the discussion of the negotiation of identity.

FROM TELEPHONE CALLS TO NEWS DISCOURSE

My strategy in this book is to open with this discussion of the implicational hierarchy in real-time social interaction of situation, identity, and topic as reflected in the Maxims of Stance. Beginning in the next chapter, I will argue that the power alignments which are negotiated, the identities which are constructed, and the topics which are introduced in news discourse, whether it is on the production side of the journalists or on the receptive side of the readers and viewers are negotiated and constructed within the same social practices we have just discussed in this study of business telephone calls.

From the point of view of the production of news discourse, I will argue that the broadest domain in which power is exercised is the power to frame communicative events. This exemplifies the first maxim to attend to or construct the channel or situation. Within that is the power to position participants in relationship to each other. This positioning is done by delegation of both the rights to speak or write, as is done by editors and presenters, and the rights to topics, as is done by reporters with regards to newsmakers.

As I will argue, beginning in Chapter 3, the relationship between the producers and receivers of news discourse is that of spectacle and observer. While the journalists are primarily engaged in producing a spectacle for the observation of readers and viewers, I will argue that the primary social interaction, that is, the interaction in which they are entrained as participants in real-time social practice, is primarily among themselves. I will argue that this is the same sort of spectacle-for-observation which is played out on sports fields among players of games for the observation of both live and broadcast spectators. Although the game is played *for* the spectators, it is played *among* the athletes, referees, and other on-the-field performers.

Because my argument depends upon this spectacle–observer relationship, in the following chapter I will first take up the social practices of observation in an analysis of reading and watching as social interactions among readers, watchers, and others socially co-present with them. Following Sartre (1969 [1943]), Burke (1945) and Goffman (1974), I will argue that a dramatistic metaphor of performance-for-observation is a productive way of reconceptualizing the now tired and misleading sender–receiver metaphor of communication (Reddy 1979). It is to this analysis of acts of reading and watching I now turn.

NOTES

1. Here I should hasten to indicate that Goffman's characterization of the 'with' is largely relevant to 'withs' constructed in North America among hearing participants. Japanese may orientate their bodies towards a common vanishing point as if they are all watching a game or other spectacle and 'withs' using sign language may remain at a considerable distance from each other as long as a straight line of sight can be maintained.
2. Engeström (1997) has cogently argued that no principled distinction can be made between conceptual tools such as a language and concrete tools such as telephones.
3. Elsewhere I have used the term 'discourse system' in what may appear at first sight to correspond to 'community of practice' (Scollon and Scollon 1995a). In this case if I were to talk of a 'banking discourse system' I would mean a much broader discourse in the Foucaultian sense of an order of discourse in which bankers world-wide might participate. Here I mean to focus more closely on a probable (though in this case not attested) group of people who often work together, who know each other on a face-to-face basis, and who recognize each other as members of the same group.

THREE

Acts of reading and watching: observation as social interaction

METHODOLOGICAL HEURISTICS

A newspaper story or a television news story are just two of the many kinds of text we read and watch. In this analysis I do not want to focus only on printed text, however, but also mean to include television programming, commercials, printed advertisements, hand-bills, and any other of the semiotic genres that might be included within the broad spectrum of communications. For ease of exposition I will adopt the practice of media and critical studies (O'Sullivan et al. 1994) of referring to all of these forms of text simply as 'texts' from words to images, whether printed or video or audio, and only when necessary specify the particular kind of text such as 'news-paper story' or 'commercial text'. I will also use the single verb 'read' to cover the wide range of interpretive processes from reading printed texts to watching a television movie.

My analysis of business telephone calls in Chapter 2 presented three hierarchical social practices which interpolate social practices of power into the common task of telephoning. At the broadest level there is the social practice of defining the situation or of fram-ing the event. I worded this as the maxim: Attend to the channel. There I suggested that the power to construct the channel is the unilateral power to pre-empt anything carried on that channel. Whether it is a personal telephone call among friends or a telephone summit between heads of state, whoever has the power to disrupt the line transmission has the power to intervene between the callers, at least temporarily to disrupt their relationship positioning, and to disrupt their topic. This is attested by telephone callers when the line is broken. When transmission is resumed they engage in res-toration of the relationship positioning ('You didn't hang up on me, did you?' 'No, it must have just been something wrong with the system.') as well as in topic restoration ('Well, as I was about to say . . .'). Perhaps for this reason heads of state have 'secure' telephone lines which in this case means that they entrust the care of the telephone lines to official branches of the government to be protected by state military power.

I would like now to rephrase this first maxim somewhat more broadly so that we can include not only telephone calls across a technological channel but also all forms of social interaction as was originally done by Schegloff (1972). I would like to focus on the definition of the situation or the communicative event (Gumperz and Hymes 1972; Saville-Troike 1989) and to rephrase this first maxim as:

1. Attend to the definition of the situation (including the channel).

The second and third maxims may also need rephrasing as we go along, but the essential focus remains the same. Subordinate to attending to the definition of the situation, the participants attend to the positioning of their relationships and, again, subordinate to that, they take up the texts, topics or communicative focus of the situation. Having said that, it is important to make it clear that I do not mean to be suggesting that these three social practices do not interdiscursively interpenetrate each other. It could be argued, for example, that the sole function of particular topics or the introduction of particular texts in a situation is to negotiate the positioning of the participants or even to negotiate the definition of the situation. I do not mean to suggest that these must follow in any chronological sequence in any particular event, though the literature on conversational analysis and my analysis of news stories below both show quite regular sequencing. What I argue is just that there is an implicational hierarchy among these three levels of social practice. One can change topics without disrupting the sense of the situation but it is much more difficult to argue that one can change the situation without in some way disrupting topical continuity.

Now what I would like to suggest is that as a methodological heuristic it is useful to begin an analysis at the level of the broadest of these maxims. In a way, of course, that is what I have done in Chapter 2. I rather unilaterally defined the subject of analysis as business telephone calls. That is, I presupposed the fundamental question: What is the situation here? What is the mediated action taking place in which the participants are engaged and which I am going to analyse. I simply named it business telephone calls. In any case one might always do otherwise and it is a recurring methodological problem to know at what level to define the situations one studies. Here I am suggesting that the framework we are using here poses the mediated action as the primary unit of analysis and so the analysis most naturally unfolds from that point. Thus I propose as a methodological heuristic that we begin our analysis in the same place. I argue that participants must begin by asking: What is going on here? What sort of mediated action is taking place? What sort of situation are the participants in and how do they signal that among themselves and come to at least a standing agreement? From this will follow the other questions of what mediational means are being used, how those mediational means support or undermine their actions and how those mediational means are instrumental in interpolating sociocultural practices into the ongoing event. To put it another way, the first concern is always a concern with what is somewhat misleadingly called 'context'.

METAPHORS OF CONTEXT

Kenneth Burke was one of the first of contemporary analysts to call our attention to the role of context in interpretation. In one of his late essays he wrote, 'Let us suppose that I ask you: "What did the man say?" And that you answer: "He said 'yes.'" You still do not know what the man said. You would not know unless you knew more about the situation and about the remarks that preceded his answer' (Burke 1989: 77 [Originally published 1973]).

Researchers have focused on at least two aspects of contexts, what Burke (1945) in much earlier work called the situation[1] and what Shannon and Weaver (1949) called the channel. In such studies the situation (scene, or setting) really refers to anything which participants might call upon to make sense of what is said from the time of day and the place to the manner in which the participants are dressed or their tone of voice (Saville-Troike 1989). The five elements put forward by Burke (1945) – act, scene, agent, agency and purpose – formed the basis of Hymes's (1972) categories for the study of the ethnography of communication. Like Burke, Hymes was concerned not simply with a journalistic analysis of the five Ws – Who, What, Where, When and Why – but was concerned with the ways in which any communication must be interpreted against

the stance taken in the implied author). These distinctions are also discussed in Ong (1982) as underlying any understanding of how the written form transforms not only the language but the person in communicative events.

While the distinction between real and implied communicative roles has been a very stimulating insight, the problem remains of coming to understand just how such implications or conventionalizations come into force. In face-to-face interaction it has been argued that these face relationships are negotiated in an ongoing, real-time process of conversational inference (Gumperz 1977, 1992). What is more difficult to analyse as *social interaction* are the processes by which such stances come to be more rigidly stabilized, that is, conventionalized.

This same conventionalizing aspect of written communication has been couched in somewhat different terms, but with the same conceptual force, in the term audience design used by Bell in his analysis of the language of news media (Bell 1991). That is, a writer writes to an assumed audience with certain assumed characteristics of education, class, gender, age, social group membership, attitudes, and interests.[8]

Two problems with this phrasing of the reception metaphor have been discussed in the literature. In the first place, Duranti and Goodwin (1992), in using a very similar term, recipient design, have argued that all communications, written or oral, face-to-face or mechanical, display characteristics of recipient design. This, in fact, is another, and perhaps more general way of phrasing the earlier concerns with face relationships. The difference, however, is that it is coming to be recognized that not everything that happens in face-to-face interaction is negotiated on the spot; many aspects show the same sort of scripting, formulization and conventionalization that has been analysed in written communications. In other words, one has still not come to account for just *how* such conventionalizations come into existence.

Furthermore, Bell has introduced the term 'referee design' to argue that often communications are couched in terms not of either the producer or the receiver but of some non-present third party. Common examples are seen in, but not limited to, advertising in which a language is used which is not the language of either the producer or the receiver for various effects such as the use of English in Japanese advertising, Italian in Hong Kong advertising, or French in American advertising to signal prestige or internationalization.[9]

The channel or conduit metaphor mentioned above (Reddy 1979) proved to be productive in certain areas of study such as raising the light on problematical aspects of establishing the basis for communication. The face metaphor furthered the agenda of more closely examining ways in which the language used in communication is reflective of as well as constitutive of the relationships among the participants. Dodging problems of the interpretive context through using terms such as conventionalization and through the scheme of using the metaphor of scripts and schemata has only postponed dealing with these issues. Once we have seen that the context itself is not simply the mechanical frame placed upon communication nor the mechanical conduit through which it occurs, it becomes necessary to face up to the socially constructed nature of these frames and contexts themselves. As Schegloff has recently put it, 'If context is *in* the conduct itself, if it *is* in a sense the conduct itself, then rethinking context is the omnipresent job of analysis' (1992: 215).

But are we likely to escape from the use of metaphor? We are not, but I would argue that we must use our metaphors with caution, asking of each in turn not only what is being highlighted, but also what is being obscured. The metaphors of communication based upon messages, channels, and contexts tend to keep the focus on the message itself. That is, when context is used as a metaphor to mean 'what is around' (but what is not *in*) the communication, our attention is diverted from the social aspects of communication. The message or informational aspects of communication are highlighted no matter what attempts are otherwise made to focus upon other aspects of communication such as the relationships or the identity of participants, which are my central interest. For that the metaphor of the theatre of discourse seems more productive.

My concern with the social construction of the person in the public discourse of newspapers and television goes considerably beyond any concept of the person which can be encompassed within terms such as writer and reader. On the production side there is a wide range of persons from newsmakers, their speech writers, their agents, and their spokespersons to journalists including stringers who work in the field for various news-gathering organizations and on-the-spot reporters to news agency writers and editors and local news organization writers and editors. Still on the production side are various animators (Goffman 1974, 1981) of the texts, including printers, along with the mechanics who repair the word processors and printing presses. Intermediate between the producers and the receivers are distributors, news-stand sellers, and home delivery agents. Among receivers are, again, a wide range of users from children who read only the youth pages, shippers who concentrate on the shipping news, and those whose only interest is the daily crossword puzzle. There are those who read a story and then tell others about it. Furthermore, there are those for whom the daily newspaper is packaging material, material on which to lay out vegetables in the market, and teachers for whom daily editorials are the stuff of lessons in grammar and even discourse.

In his 1972 essay, upon which most work in the ethnography of communication has been based, Hymes used Burke's (1945) dramatistic-rhetorical view of communication as his organizing metaphor.[10] Hymes points out that this shift in rhetorical base which Burke had brought about signalled more than just a shift in terminology. He showed that the shift to a dramatistic view of communication signalled a shift from a focal emphasis on persuasion to identification as the key concept in rhetorical and communication studies. Burke's own way of speaking of this dramatistic perspective was not as a metaphorical base but as a 'representative anecdote' (Burke 1945). For Burke, and therefore for Hymes, the key question driving an ethnographic analysis of communication is not so much 'What is being said and how do we interpret it?' as it is 'What identities and memberships does one signal by speaking in this way rather than in another?' Though one aspect of communication can never be entirely separated from another, the representative anecdote of the theatre of discourse is a story about who we are more than about what we are saying.

The analytical method of the representative anecdote, while first associated with Burke as a method in literary criticism (1945, 1950) was a major influence on the sociologist Goffman, especially beginning with his study of the presentation of self in everyday life (1959).[11] This use of dramatistic analysis was not so much a matter of introducing anthropology into rhetorical or critical analysis as recognizing in ethnographic studies the presence of elements of rhetorical analysis (Burke 1989). For both Burke and Goffman the primary representative anecdote was the theatre, though they used this approach in rather different ways. Gusfield (1989) points out that for Goffman theatre was not a metaphor for life, it was life itself. As Gusfield puts it, Goffman's title *The Presentation of Self in Everyday Life* might as well have been worded 'How to Convince Others That You are Who You Claim to Be' (1989: 22). It should be further noted that Goffman used the term 'dramaturgical' rather than 'dramatistic'.

Burke used the dramatistic representative anecdote to signal that the language by which we critically describe theatre is also an effective language in which we can describe day-to-day human action. It is a language of actors, scenes, motives, roles, and even of tragedy and of redemption.

Finally, there is in the use of the representative anecdote or the metaphor of the theatre of discourse an interest in understanding point of view. Again, the concern is with seeing communication from the point of view of human actors who are using communication to position themselves and others within a discourse as particular kinds of person who are making particular claims about themselves and about others. Such questions of point of view in discourse have recently been studied under the influence of new translations of the critical writings of Bakhtin (1981a).

While the study of the dialogic or heteroglossic nature of discourse is currently attributed to the writings of Bakhtin, it should be observed that there is a convergence here of two lines of research and two metaphorical bases, the dramatistic/critical (Burke) and the dramaturgical/sociological (Goffman) on the one hand, in which theatre is taken as the primary representative anecdote, and the novelistic/critical writings of Bakhtin, in which the novel is taken as the representative anecdote on the other. The confluence of these two lines is not far to seek. In Goffman's (1974) very influential, but perhaps not so widely read, *Frame Analysis*, he registers his debt to Uspensky (1973).[12] Uspensky, for his part, registers throughout his book a deep indebtedness to, among others, the writings of Bakhtin. One might suppose, therefore, that the apparent convergence of the dramatistic/dramaturgical and novelistic/critical lines of thought were less a question of accidental convergence and more a matter of influence.

These several lines of thought, critical writing, scholarship, and research[13] have now all but completely converged under a wide variety of headings. One finds a lifetime ethnographer, Geertz, writing of 'authoring selves' (1986). On the other hand, one sees a recent book of essays called *The Ethnography of Reading* (Boyarin 1993) which a decade ago would have been thought primarily critical or literary in nature.[14]

The metaphor of a theatre of discourse has brought with it not just a change in the focus of research/scholarship away from a focus on the message, its information content, and the interpretive process towards a focus on the social construction of identities and member-ship, it has also brought a considerable interdiscursivity of analytical methodology.[15] I have already mentioned the method of the repre-sentative anecdote. As Goffman described his method, he argued that the examples he gave could not be said to be true either in some large categorical sense or true in some statistical or probablistic testable way for some population. He felt that they could be said to have been true at least once – in the case he had analysed – and also that they could be hoped to be true in some broader logical sense that they would stand the test of critical analysis. It should be clear that this standard of veracity places such ethnographic work considerably closer to the practices of literary criticism and rhetor-ical analysis than to the quantitative methods used by many other sociologists.

Hymes in a similar way has argued that at least in some cases – he would never allow this as one's only method – it is justifiable to engage in what he calls 'sociolinguistic restatement' (Hymes 1972: 51, but also see Hymes 1966). The ethnography of communication, or, as I am narrowing the scope, the interactional sociolinguistic study of mediated discourse, relies on a wide variety of sources of observation from carefully recorded, transcribed and analysed field data of instances of discourse which owe their methodological rigour to standard methods used for well over a century now in linguistic field studies to careful reading and sociolinguistic restate-ment of historical studies and even contemporary popular culture. The key lies in the concept of sociolinguistic restatement which we can take to mean testing any concepts, data or observations from any source in a contrastive[16] ongoing ethnographic analysis of the field of discourse whether they be a direct observation made by the researcher, a statement in a published history of the subject, a transcribed strip of conversation, a dictated life history of a tribal elder or, indeed, today's newspaper or a moment from this evening's television news broadcast.

'THE LOOK' IN THE SOCIAL CONSTRUCTION OF SELF

Goffman argues (1981) that the social nature of virtually all of our behaviour can be seen in the *oops*, *eeks*, and *whews* we utter even when alone. One walks along the street, trips over a crack in the pavement, mutters a curse, and then turns to examine the spot as if calling on all other observers to support us in our view that we have been tripped up unjustly and through no carelessness of our own. We behave, even on our own, as if we are being seen by others. We behave, in Goffman's analysis, like we are under the requirement to move through spaces in socially appropriate ways whether or not it is obvious that others are watching us.

It is not clear to me if Goffman intended to resonate in his analysis with Sartre's (1969 [1943]) study of 'the look'; though Kendon, an analyst close to Goffman in spirit at least, does specifically reference *Being and Nothingness*. Sartre writes of the voyeur who, secretly looking through a keyhole at some scene, starts when he hears footsteps. His heart beats faster, he assumes some other posture to disguise his voyeuristic activities in the hopes that he will not be caught, and only when the noise proves not to be another person, a second person secretly observing *him*, does he go back to peering through the keyhole. But in this second instance of looking, Sartre sees the primary situation – one has one's being brought into existence, whether as voyeur or simply as a person – through the 'look' of the 'other'.

More recently, Foucault has argued that the consciousness of self as it has developed in Europe owes much to 'the gaze' of professional, authoritative and expert others. Thus he argues that the human sciences themselves are predicated upon the clinical gaze of such professionals as psychiatrists and ethnographers (1973a, 1973b), the rule of law along with its punishments are equally predicated in the disciplinary view of authority (1977), and that both the contemporary concept of law and the contemporary concept of scientific observation are rooted in the 'pastoral gaze' of the confessional of the pre-Renaissance church (Gordon 1980). Goodwin (1994) much more recently shows how the authoritative vision of the other is socially constructed in the activities of professional training and practice in two quite diverse professional fields, archeology and forensic legal witnessing.

For Goffman, Kendon and Goodwin, as for Sartre before them and their contemporary Foucault, the human reality is a social reality and as a social reality it comes into existence by the interaction of observation by others and the awareness of being a third person, an object in the perception of others in the social world. Goffman (1974) takes a dramatistic view of this reality, arguing that our lives as humans are played out as a kind of theatre on the stage of the perceptions of others. He believes that 'a central function of talk is to provide the talker with some means of taking up a self-saving alignment to what is happening around him even while he forgoes any immediate effort to redirect the situation' (Goffman 1974: 501). For Goffman, the human self is not the atomistic, independent, autonomous, and internally motivated entity out of which society is constructed. 'Self, then, is not an entity half-concealed behind events, but a changeable formula for managing oneself during them' (1974: 573). Goffman's view of the self is that it is largely derived from the social circumstances in which we play out our roles. As he puts it elsewhere, 'Whenever we are issued a uniform, we are likely to be issued a skin' (1974: 575).

While it may seem a bit far afield from this discussion to look into Chinese etymology, there is some evidence of a very similar understanding of the nature of the self being constituted in reference to the observation of others. The word *xing*,[17] for example, carries a range of meanings including 'to examine oneself critically' and 'to visit parents or elders'. It seems clear that from Zhou Chinese to the present there have been associated two not entirely polysemous meanings which suggest that critical self-examination is fostered within the environment of one's parents or elders.

There is further ethnographic evidence that contemporary Chinese are well aware of the potential of which Sartre writes, that the voyeur himself may be observed, that is, of 'the look' itself being subjected to 'the look'. In a discussion of ethnographic observation of Goffman's 'withs' (Goffman 1971) I had with two research assistants, both of them Hong Kong Cantonese–English bilinguals in their twenties, I commented that we were interested not only in making ethnographic observations, but in our own activities as observers. This latter was to include noting to what extent we ourselves were being observed and to what extent that higher framed observation might have an impact on our own perception of the situation. One of these research assistants said to the other *'tohng lohng'*. The other nodded immediate understanding. The full phrase being referenced is,

Tohng lohng bouh sihm, wohng jeuk joih hauh. (Cantonese)
Tang lang bu chan, huang que zai hou. (Putonghua)
mantis stalks cicada, oriole at back
'While the mantis stalks the cicada, the oriole behind stalks the mantis.'

This *chengyu* or common phrase is found in most Chinese dictionaries of such common phrases and idioms. It is attributed to Zhuangzi (Chuang Tzu) (Wang 1987), giving as the primary meaning that it is dangerous to plot against another as one may find that one is oneself being plotted against.

Whether one argues from the sociology of Goffman, the existential philosophy of Sartre, the postmodernist thought of Foucault, the social scientific analyses of face-to-face interaction of Kendon and Goodwin, ethnographic awareness of the paradoxes of participant observation, Chinese etymology, or Chinese folk tradition, the point I wish to call attention to here is that it can be argued that the human self, to the extent that it is social, is constituted in the fact as well as the potential of observation by others. To put it more succinctly, we are what we are seen to be.

POSING AND WATCHING

As one social site within which to examine the social construction of the observer, I have conducted a study of the taking of photographs in public settings. The heuristic question is: What is going on here? or What kind of situation is this? I will argue that from the participants' view at the broadest level it would be called going out for a walk and within that taking a photo in one type of event I have studied or in the other type of event it would be called the formal outdoor wedding photo.[18]

From these observations I will argue that one can distinguish a kind of social activity, watching, in which a particular kind of posed or conventionalized self is constructed through socially formulated observation, the photographed person. My general purpose here is to provide a basis for understanding the social construction of a much wider set of observers from readers of newspapers and viewers of television to spectators at ball games and ethnographers.

Goffman's 'with'

Goffman (1971) defines a with[19] as follows: 'A with is a party of more than one whose members are perceived to be "together"' (p. 19). The with contrasts with a 'single' which is a person operating as a social isolate. Perhaps it will be useful to bear in mind that a with is a temporary grouping of two or more people; it is not a permanent grouping nor one that has status beyond the current social interaction. That is, it is not a community of practice (Lave and Wenger 1991).

Withs normally display 'ecological proximity', that is, the members maintain a degree of closeness which may be read by others socially present that they are together. A with excludes non-members through what Goffman (1971) calls 'civil inattention', that is to say, non-members though they may be within visual and other perceptual fields are treated as not having currently ratified communicative status with members of the with.

A corollary of the communicative distinction between members and non-members of withs is that members have the right to initiate talk among members and the conversation of any is potentially accessible to all. Of course, several side conversations may be taking place simultaneously in a with of four or five, as often happens at dinner parties or in travelling groups. In such circumstances any member may jump between conversations or ask for portions to be repeated without having first to establish a state of communication. Therefore, a with engages in ritual practices for joining and for withdrawing, such as greetings and departures. Outsiders wishing to join a with, then, recognize that they must defer to the priority status current members enjoy in relationship to each other. Finally, members of a with generally enjoy greater latitude in their behaviour than any of them would enjoy as singles, while in exchange for this greater latitude comes being subjected to shared judgement of their behaviour.

The 'togetherness' of a with is seen through what Goffman calls 'tie-signs' (1971). Two teenage girls are walking through a crowded shopping centre. I aim to pass between them and then notice that each of them has one end of stereophonic earphones from a walkman in her ear. This rather literal electronic and presumably musical tie between the two girls goes beyond the tie-signs written of by Goffman in pre-walkman days, but it illustrates just one of the many ways in which withs may be perceived as being together.

There are two aspects of withs which are of interest to me in this study of watching. The first of these is that in any with, members repeatedly negotiate exchanges of observer status. Researchers such as Kendon (1994), Goodwin (1981, 1986b) and Duranti and Goodwin (1992) argue that the recipient role is crucial to the definition of both the communicative situation and the producer's role. That is to say, the social statuses of observers in withs cannot be studied in isolation, but must be seen to be jointly constructed in interactions among members of withs. Most studies of communicative statuses have been studies of withs whether or not this terminology has been used, and so any study of observers is to some extent a logical extension of the studies of withs.

A 'watch'

Studies of withs have prospered because members of withs engage in constant, active and mutual processes of feedback among members. This allows researchers to go beyond analytical inferences about what tie-signs mean, for example, by checking their inferred meanings against the progress of the social interaction. A touch might be inferred to be a tie-sign of the change signal type, a person making an 'advance' upon another. This interpretation can be greatly strengthened if subsequently the touched party moves into closer proximity and engages in reciprocal touching. The same inference would likely be justified if the second party backs away or slaps the first toucher.

My interest, however, is in social interactions in which the idea of social interaction involves polarization between a primary watcher or watchers and a poser or posers, what I will call the spectacle. When a person sits alone reading a book, can this be thought of as a social interaction? Although a number of writers talk loosely of interactions between writers and readers, I would like to have a common framework for understanding the whole range of possible watchings from a person reading a book to a large crowd watching a football match and even including one or more watching that same match on television. I want a framework for talking about readers of newspapers, listeners to an academic lecture, hecklers at a Hyde Park political speech, passersby glancing at a street brawl, or in this case photographers taking a few pictures of their friends or children in front of the old Kowloon–Canton Railroad tower in Tsimshatsui.

The strategic problem is that in many of these cases there are limits on feedback which are either socially or technologically grounded and I am not yet convinced that there is a theoretical reason for treating these two types of limits as different cases. We know of course that the ordinary television viewer cannot interrupt the presenter by saying, 'Wait a minute, I don't quite see what you mean there'.

Of course this technological barrier to actual social interaction can be exploited by viewers making apparently real interactive commentary to the spectacle. On the other hand, conventions of social interaction may provide an equally inpenetrable barrier to the give and take between co-present participants in some cases. Jurors are a fairly clear example of participants in a social interaction who have highly restricted opportunities to interrupt or comment interactively within the framework of courtroom discussions, even though they are significant players in the scene.

Furthermore, it seems that in some cases, such as watching television sports, there is often a fairly high level of synchronously entrained social activity between the producers of the spectacle being observed (the players of the game) and the watching participants, even though the communicative activities of the watchers is not accessible to the players and so cannot be thought of as social interaction between players and observers. This is the case, in fact, whether or not the spectacle being observed is a game on television or a fireworks display which elicits highly synchronous cries of 'Waaaa!'

A watch, then, may be defined as

> any person or group of people who are perceived to have attention to some spectacle as the central focus of their (social) activity. The spectacle together with its watchers constitutes the watch.

The person or people of the watch may consist of a single (reading a book) or a with (a couple watching a film) or indeed many withs (a football match). The spectacle may be a wide range of things which may be looked at whether static (an historical monument) or active (a fireworks display), present (a university lecture) or mediated (a movie), 'live' (a news broadcast) or 'canned' (a documentary), or any combination of these (a video display used by a lecturer within a lecture).

For the moment I see no reason to make any separation among spectacles in wholly mediated form (books, films, videos, recordings, photos, paintings, monuments), partially mediated form (lectures, concerts, public forums with microphones and amplification) and without mediation (passersby, brawlers, families out for a

Sunday stroll, lovers on a park bench, or ethnographically observed 'natives'). From the point of view I am taking it is the socially constructed polarization of interactive statuses between the spectacle and the watchers which is crucial in defining the watch, not the technology of the barrier.

Nevertheless, it might later be necessary to consider cross-over behaviour as when the fans at a football match pour down on to the field to interrupt the game. In the definition above the word 'social' is put into parentheses because it remains to be argued that the activity of a watch is, in fact, a form of social activity.

A watch may consist of a single, a with, or multiple withs; in any event the social status of the single or with, as with, is different from that of the with or its members as a watch. To make this distinction clearer it will be useful to talk about 'view-signs' to distinguish them from tie-signs.

View-signs, like tie-signs for withs, are the evidence one might use to decide that one was observing a watch. Laughing in synchrony with the studio audience (or recorded laughter) on a television sitcom would be a potential view-sign. The most obvious, of course, would be body orientation and gaze directed towards the spectacle; though this in itself is hardly sufficient evidence that one is a member of a watch as any lecturer or theatre performer can attest.

That a watch is a special form of social interaction, though certainly not discontinuous with the with, can be demonstrated fairly directly. For example, a couple may simultaneously be a watch (i.e., watching a movie in a darkened theatre) and display such view-signs as laughter with jokes or crying with sad moments, but at the same time display tie-signs as a with by holding hands. One can also imagine conflict between watch-connected behaviour and with-connected behaviour. One of the members of the watch/with party at the movie may give dominance to the watch (primarily enjoying the movie) while the other gives dominance to the with (primarily enjoying the hand-holding) to the mutual irritation of both.

From with to watch

A young couple walks along the waterfront in Hong Kong's Tsimshatsui on a Sunday afternoon. They are clearly a with. They stroll almost exactly in step, going forward together, pausing together, turning their faces towards each other when they exchange speaking turns, laughing together, and when one points towards something the other orientates towards the place pointed out.

This couple comes to a long fountain pool. She sits down along the bordering wall and he backs away a short distance, raises his camera and begins the preliminary operations of taking a photo of her. She meanwhile adjusts her body and clothing and begins to set a pose. They chat back and forth about postures and the like. He asks if she's ready, counts 'one, two, three . . .', while she holds a posed smile and he snaps the photo. At the snap she breaks the pose turning her head away, smiles, gets up and the couple continues strolling along.

We have observed the transformation of a with into a watch. For the brief moment of the snap one member of the with has become a spectacle by taking on this specialized posing role; at the same time the photographer has become a watcher by taking on this specialized observing role. In this transformation from with to watch and back we can outline the basic aspects of watch status as well as the differences between watches and withs.

PHOTO-EVENT FRAMING

Three frames are analytically separable in the photo-event: the setting frame the adjustment frame, and the snap frame. As these frames take place through the linear flow of time, they have both opening and closing phases and could be represented as nested brackets:

[{ ( ) }]

These brackets could be labelled:

with [setting {adjustment (snap=watch) break} setting close] with

Setting frame

Another with is a family consisting of a mother, father and two girls, one of them about six years old and a younger sister of about three years old. As a with they are enjoying the carnival, the harbour view, and the many spectacles of others taking photographs of

each other. As they enter the setting frame there is much mutual discussion about where the photo should be taken, who should be within the photographed frame, what the backdrop should be and the like. Together as a with they begin the preliminary sorting out into watchers and spectacle; members of the with begin to take on potential spectacle status along with the backdrop of the Hong Kong Cultural Centre steps, a merry-go-round in the carnival, or the view of Central buildings across the harbour. At the same time other members (most often just one) take on watcher status as the with discusses where he/she should stand and how the spectacle should be viewed in the photograph.

The setting frame, then, consists of all the preliminary activities (both talk and movements) by which the with comes to agreement about how they will polarize into spectacle and watcher. In other words, the setting frame is the discussion and behaviour among the with which characterizes what sort of a watch they are creating. These are the discursive movements by which they integrate the social practices of producing a photo (Berger 1972; Sontag 1979; Bourdieu 1990; Wells 1997) into their social interactions.

Adjustment frame

This family has decided that the mother will photograph the father and the two girls sitting on the Cultural Centre steps. Having polarized the with as spectacle and watcher, the spectacle takes up position on the steps while the mother with her camera backs down a few steps facing them and begins to adjust the camera on the one hand and to give orders to the spectacle about how to sit. For their part, the spectacle gives over attention to constructing a pose by adjusting clothing and bodies. They also begin to set smiles on their faces.

Their activities begin to show considerable asymmetry in the adjustment frame. The spectacle becomes much less active, more frozen or posed in movement. The father and older sister begin physically to restrict the movement of the littlest – he puts his arm around her which both consolidates the spectacle and holds her within the photographic frame. The photographer, on the other hand, has an increased latitude of movement and authority. She moves forward and back, from side to side; she issues orders: 'to the left',

'closer together', 'stop wiggling', 'straighten out her hair'. The status of the photographer becomes the dominant status with rights to dispose of the spectacle however it might suit the framing of the photograph.[20]

In the adjustment frame, then, both spectacle and photographer begin to display asymmetrical social rights with dominance being given over to the photographer who choses the final framing of the photograph as well as the moment in which to snap the picture. For their part the spectacle ratify this asymmetry by acquiescing quickly in carrying out the instructions of the photographer. The youngest sister, who is less socially adept in constructing her portion of the spectacle, is brought into line with subtle physical and psychological force by father and older sister who from time to time frown or laugh at her immature levels of competence.

Snap frame

At some point the photographer becomes satisfied that a suitable spectacle has been prepared for photographing. She indicates her satisfaction by saying, 'OK, are you ready?' The focus now turns towards freezing a pose. Interaction between the photographer and the spectacle becomes highly stylized or conventionalized. She puts her face behind the camera; they take on and hold smiles and frozen body postures.

None of the watches I observed had any technological reason for socially freezing the snap frame. They were all using very new, up-to-date cameras. The outside lighting was bright which would ensure that their automatic cameras would select a fast shutter speed – certainly fast enough to automatically freeze body motion into a sharply focused photograph. In the days of slower films and non-automatic cameras there might have been cause to ask the spectacle to freeze, but none of the people I observed lived in those days. I believe it can be argued that the reasons for the frozen snap frame are more socially than technologically motivated. The snap frame is the few moments in which the highly conventionalized pose is struck. Together the spectacle and the photographer reproduce the photographs of family (Sontag 1979) and fashion (Chun 1996; Wells 1997). The freezing of postures becomes a view-sign of this moment of appropriation from the broader discourses of the public media.

Closing the snap frame

There are two primary ways in which the close of the snap frame is signalled: the sound of the shutter and the flash. Most of the photographing I observed took place without flashes and therefore it was the click of the shutter which opened the closing of the snap frame.

The click is, however, only the technical signal of the closing of the snap frame; there are also social closings. Most salient are that the spectacle break their poses and the photographer drops the camera away from the face. Both of these moves are normally accomplished as short, quick and decisive gestures which signal spectacle to photographer and photographer to spectacle that the snap frame is closed.

I do not mean to make much of the word 'gesture' in this case other than to say that these are body movements which are somewhat more decisive and sharply delineated than appears necessary by simple relaxation of held postures. It becomes clear in the closing of the snap frame that the posed smiles, however radiant they may be,[21] are, in fact, posed. The eyes turn away, the head is thrown back, the body twists, shoulders orientate away and the smile becomes very subtly but perceptibly a different smile. The posed smile becomes a 'natural' smile; the view-sign becomes a tie-sign. In this subtle shift the watch begins to be decomposed again into a with.

Further evidence of this decomposition from watch to with is seen in the activities of the photographer. She moves a pace closer to the spectacle, withdraws the camera, smiles. By issuing these tie-signs she begins the formal closure of her separate and asymmetrical status. In all of the photographic watches I have observed there is a very high level of synchrony in the closing of the snap frame. It seems that there is little doubt about both how and when to dissolve the watch back into a with.

Closing the adjustment frame

Yet there are occasions on which the watch does not dissolve immediately or entirely into a with but simply returns to the adjustment frame. Photographers often take multiple pictures and so after the snap, while spectacle and photographer alike signal

partial with status by the resumption of tie-signs, they normally continue to hold their general positions and take up a bit of discussion. Spectacle participants often ask, 'Did you get it?', 'Is that OK?', 'Do you want another one?' In most cases this line of question clearly maintains the spectacle–watcher asymmetry. That is to say, one rarely hears the photographer asking whether that is sufficient.

But there are cases where the photographer does, in fact, ask the spectacle if another photo should be taken or another pose given. That is to say there are cases in which the dominance in this asymmetry appears to be on the side of the spectacle, not the photographer.

A group of three women are taking various pictures of each other in pairs. They go through all of these frames as they create spectacles to be photographed. But they want a photograph of the whole group. To accomplish this they first set themselves as a spectacle by figuring out where they want to pose, what the frame should be, and so forth. Then, having set themselves, they wait for someone to pass by who looks friendly enough to be asked to photograph them. I happen by and they ask me if I will take their picture. I agree and they then take on both roles, spectacle and photographer. They tell me where to stand, how they will pose, how to shoot the picture. After I have snapped the photo I ask, 'Is that OK?' They say, 'Could you take one more?'

This example suggests that the polarization between spectacle and watch are, in fact, situational roles not unlike Goffman's (1974, 1981) 'animator', 'author' and 'principal' – roles which might often be combined in a single person but which are not necessarily distributed in that way. The role of watcher in this case may, in fact, be analysed as consisting at a minimum of a 'director', who organizes the spectacle from choosing the participants to setting up the backdrop and taking artistic responsibility, and a 'cameraman' who does little more than operate the camera. In most of the cases I have observed, these roles are somewhat shared out among the with during the setting frame and then become polarized during the adjustment frame and finally completely polarized in the snap frame. In the case of the non-with passerby who takes the photo, only the camera operator role is distributed to a person outside the with as it becomes transformed into a watch. When the passerby has completed the camera operation at the end of the snap frame, he acknowledges that he has reached the end of the social authority which has been delegated to him and awaits further instructions

from the executive authority which has been retained in this case by the members of the spectacle.

Closing of the setting frame

When it is negotiated that no further photos will be taken at that place or in that moment, the watch finally dissolves itself and takes up again full with status. Again, high levels of synchrony are displayed at this point as the photographer moves towards the spectacle, the spectacle breaks up into members of the with. When the with is a group of people it is often the case that they then almost immediately begin to reset themselves as a different spectacle–watcher constellation. In other words, one hears, 'Now let's get one with you in the picture. I'll take it', as someone breaks from the spectacle group, moves towards the photographer, hand outstretched to take the camera, and to take up the photographer's position and role.

In most cases the closing of frames is quicker than the opening of frames, the resumption of with status appearing to be something only temporarily held in abeyance by the exigencies of getting the photograph taken. The quickness of the closing of the three frames, setting, adjustment and snap, should not blind us, however, to the sense of needing to close them which participants display. One sees this necessity in violations.

The pose is set, the camera raised, but no snap is heard. Members of the spectacle with frozen smiles like ventriloquists ask, 'Did you get it?' Until the snap is heard and the camera lowered, they display considerable hesitation in entering back into the less polarized social interaction of the adjustment frame. Likewise, after the photo is snapped, the father smiles and releases slightly the pressure on the littlest sister but does not otherwise break the set spectacle posturing in case a second photo is to be taken. Feeling the released pressure, the little girl jumps up and skips off while the father and older sister call her back while at the same time seek confirmation from the photographer that it is acceptable to break the adjustment frame. Finally, there is often a bit of lingering among the reconstituted with about the scene of the spectacle and even a bit of discussion of the now closed photo-event. Members of the spectacle may take up the position of the photographer to have a look at what the picture might have been before finally moving on to some other setting.

PHOTO-TAKING RELATIONSHIPS

Not all withs undergo a simple bipolarization when becoming a watch. A family of mother, father, older daughter and younger son comes along and sets up to take a picture. In this case the spectacle is to be the two children, the father is the photographer and the mother takes on a secondary or assisting role. She is neither spectacle nor photographer but lends her support to the construction of both activities. She is now over by the children arranging them, helping them to adjust their clothing, and encouraging them to settle into an acceptable pose. She is then over by the father smiling, waving, clapping, calling the childrens' attention and gaze to the father and the camera. But she is also not simply subsumed to the photographer's role as an assistant either since she issues directives to him to stand further back, to be sure to frame the fountain, to watch out because somebody is about to pass between the spectacle and the camera.

Finally once things are set and the adjustment frame is nearing completion she may step back a pace or two to remove herself from the watch. In fact, this watch of father-photographer and children-spectacle as a unit becomes a spectacle in her watch. As a single she can be seen to have taken a major role in creating the spectacle of father-photographing-children for her third-party observation.

Thus we can argue that there are layers of participation or frames within frames. The primary relationships between photographer (watcher) and subject (spectacle) may themselves be subsumed as a spectacle, a subject, for the active social constructive work of another observer. The original with has become a set of box-framed watches.

But this is not the only set of relationships which can obtain in the reconstruction of a with into a watch or set of watches. In larger withs it happens that one or two members set themselves off to the side from the beginning and take no role in either the primary watch construction nor in the secondary watch construction. As tertiary watchers they may include within their spectacle not just the children being photographed and not just the father–children spectacle being watched by the mother; they may also include the carnival, the scene on the Cultural Centre steps, and other aspects of the general environment. For these tertiary-level observers, the spectacle is more a happening which they watch than a spectacle they interactively assist in framing.

In such tertiary watches the three frames – setting, adjustment and snap – are more diffusely constructed and dissolved. As the with begins to evolve into the primary watch, tertiary watchers tend to drift away towards the margins, taking a wider-angle view so to speak. By disengaging from the activities of setting up the primary spectacle or the activities of the secondary watcher in moving back and forth between them, they signal during the setting frame that they intend neither to be part of the spectacle nor the watch itself. Thus they show no interest in camera settings or posings. The primary view-signs they display are taking up a position which is neither within the angle of view of the camera nor on a line with the camera towards the spectacle. Most often they take a position at oblique or nearly right angles to the most direct line from the camera to the spectacle. This position is different from the secondary watcher who is usually positioned just outside the camera frame on the spectacle side or quite near the photographer on the watcher side.

These tertiary watches further set themselves apart by establishing within-watch withs. They display a variety of tie-signs which include orientating towards each other and chatting softly so as not to be overheard by the spectacle. These tie-signs set them interactively apart from the other members of the former with which is now reconstructing itself as a watch.

Beyond tertiary watches are quaternary watches consisting of those who are watching the whole scene as a spectacle but are not in any way associated with the original with of which these more primary watches are constructed. These quaternary watches display view-signs such as not undertaking any form of social interaction with any members of the original with. Furthermore, they tend to use civil inattention; that is, if members of the original with look their way or focus their attention upon them, these quaternary watchers will look away or display manifest attention to something other than the spectacle. To put this another way, quaternary watchers will treat all of the participants in the spectacle as spectacle, but disallow individual attention to separate members and thus maintain an effective social barrier to further interaction.

One form of momentary watch arises when a single or a with is walking along and discovers that they are in danger of passing into the territory of a watch then being constructed. A person walking along sees somebody off to the right setting up a pose. To the left is a person with a camera. There is a momentary assessment of whether this watch is within the setting frame, in which case passage is allowed, the adjustment frame, in which case passage is questionable, or the snap frame, in which case circumnavigation is expected. The passerby thus engages in a momentary watch with the picture-taking watch as his or her spectacle. In my observations it is often the case that once this person (or with) has passed by (or halted to avoid disrupting the snap frame) he, she, or they will pause and continue to watch until the setting frame has been dissolved.

FRAMED OBSERVATIONS AND CHAINED OBSERVATIONS

But is it useful to distinguish what might be called framed observations from chained observations? Or might a watcher single out any portion of the spectacle for special attention rather than having the entire watch remain as a unitary spectacle?

In some cases a person sitting on the Cultural Centre steps watches another person. These two are related as a watch, although, of course, not one which has arisen from a former with; they are strangers to each other. Normally, if the spectacle notices that he or she is, in fact, a spectacle for the watcher, some corrective action is usually taken. Our society[22] does not accept unmitigated staring at somebody except under circumstances in which the person being stared at has been socially transformed into an acceptable spectacle. For example, as the spectacle moves into the snap frame it is quite common for all kinds of passersby to stop and unabashedly stare at the person or persons being photographed.

I have observed two types of corrective behaviour. In the first case the person observed looks back at the observer, the observer directs his or her attention elsewhere and the denial of watch has been achieved. That is to say, the spectacle has displayed by this challenging return look that he or she does not accept spectacle status. Normally, shortly afterwards there is a second glance by the nominated spectacle to see that the rejection has been accomplished. If the watcher has moved on to other sights, nothing further happens. If, however, the spectacle sees that the watcher continues to look, he or she takes further action to reject spectacle status. This is most commonly to turn about completely or to walk away.

In one case I observed the nominated spectacle did not have the option of walking away. He was a government worker who was cleaning up the steps. I noticed a tourist setting up to take a picture of this man. The man noticed he was being selected as a spectacle and turned slightly. Glancing back again he noticed that the photographer was still preparing the adjustment frame. The cleaner then took off his hat, pulled out a handkerchief and began to wipe his face and continued to do so until the photographer lost interest and left. As it was a rather cool day, the worker was far from overheated, and the face wiping lasted for nearly two minutes, it seems clear that this should be understood as a kind of anti-view-sign, a rejection of potential spectacle status.

The other form of corrective behaviour I have observed when a person is selected for spectacle status is for that person to redirect his or her attention to the spectacle he or she is observing. Thus I have observed a wedding party being photographed by what appeared to be a professional photographer. That watch, in turn, was being photographed by one of the tertiary members of the wedding party. That whole group was being photographed by a passing tourist and I photographed those three photographers and their spectacles as my spectacle. Turning around I noticed on a walkway up above the entire scene several tourists taking wide-angle photographs of the entire scene.

What seems to legitimate such focused observation is that the spectacle accepts the negotiation through the setting and adjustment frames to enter the snap frame. Even within the adjustment frame, much otherwise unacceptable observation by unassociated observers is tolerated as attention is given over to the construction of the snap frame.

Framed observations can then be distinguished from chained observations. In a chained observation, someone might be observing an observer without taking an interest in what that observer is himself or herself watching. That is, the interest is not in that person as part of another watch but as a single as his or her own spectacle. In some cases one observes a person, at first without awareness of their status as participants in a watch (either as spectacle or watcher). Then one becomes aware of the other frame, and that resets one's own interpretive frame. Further, the behaviour of the members of the spectacle is different depending upon their own perception of the situation. There is a cline of engrossment from greatest for primary spectacles to least for quaternary observers such that primary spectacles almost never let secondary, tertiary or quaternary observers distract them from the primary watch frame. Their gaze does not wander from the camera except at moments of adjustment of equipment, body and clothes. Their concern for other observers and watches of which they may unwittingly form a part is not that they are observers but that they are potential disturbers of the primary watch; they might move between the spectacle and the camera and become part of the photograph.

Thus these outer observers are themselves subject to observation by the primary spectacle and photographer, but only to the extent that they are confirmed to be accepting their observer roles. On the outer frame, watchers who see themselves being observed may either deny observer status (rare) by looking away from the primary scene, or ignore their own spectacle status by continued looking at the spectacle. They may go further to readjust their own position to be seen to continue their watch unobstructed. Thus the pose of the watcher as spectacle is that of an interested observer. Once this pose is taken, no further denial of spectacle status takes place. These constitute framed observations.

In a chained set of observations, when an observer becomes aware of being observed, his or her first concern is to display his or her own observer status by taking an observer–spectacle pose and reorientating to the primary (or lower frame) spectacle. If he or she then notes that the chained observer maintains his or her interest in him or her (but not as being within the watch), then a refusal occurs, turning a back, staring down the observer, and so forth. What seems crucial in the distinction between framed and chained observations is that the observer–spectacle checks to see if he or she is being individually framed for focused observation or as part of a watch. It seems that being part of a watch is easily accepted but to be singled out as a spectacle is rejected.

POSING

Primary spectacles

Much of what I want to say about posing has already been said or implied. A primary spectacle, a person or a group, works at accomplishing a pose during the adjustment frame and then holds that pose during the snap frame. While I will not elaborate on it here, the mediational means appropriated in this posing, at least in Hong Kong, are the ubiquitous fashion photos in magazines, newspapers, and on light-box posters in the Mass Transit Railway. Chun (1996) argues that the development of the fashion industry and the accompanying film entertainment industry in Hong Kong was undertaken as a means of opening up a non-political sector of public involvement, in part to diffuse the potential for conflict between Mainland and Taiwanese interests after the 1949 establishment of the People's Republic of China. Thus we see in this fashion posing the naturalizing of a sociopolitical discourse in the social practices of family groups on weekend outings.

When timers and tripods are used some effort needs to be expended for at least one person to act in both photographer and spectacle roles. This person must accomplish an interrupted adjustment frame, posing himself or herself, triggering the camera's timing apparatus, and then rushing back to assume the pose in time for the snap frame. Such movement between both frames and roles indicates that we should not come to think of either frames or roles as fixed upon persons.

Within the primary spectacle frame there are at least three types of poses: unposed (i.e., candid), frozen posed and candid posed. In the first case one finds pictures taken largely without the awareness of the spectacle. Setting, adjustment, and snap frames are accomplished by the watcher without negotiation with the spectacle. But this should not be accepted simply upon face value. It is often the case that the setting and adjustment frames are deceptively negotiated. That is to say, the photographer enters the social scene and disguises his or her intentions of taking a photograph. One observes photographers setting exposures, focus and stops on a neutral object at the same distance as the potential spectacle and then quickly turning to enter the snap frame before the spectacle has time to adjust or negotiate.

The frozen pose is the most common in my observations. What may vary from watch to watch is more the keying of the pose than the basic framing. Some spectacles key in smiles and openness, others key in sultry or distancing gazes into the distance. In most cases, however, the adjustment frame is keyed as serious activity with the smile (or its alternative) being keyed in just in the transition to the snap frame and then altered or dropped quickly in the closing of the frame.

Within the primary spectacle there are also what I would call posed candid shots. The participants in the watch go through the setting and adjustment frames but then continue their interaction into the snap frame, leaving it entirely to the photographer's judgement when to snap the actual picture. Thus the large physical frame is posed with relatively little movement but the face remains mobile until the snap is taken.

Observer poses

I have noted above, however, that it is common for observers in watches to themselves become the spectacle of inclusively framed watches. Thus there is a kind of observer pose. This pose is characterized by heightened attention to the spectacle within that observer's watch. One poses to be seen seeing. This includes an intent gaze and even some irregular alignment of the body to overcome intervening obstacles to one's line of vision. Often the observer pose will include rather uncomfortable craning of the neck as a view-sign of that person's membership in a watch.

CULTURAL ASPECTS OF PHOTO-EVENTS

My observations do not allow significant cultural statements; nevertheless, I can offer up a few suggestive observations. I have mentioned the Hong Kong frozen smile pose. One might think of this as a fashion-model or entertainer pose. One finds it very widely used around suitable photographic sites in Hong Kong, especially by young women spectacles. But without rather intensive further interviewing one could not insist that it is Hong Kong people taking on these poses. It could well be Chinese from elsewhere or other Asians who feel this is the appropriate pose to take while in Hong Kong.

In contrast, however, further observations in Beijing did not turn up examples of this entertainment-star pose. In Beijing what I observed could more readily be divided into two types: the 'heroic' pose and the 'stern' pose. In the heroic pose the spectacle stands in a posture suitable for casting in bronze; the body is fully erect, slightly tilted back, the chin is pulled in, and the eyes gaze off into the distance focused to one side of and above the position of the camera.[23] In the stern pose the body is still erect but much closer to a neutral tone. The face takes on a serious, but not grim, cast. The gaze is towards the camera but does not seem so intently focused as in the Hong Kong star-pose.

It must be understood that my observations in Beijing took place largely in places of heroic dimensions, before the Mao mausoleum, Tiananmen Gate, the Great Hall of the People, and the Revolutionary History Museum. The weather was bitterly cold (well below freezing) and it was a gray winter day. My observations in Hong Kong took place on the steps of the Cultural Centre where many wedding couples were being photographed, there was a carnival operating within the same space, and it was a bright, warm, late-autumn day. These differences may not account for all of the differences observed, but they should not be ignored.

What does appear significant, however, is a behaviour that I observed in only a few cases. In almost all of the photographs of what in Hong Kong are often called 'expats' with the understanding that one is talking about caucasians, I observed that the spectacle engaged in rather exaggerated clowning during the adjustment frame. During the adjustment frame expats took on exaggerated 'Hong Kong smile' faces, 'Mainland heroic' postures, and a variety of other keyings of the situation as either humorous or embarassing. These instances of role distance contrast strongly with the generally serious and cooperative stances taken by all of the other spectacles which I observed.

These observations should be coupled with further observation that in the great majority of cases where I observed an expat in a watch, the role of the expat was as watcher, not as spectacle. That is to say, there seems to be a general preference among expats to take either candid photographs or wide-angle photographs of the whole scene, but not to create negotiated watches from among their withs. There is apparently some awareness of this preference in the comment often made by westerners that Asians always and only take pictures of themselves wherever they go.

POSING AS CONVENTIONALIZATION

In the view I have developed here, the conventionalized poses of the spectacle are integrated into the ongoing social interaction of the observers. In making such poses and in taking such photographs, interactional withs interpolate the social practices which reproduce the texts of the broader social discourse. Spectacles take on the poses needed to reproduce photographs like those they have seen in the public fashion displays or elsewhere in the public discourse. Observers for their part take on the director and photographer roles required for the joint reproduction of this discourse in their own day-to-day discourses. Thus I am arguing that there is a continuity of practice from professional production of public discourse on the one hand to the casual making of a family photograph on the other.

From this point of view I have focused on how one set of publicly available texts, fashion and other photographs are interpolated into the social practices of common discourse. In Part III I will take up in more detail the social practices by which the texts of public discourse, especially news discourse, are constructed. In what follows I will focus on the social practices of observation when the posed text, the spectacle is even more distantly removed from social interaction with the observer, the reader of a daily newspaper, a magazine, or a book.

WHAT IS READING?

'I carry Kierkegaard, what do you carry?'
 – Dylan Thomas, *A Few Words of a Kind*[24]

In the 1950s, the poet Dylan Thomas satirized shallow intellectuals by suggesting that they were more concerned with being seen to be readers of Kierkegaard than with doing any reading. In a recent episode of the American sitcom *Roseanne*, Roseanne's daughter retreats to her room where she is shown holding, but not reading, J. D. Salinger's *Catcher in the Rye*. She suggests to her aunt that if she would like to read there is 'some Vonnegut' over on the shelf. Times, titles, and authors have changed, but this use of the act of reading to display something about oneself to others has not.

The act of reading is a kind of social interaction, a way of being socially present in the here-and-now, which places participants in quite specific webs of mutual obligation to others who are socially present. This social-interactive aspect of reading is quite apart from (and in addition to) the cognitive aspects of decoding text, the cultural and historical aspects of where and how literacy is embedded in the society as a whole, and the ideological aspects of the interpretive stance taken by the reader or implied by the writer.

The use of the act of reading to display or claim social position could be analysed within Collins's (1981a, 1981b) notion of the cultural or institutional resources one accumulates to display one's membership within social groups (Grimshaw 1994), though it might be an extension to do so as I read this literature. Such resources would lie in the knowledge or information contained within the text as something one would have as tokens for social exchange. Perhaps the act of displaying one's reading matter for others to see would be analogous to driving the latest prestigious car or living at the right address, not as the capital in itself, but as the display to others that one does, in fact, have access to such riches.

Another direction from which reading has been approached is reading as a cognitive or perceptual activity, and while there is much work to be done in this area, perhaps it is fair to say that until fairly recently, most studies of reading were of this type. That is, most studies of reading have concentrated their focus by separating the cognitive, social, and even cultural consequences of reading from the act of reading as a socially situated action. In the past 20 years, however, a number of studies have begun to place reading into a sociohistorical context. Scribner and Cole's (1981) rigorous cross-cultural, cross-linguistic comparisons demonstrated how literacy is differently grounded in social practice. Heath (1983) drew clear contrasts among literate practices within the same English-using speech community. The articles in Cook-Gumperz (1986) showed both that our current conceptions of literacy have been constructed historically and that much of this construction is carried out in day-to-day practices, especially in schools. Street's (1984) theoretical analysis of the study of literacy itself pointed to the role of the researcher's own ideological position in constructing theories of literacy.[25]

Keller-Cohen's research (1993a, 1993b, 1993c) within this same tradition has made it clear that literacy as currently constructed, at least in North America, has undergone significant change since the colonial period, particularly in the increasing development of the idea of isolated, individualized reading. Her studies and those of others suggest that we can no longer ignore the multiple social faces of literacy and of reading (Cook-Gumperz and Keller-Cohen 1993; Keller-Cohen 1993d).

From the historical perspective, Howe (1993) has argued in his study of reading in Anglo-Saxon England that such reading was primarily understood as a social activity, not the activity of an isolated individual. Reading alone, the proto-typical contemporary conception of reading,[26] is a peculiarly modern phenomenon, in Howe's analysis. He comments on Augustine's description of the silent reading of Ambrose, Bishop of Milan, which is frequently noted by other scholars as well as being the salient case in the European literate tradition of the departure from socially-grounded reading. Howe comments (1993: 71) that in Caedmon's monastery 'reading necessarily involved the element of oral delivery, of reading aloud, and also of giving counsel or advice. . . . To read meant to expound to other members of one's textual community.' As he puts it in another place: 'Quite simply, no Anglo-Saxon learned to read in order to read alone, late at night, in a quiet house and a calm world' (1993: 71).

The studies collected in Boyarin (1993) are useful in coming to understand the historical bases of wide cultural diversity in reading practices. To these might be added the sequence of more anthropologically orientated studies conducted by Besnier (1988, 1989, 1991), in which he clearly demonstrates that literacy, including reading, functions in significantly different ways in different societies.

In a very different line of research, media analysts have taken an interest in reading as a social phenomenon. We know a good bit about readership from media studies which focus upon audience measurement and audience response (Brown 1994; Kent 1994), but those studies are more likely to tell us who buys a newspaper than who reads it, and where they do tell us who reads it they are, with only a few notable exceptions, virtually silent on the question of how and where it is read. While media studies of television viewing (e.g., Moores 1993) are somewhat more interested in how television is watched, in general media studies are broadly-surveyed quantitative analyses based upon presence of the specified reading material or television broadcast, or simple self-reporting and thus of little help in coming to understand the social-interactive processes of the act of reading.

READING AS SOCIAL INTERACTION, THE 'WATCH'

Reading as a kind of watch proves amenable to an analysis similar to the one I have developed above regarding photographs. The spectacle, the newspaper or book, is more fixed in its 'pose' than any person posing for a photograph, of course. On the other hand, the watcher – the reader – alternately directs his or her attention to the text and to the other individuals in the immediate environment. The reader seems to give particular attention to potential violations of his/her territory in the form of those who would read over the shoulder. We see, for example, that on the train a reader glances up and sees someone next to him[27] reading his text. He makes a slight reorientation of the text so that the focal length and angle of the paper are exactly suited to his own reading and not to that of the interloper, thus indicating through this publicly available display his claim to exclusive territory. This territorial claim is ratified by the interloper as well, who when she is caught out looking over his shoulder, quickly looks away, feinting interest in an advertising poster along the top of the car.

Many observations such as this one indicate that readers as well as others in their vicinity recognize that readers may make specific claims to the right to exclusive observation of the spectacle, to non-interference in implementing this right, and the right to object to others who violate these claimed rights and territories. But not only do readers claim interactional and territorial rights, they display their claim to greater latitude in external emotional displays than non-readers. A reader may chuckle, laugh out loud, scowl, look troubled, or even cry in public places in a way that the same person without a text on display would not be able to do. To put this another way, behaviours such as these, which openly display emotional responses, find social legitimation when a text is presented as the 'explanation'. When a text is not present, such behaviours produce greater social spaces, such as giving the person a wider berth or looking evasively away from them. It is important to notice that what gives rise to the emotional displays is, perhaps, equally cognitive or internal in either the case of the reader or the non-reader. What differs is the social-interactive code exempting readers from censure.

One final aspect of the greater latitude granted to the watch is also by comparison to the single. Based upon the reader's claim to non-interference and upon the nested frames by which concentrated reading is claimed, it is understood that a person reading a book is fully occupied socially and, therefore, is not, in fact, a single as a person alone in public would be if not immediately interacting with another person. Thus people (perhaps more women then men) who find themselves alone in public, such as when they are travelling on planes or sitting in waiting rooms, may strategize to avoid being accosted in unwanted ways by making a display of reading. Having a book in hand allows one to temporarily close the snap frame of actually attending to the text to look up and say to a potential intruder, 'Excuse me, but I must finish this before this afternoon'. Without the book it is much more difficult to say, 'Excuse me, but I must stay alone during the next 30 minutes'.

READING AS VIEW-SIGN

There are, of course, many kinds of reading. One might want to distinguish among focused, textual reading which would include newspapers, periodicals, books, letters and many other forms of extended texts and non-focal or subsidiary reading, such as what one does as the bus passes and one almost unconsciously notes an advertisement along the side. Another category which might fall across either focal or non-focal reading categories might be called instrumental reading. By this I would mean the very large number of things one reads to navigate through the ordinary day. This would include reading the can to determine one had the tea one wanted for breakfast or noting the room number as one looks for the classroom in which one is to teach. Many of these uses show it is difficult to separate textual aspects of recognition from non-textual aspects such as colour, shape and placement. Much of the text one sees in the course of a day, from television advertising logos to road signs, may be treated either focally as when it is crucial to make some momentary but significant distinction, or non-focally as when one is riding on a bus and watching the road signs and adverts pass by.

In my research I have largely focused on focal reading of non-instrumental texts such as newspaper articles. But in doing so I would not want to suggest that similar claims upon social interaction are not being made in those categories of reading, though I do imagine they will differ in significant ways. For example, in insightful research concerning APIs (Announcements in the Public Interest) concerning AIDS, Jones (1995) has described a television commercial (API) in which we see, from behind, a heterosexual couple holding hands on an MTR (Mass Transit Railway) station platform in Hong Kong. Across the tracks in front of them is a large, lighted advertising box with an AIDS awareness announcement. We only see this announcement for a quick second on the screen but are given to understand that we are watching the couple as a watch who are focused upon this announcement. We then see the couple momentarily squeeze each other's hands. Thus the tie-sign of this with is transformed into a view-sign by which we are to infer that they are seeing and interpreting the announcement before them.

In this case it seems clear that a with (a couple in the train station) may be embedded within a watch (they show themselves to have focused their attention, however momentarily, on the announcement) and that the with/watch may itself be framed as spectacle for our watching on television at home. Further, since Jones has described this entire scene for us, it all becomes spectacle for his watch, and his text becomes spectacle for our reading. This Goffmanesque framing of frames (1974) demonstrates, I believe, that even the most momentary readings of non-focal texts are likely to be amenable to the kind of analysis I am developing here.

As an example of multiple framing, reading may be used as a view-sign of watch involvement in another kind of watch. In a lecture we note a range of signs of involvement from some members of the audience who assiduously follow the lecturer's handout as a sequence of points is made, to those who gaze about the room with marked inattention. As I have suggested above, the spectacle has rather limited rights of interaction – the spectacle is limited to striking the pose – but the watcher is relatively unconstrained in his or her attention to the spectacle. Thus the lecturer may attempt to reduce the watchers' freedom by using an overhead projected transparency with another paper to block portions of the text. Using a kind of progressive disclosure of the text, he or she attempts to take some measure of control over the watchers' reading. Such progressive disclosure is, of course, the essence of such mediated texts as sub-titles or scrolled screen texts. Perhaps it is this attempt to limit the freedom of the viewer which contributes to the popularity of home videotaping which restores viewer latitude.

Writing as well as reading may be a view-sign of the lecture watch. For example, in a lecture, one of the participants is writing as the lecturer speaks. Of course we do not know whether this should be construed as a view-sign or a watch-distancing sign. Perhaps he is writing his own lecture notes or a note to the person in the seat next to him. But then he drops his pencil and it falls behind the seat of the person in front of him, a stranger. She has heard the clatter and turns slightly. He taps her on the shoulder and points downward. She bends, picks up the pencil and, as they both smile, she hands it to him. They both then strike poses as watchers by giving the lecturer's handout a careful examination. In this latter bit of reading, they have displayed their apologies to those also concerned with the lecture for their momentary disruption as well as displayed themselves as giving attention to the lecture as their centre of focal attention.

Reading may also function as watch-distancing. One follows the handout or cooperates with the lecturer's progressive disclosure to signal attention. In contrast, we see bored listeners in a conference lecture who pick up, not the lecturer's handout, but the conference programmes at which they look from time to time, thus displaying inattention to the spectacle being posed before them.

Finally, reading as a view-sign can be used to display changes in the frame itself. At the beginning of the lecture, the lecturer makes a few introductory and orientating remarks. She then turns to the main portion of her lecture. At this point participating watchers turn to their handout to orientate themselves to the core of the lecture. This reading displays their marking of the shift from adjustment frame to the snap frame of the lecture.

In a corresponding way, as the lecturer nears the end of her lecture, she says, 'One point I would like to make in concluding'. As this registers on the listeners, we see many of them beginning their return to the adjustment frame. They pick up their conference programmes, perhaps to see what is next on the programme. They put their lecture handouts into portfolios or briefcases, they adjust their belongings, put away pencils and pens, some even put on coats and jackets. In this array of adjustment frame closings, their shifting their attention from the handout to the conference programme is just one of a number of the view-signs given which display the changing frame of the watch.

SOCIAL LICENCE TO READ AND WRITE

Because reading as well as writing make claims on the social space which asks others who are immediately present to ratify those claims through their own behaviour, the rights to make such claims are not entirely evenly distributed in society. We note, for example, that very rarely does one see anyone writing in a public setting. Those who do write are policemen, inspectors, reporters, the odd ethnographer and others who claim the social power to write down publicly what they see in the presence of others. Having a clip-board or notebook and pen in public becomes in itself a claim of assymetrical rights to observation and annotation.

Waiting at a bus-stop for the driver of a bus which is parked there, I think of a point to put in this very chapter. I take out my notebook and pen and begin jotting down the point. The driver comes along the queue towards his bus, sees me writing, slows his walk almost to a stop, looks very carefully at me, at my notebook, tries to determine what I am writing, looks back at me, and then slowly gets into the driver's seat. Again, when I board the bus, he examines me carefully. Of course, in this case I cannot say what has caused this response as I did not interview the driver. Nevertheless, at that bus station all of the other observers with notepads and pens were official bus company employees working on dispatch and other company duties. I uncomfortably crossed this frame by carrying out a literacy task which was common enough in that scene, but as a non-uniformed member of the public. I believe it is sufficient to have caused his reaction that I had blurred the clear demarcation between authorized company writer and public bus rider.

Power to read (or write) in the presence of others is not just a question of corporate authorization. In Hong Kong, for example, at morning tea in the tea shops one finds men and women around a table. There is a gender-based distribution of activities, on the whole, with men holding large newspapers to read and women chatting together without reading materials. Some informants have said that they, as women, do not like to read newspapers because the news-print and ink dirty their hands, but men do not mind that. Others comment that, as women, they do not feel they can take up so much space at the table. Whatever explanation is given, it is clear that these men are interpreted as using the view-sign of reading the morning newspaper as a clear claim to occupying a social territory.

This observation is further corroborated in that as the women speak in their withs, they exchange turns freely and show the other tie-signs of with involvement. The men, with their newspapers, display themselves as watches, unconcerned with these conversa-tions going on in their immediate vicinity until a point arises on which they have an interest or something to say. In this case, they are observed to drop their papers, interject their comment, and then quickly resume their territorial marking as having withdrawn from the conversation.

Reading can be analysed as a kind of social interaction. A reader makes claims about social territory, the space between himself or herself and the text, makes claims about rights to non-interaction with others co-present, requires ritual awareness in taking up a watch and in terminating it, and may, therefore, take on a variety of other social functions which are based upon these primary conditions. Thus, a reader may be a legitimate social entity where a single is not. A reader may also use reading to signal either attention or disattention to other potential spectacles. The rights to use reading as a claim to power in social situations are differentially distributed with men, in some cases, being able to claim the right to read as well as the reader's attendant territory which is denied to women.

The act of reading, in my analysis, embodies not only a wide range of cognitive, social-analytical skills and interpretations, it also embodies a set of social claims to a person's position in the ongoing social situation. While in this brief sketch of possibilities I have no more than suggested a few ways in which the study of reading may prove of significance in studies of social interaction, I believe that this analysis calls into question the assumption that primary *social interactions* are between the writers and the readers of texts. From the point of view of interactional accomplishments, reading needs to be understood as one of the ways in which communicative behaviour is grounded in the moment-by-moment social interactions of daily life.

WATCHING TELEVISION

Watching television is much more than focal attention to the screen for the purpose of making an interpretation of what is being projected there as media researchers and critiques have argued (Hall 1980; Morley 1980, 1990; Livingstone 1992; Moores 1993; Ang 1996) From the point of view I am developing here, the main concern is to ask what kind of mediated action is taking place and then from that point of view, how is the spectacle of the television appropriated as part of that mediated action. To be sure in some cases, the mediated action is, in fact, someone watching the news to find out what happened, or is said to have happened, that day. More often, however, our research (R. Scollon and Yung 1996, R. Scollon, Bhatia, Li and Yung 1996) tells us that what is going on is much more complex than that. More often living-room events are much as Roddy Doyle (1993) has characterized them in his novel *Paddy Clarke Ha Ha Ha*.

> Da thought he was great because he could sit in the same room
> as the television and never look at it. He only looked at The News,
> that was all. He read the paper or a book or he dozed.
>
> (1993: 188)

Here Da makes it a matter of some pride that he can ignore the television broadcast while others in the family are captivated by it. For others, however, the television broadcast is taken as a legitimate reason for not otherwise engaging in conversation.

> They said nothing for long bits but that wasn't bad; they were
> watching the television or reading, or my ma was doing a hard
> bit of knitting. It didn't make me nervous; their faces were okay.
> My ma said a thing during The Virginian.
> – What did we see him in before?
> My da liked The Virginian. He didn't pretend he wasn't watching.
> – I think, he said, – I'm not sure; something though.
>   Sinbad couldn't say Virginian properly. He didn't know what it
> meant either, why they called him the Virginian. I did.
> – He comes from Virginia.
> – That's right, said my da. – Where do The Dubliners come from,
> Francis?
> – Dublin, said Sinbad.
> – Good man.
> Da nudged me. I did it back, with my knee against his leg. I was
> sitting on the floor beside his chair. Ma asked him did he want any
> tea during the ads. He said No, then he changed his mind and
> shouted in Yes.
>   They always talked during The News; they talked about the news.
> Sometimes it wasn't really talk, not conversation, just comments.
> – Bloody eejit.
> – Yes.
>   I was able to tell when my da was going to call someone a bloody
> eejit; his chair creaked. It was always a man and he was always
> saying something to an interviewer.
> – Who asked him?
> The interviewer had asked him but I knew what my da meant.
> Sometimes I got there before him.

– Bloody eejit.
– Good man, Patrick.
My ma didn't mind me saying Bloody when The News was on.

(1993: 226–7)

Da is not only watching TV here but he is posing before the kids and wife as watching. Much like the spectacles we have just observed in getting their photographs taken, Da is setting a pose, taking on a conventionalized expression of himself as disinterested in anything but *The News*, intelligent critic of what political figures are saying in interviews, and concerned mentor of his male children. He is the watcher of the spectacle of *The News* on the one hand and he is the spectacle posing for his family on the other.

In this living-room scene Doyle portrays both reading and watching *The News* as linked chains in spectacle–watcher social intersactions. Da reads but, except for *The News*, does not watch. But he is watched in his not watching. And the talk which takes place is a kind of posed, conventionalized interaction between Da and the television spectacle or it is side-play comments by the others.

FROM READERS AND WATCHERS TO SITES OF ENGAGEMENT

It would go beyond the scope of this book to enter into an extended treatment of the nature of these chained observations in respect to newspaper reading and television watching. I will, however, return to the social practices of reading and watching and especially the interdiscursivity between reading/watching and the social practices of production in Chapter 8.

My goal in this chapter has been to make the argument that if we approach the analysis of reading and watching from the point of view of mediated action, we shall see that the role of the text, television or newspaper is as a mediational means by which participants in the social interactions of being a family together for an evening or of reading a newspaper on a train construct the ongoing social interaction. The television programme may be significant as the topical centre of the conversation or it may be quite peripheral as the footing shifts to a quasi-pedagogical discussion of how people from places such as Virginia and Dublin are named. It may even be most crucially used as a foil for the display of inattention as when Da thinks he is great because he can act as if he is ignoring it.

As I shall argue in the following chapter, the texts which we appropriate for mediated actions, whatever internal meanings may be constructed for them – and I should reiterate that I do not consider that an insignificant process – must also be understood as the sites upon which social interactions are constructed. Those sites of engagement are the primary focus of the social-interactional view of mediated discourse which I take up in the following chapter.

NOTES

1. Burke was not, of course, the first to call attention to the necessity of understanding the context. He was preceded by the anthropologist Malinowski (1923) who argued for the study of both what he called the 'context of situation' and for seeing language as human action rather than as abstract symbolic structure. A comprehensive and thoughtful review of the problems raised by the study of context is Goodwin and Duranti (1992).
2. Strong views of the psychological and sociological consequences of the differences between spoken and written communications were put forward by Goody (Goody and Watt 1963; Goody 1977). For an even-handed critical review of this literature, see Gee (1986, 1990).
3. Littlejohn (1992) is a particularly comprehensive introductory survey of theories of communication which includes a thoroughgoing critique of early systems theory.
4. But such insights must be viewed with considerable caution when crossing cultural or sociological boundaries. Athabaskans, for example, tend to assign the right to introduce topics to the responder rather than to the initiator of a communication (Scollon and Scollon 1981) and in Asian communication a period of facework is sometimes introduced between the identification sequence and the sequence in which topics are introduced (Young 1982, 1994; Scollon and Scollon 1991, 1995b).
5. Such an awkward phrasing as non-real-time communications is used because I intend to include in this statement such distanced communications as radio and television in which there is little or no feedback loop between productive and receptive participants.
6. The face metaphor was introduced by Goffman (1967) who referenced Hu (1944) as his source. Of course this metaphor has been used commonly in English for much longer (Oxford Universal Dictionary).
7. Ferguson (1994) is an insightful review of the various domains of sociolinguistics in which the unsatisfactory notion of conventionalization has been used.

8. The burgeoning literature on scripts and schemata is a further attempt to account for such conventionalized interpretive schemes (Schank and Abelson 1977; Kintsch 1977; Kintsch and Greene 1978). This approach has been particularly popular in studies of reading (Carrell 1983, 1984a, 1984b, 1989).

9. One could add to these advertising examples many religious communications such as public prayers in archaic English, Latin or Arabic, understanding that participants may well be divided on the question of whether the referee, the divine figure, is or is not to be understood as actually present to the communication.

10. Hymes gives credit to Burke as a major influence in the ethnography of communication even more clearly in Hymes 1974, especially Chapter 7.

11. For further discussion and illustration of Goffman's sociological and sociolinguistic methodology, see especially Goffman (1974, 1981) and Verhoeven (1993a, 1993b).

12. This reference is to the published edition. Goffman's reference in *Frame Analysis* is to a pre-publication version of this text. One might assume that Goffman's possession of a pre-publication version would indicate that someone understood how closely Goffman's and Uspensky's (and therefore Bakhtin's) work were in sympathy.

13. I offer the reader a choice of several terms here making reference to Goffman's claim not to have ever done 'research' but only 'scholarship' (Verhoeven 1993a, 1993b). In the cited interview Goffman distinguished research from scholarship at least partly tongue-in-cheek by saying that research is funded by means other than the researcher's paycheck and provides research assistants, scholarship is done within the scope of a scholar's day-to-day worklife without assistants or machinery.

14. One even finds novels such as LeGuin's *Always Coming Home* (1985) cast in the format of an ethnography. For further discussion of the merger of ethnographic writing and imaginative fiction see R. Scollon (1991), Atkinson (1990), and Fiske (1991).

15. I must go against the current of my own enthusiasm for the metaphor of the theatre here and sound a caution that this metaphor may carry with it a culturally grounded position. Spence (1992), in reviewing Dennerline's (1988) monograph on the Chinese philosopher Qian Mu, notes that Dennerline reports that Qian sees the difference in the Chinese pattern of history and that of the West as the difference between a poem and a drama. Dennerline puts it this way:

> The one develops in a meter from rhyme to rhyme, always by the same rules; the other develops in stages, from act to act, always with a different plot. The one expands to fill a space when it is ordered and disintegrates when it is not. The other progresses from conflict to conflict toward some inevitable tragic conclusion.

> (Dennerline 1988: 66)

Spence goes on to say that Qian argues that Westernized intellectuals always presume the 'universality of the dramatic form'. I am not prepared at the moment to pursue the metaphor of the poem as a venue for contemporary Hong Kong public discourse, but as with any metaphor, the concept of the theatre of discourse should be used where useful and at the same time watched carefully.

16. Some researchers prefer to use the word 'triangulation' for such a cross-methodological verification of observations.

17. *xing* (also: *sheng* (Md.); *sing, saang* (Cant.)) is defined as follows in three dictionaries of Chinese ranging from Early Zhou Chinese of the bone inscriptions of the fourteenth to eleventh centuries BC to contemporary Putonghua (Mandarin):

> 'to inspect', 'to examine', 'to scrutinize' [*Dictionary of Early Zhou Chinese* (1987)],

> 'to examine (oneself, etc.)', 'to reflect', 'to introspect', 'to consider'; 'to understand', 'to know'; 'to visit (one's seniors, etc.)', 'to test', 'an examination'; 'memory' [*Far East Chinese–English Dictionary* (Chang 1992)],

> 'examine oneself critically', 'introspect'; 'visit (esp. one's parents or elders)'; 'become conscious', 'be aware' [The Pinyin Chinese–English Dictionary (1981)].

18. The primary site I have studied is the area between the Star Ferry and the Hong Kong Cultural Centre, both in Tsimshatsui, Kowloon, Hong Kong, on Sunday, 18 December 1994. Within that same area at the time was a holiday carnival with a merry-go-round, a ferris wheel, and a variety of other carnival rides and activities. While my formal observations were made primarily in this site, I have also made other observations in the same place on quite a few other occasions as well as tourist photograph-taking in a number of other sites around Hong Kong and Beijing, as well as in Finland, the US, Japan and Ireland.

19. I will keep to Goffman's practice of not indicating the nominal usage of this word with single quotation marks hereafter.

20. See Bourdieu (1990), Berger (1972), Sontag (1979), and Wells (1997) for extended treatment of the social practices of photo-taking, including photography as a social practice for the distribution of power.

21. In Hong Kong at least there seems to be what one might think of as a movie-star-charming smile which seems rather easily adopted and held by everyone over the age of about four or five, males as well as females, though women in their twenties seem to adopt the most radiant versions.

22. There are, of course, fairly large variations across segments of any one society and across cultures in just how much and what kinds of looking are acceptable. This is a secondary issue here because I take it that it would be a rare case indeed in which a society took it as entirely

normal for anyone to stare at anyone else entirely at will. John Flowerdew (personal communication) notes that Kathy Lam, a Hong Kong teacher, has described the photo session as a way of dating in Hong Kong. Among the advantages are that the boy (normally the photographer) gets a fair amount of observational freedom, while the girl (normally the spectacle) may strike alluring poses which would not otherwise be acceptable.

23. In the ancient *Li Chi* ([*Li Ji*] Chai and Chai 1966) looks above the collar are said to indicate pride, looks below the girdle to indicate grief, and looks askance to indicate villainy. This suggests that in China not only is the traditional value placement of looks a long tradition, it is also a highly self-conscious one.

24. This epigraph is recalled by the author from a Caedmon Records recording (*ca.* 1955) of a poetry reading given by Dylan Thomas.

25. See Gee (1986) for an insightful review of this research.

26. The photographs of Kertész (1971), for example, give an elegant display of the fundamental notion that reading is a solitary act.

27. My use of pronouns in this case indicates actual genders in ethnographic field observations. I have observed the same situation across many other gender and generational pairings, however, so that the reader should not construe this gender specificity to indicate gender-distributed behaviours.

FOUR

News-stands, handbills, photographs and living rooms as stages for the construction of person

AN ETHNOGRAPHIC EXEMPLAR

On Nullah Road in Hong Kong's (and perhaps the world's) most populated urban district, Mongkok, in front of the Jockey Club, a newspaper seller stands in a downpour selling his papers – mostly the Chinese language dailies and racing papers. As there is no overhang, this news-stand is out in the weather with only the protection of the building itself. It remains an active and viable news-stand, however, because of the very high traffic of people, virtually all men, placing bets at the counters inside the Jockey Club's premises. During the rain, the entire news-stand is covered with sheets of nearly opaque plastic, through which none of the papers underneath can be seen. Nevertheless the seller stands in front of this array in a rain poncho selling papers to customers who dart out of doorways; he simply places his hands under the plastic sheets and making no mistakes pulls out the correct paper, sight unseen, even though to do so means ranging over a display which is perhaps two meters wide. The customer says two syllables, Sing Tao; *the seller slides his hand three to the left, and the paper is found.*

THE DAILY NEWSPAPER

Atkinson (1990) discusses the use of what he calls the ethnographic exemplar in the writing of ethnographies. My opening description of the news seller in Mongkok's Nullah Road is such an exemplar. As an exemplar it should be taken to be not just a single ethnographic observation, though it was, in fact, at first recorded in a

123

very similar format in my field notebook. As an exemplar it illustrates a kind of representative anecdote (Burke 1945); that is, it is a kind of hologram for many of the aspects of the analysis which the researcher intends to put forward. In the analysis which follows I will use the point of sale of the daily Hong Kong newspaper as the central stage, the site of engagement, upon which the person of the Hong Kong newspaper reader is initially constructed – where this 'person' begins to be acted out.

If we think of sites of engagement as stages in a theatre of discourse, we can highlight three aspects of discourse as mediated action: (1) these mediated actions are enacted in real-time among co-present participants; (2) the actions taken have a dialogic (polyvocal, heteroglossic, intertextual and interdiscursive) nature, that is, they incorporate the voices of others in the Bakhtinian sense outlined in Chapter 1; and (3) there is always an awareness of the 'other' as watcher of the spectacle as it is played out. As I have argued in Chapter 2, the identities imputed and claimed, negotiated and contested are constructed in part as a spectacle or pose for the observation of others.

Considering the news-stands of Hong Kong in this metaphor of a theatre of discourse, the places where one buys newspapers in Hong Kong resemble fast-food take-away shops more than five-star restaurants, if I may engage in mixing analogies for a moment. They appear designed for quick rather than considered purchase, for the convenience of the seller as much as for the buyer. To continue the analogy, they are also not buffets at which one might first look over the possible selections. Customers arrive at the news-stand, speak the few syllables of the name of the paper they want while offering payment and leave as soon as they have their paper and their change.[1] The stages for this performance are found throughout Hong Kong, rarely more than a block or two away from each other. Among the largest ones are those at the Star Ferry Terminal, but even the smallest news-stands, such as those found along Tai Hang Dong Street at the Nam Shan Estate in Kowloon, display over a dozen different newspapers. Supermarkets and convenience stores also have large selections, both in those located in streets and those located in Mass Transit Railway (MTR) stations and the stations of the Kowloon–Canton Railway (KCR).[2]

News-stands throughout Hong Kong are strikingly similar to each other in the ways in which the periodicals are laid out for display and purchase, and yet quite different from the places in which newspapers are sold elsewhere. The mapping of the stage of this theatre of discourse, then, is concerned with the structure of the point of sale, the place where the newspaper is actually sold to the public. I will discuss two aspects of this stage: the point of sale itself – the news-stand – and the player routines enacted upon this stage.

Point of sale

There are two major ways in which a customer of the newspaper company may purchase a newspaper; a paper may be bought at a news-stand or it may be delivered to the home (office, school or other organizational location) through a regular subscription paid in advance. Interviews, as well as some published statistics, indicate that the majority of the newspapers sold in Hong Kong are sold, not by subscription, but at news-stands. For this reason I have focused primarily on news-stands in this analysis.[3]

At first glance these Hong Kong news-stands are much like news-stands throughout Europe and the rest of Asia. A wide variety of newspapers and other periodicals is placed on display and sold to customers who are walking by. With the exception of North America which I will discuss below, these news-stands have much in common with such news-stands elsewhere.

As a stage for public discourse, the news-stand provides easy public entrance at a relatively low cost. In 1992, at the beginning of this research project, daily newspapers cost between $3.00 and $5.00 (40 to 65 cents, US). In October 1995 most Chinese papers sold for a cover price of $5.00 and the English papers sold for $7.00. That was followed by a price war among the Chinese papers, which at the time of writing had stabilized at about $4.00. Lower prices can be found as the day passes and sellers become interested in getting some return on their costs. There is a widespread practice of bundling together two or even three different newspapers and selling the package together at a reduced price. Such bundles are prepared in mixed combinations of papers not unlike the combination plates sold in fast-food restaurants as luncheon specials. While many combinations have been observed, I have not yet observed bundles of newspapers at ideological extremes from each other such as *Ming Pao* together with *Ta Kong Pao*.[4]

At the Star Ferry (as well as at most news-stands elsewhere) Chinese papers are laid out in an overlapping 'shingled' pattern with only the title of the paper in view on the right side. There are usually at least two rows of these with the most frequently purchased papers lying in the first bank and less purchased papers lying on a second bank above the first. While not practised everywhere, usually these banks of papers are laid out right in front of the seller so that he or she may quickly reach any paper and present it to the buyer. Rarely are these laid out so that the buyer can even reach them, let alone select a paper for himself or herself.[5]

In contrast to the Chinese-language newspapers, the English-language papers, *South China Morning Post*, *Eastern Express*[6] and *Hong Kong Standard*, are laid out with the full upper half of the front page displayed and well within reach of the customer. Foreign newspapers are displayed well away from the seller with the upper quarter of the front page displayed in an overlapping shingled layout. That is to say, whatever the front page materials might be in the two Hong Kong English papers, they are on view for the buyer to see, select and purchase. The foreign papers present the paper title and the headlines for the customer to see, select and purchase. The Chinese papers on the other hand must be purchased, on the whole, by speaking the name of the paper to the seller who hands out the paper in exchange for payment.

This overall arrangement has many variations. Some sellers prefer to sit with their backs to some wall and look over their papers towards the customer on the street. Others take the opposite position with the papers against a wall and stand or sit in the street where the customers pass. Most, perhaps, take the intermediate solution of sitting on the side of their displays with the wall on one side, the customer and street or passageway on the other and the papers arrayed in banks in front of themselves, not the customers.

In all of these arrangements it is important to remember that these sellers sell more than just the daily newspapers. There is a wide, and apparently growing, range of other periodicals sold, from comic books to entertainment and other feature magazines. These materials are mostly displayed, like the English and foreign newspapers, away from the seller and with full covers visible to the customer. Generally speaking the news-stands at the Star Ferry sell a smaller proportion of these other periodicals and a higher proportion of English and foreign newspapers than stands located in more residential neighbourhoods where the emphasis shifts towards these other specialized periodicals. Outside of the Star Ferry area virtually no foreign newspapers are sold on street or at MTR/KCR station news-stands.[7] In most neighbourhoods there are also no English-language newspapers sold. That is to say, while the displays vary little from place to place, the selection does vary, reflecting the demographic composition of the customer traffic in each area.

For Chinese newspapers (but not other periodicals) the emphasis is laid upon ease of the seller. One might assume that this is the highest volume of traffic on the one hand and the sales which require the least customer consideration. At least they are displayed in such a way that the transaction may be completed rapidly and with little movement on the part of the seller and little verbal interchange between the seller and the customer. The observations made on Nullah Road in front of the Jockey Club during the downpour with which I began emphasize the automaticity of these arrangements for the sale of the Chinese-language dailies.

Prior studies of communication which have concerned themselves with the metaphor of the channel of communication have pointed out that the channel is frequently a source of 'noise', that is, of obstructed communication (Shannon and Weaver 1949). Channel is also seen as a barrier to environmental, non-relevant noise. That is, they have seen channel as the means by which a message is focused for reception by a particular receiver. The seller who can pick out his papers from under an obscuring sheet of plastic has, through a kind of routinization, greatly lowered the amount of noise in this portion of the channel of communication between the writer and the reader. Thus, it seems clear that this form of display serves an important function of conventionalization by narrowing the range of communications necessary for the sale/purchase of a newspaper.

Hong Kong morning papers are broken down and distributed in Central sometime in the vicinity of four to five o'clock in the morning. In regions at some distance from Central, such as Sham Shui Po, by six o'clock news-stand operators can be found sitting on laid out cardboard boxes sorting and folding together the papers which have been delivered to them. The papers are delivered to them in bundles of sections which are then assembled by these sellers and their assistants into the full, folded papers sold to the public.

At six o'clock most of the news-stands which are beginning to operate stand at the doorways and entrances to morning tea houses, restaurants and markets. Even before the papers are completely folded together customers are passing to buy a paper and to go in for a combination of tea, chat and something to eat. For some this practice stands in lieu of exercise in the park. For some it is part of the morning walk and wake up routine. By seven o'clock most stands are actively prepared for sale and operating busily.

Stands in other places around Hong Kong also are timed with the rhythm of neighbourhood activities. In regions of shops and stores, the news-stands do not become active until 30 minutes to an hour before the opening of the stores – many around 10:30 to 11:00 am. Stands at transportation stations operate in rhythm with transportation systems. Finally, in portions of Hong Kong where nightclubs and other forms of entertainment dominate at night, news-stands begin their day with an emphasis on newspapers and shift towards racier publications as night-time activities increase. The point to remember here is that not only is the structure of the point-of-sale stage variable from place to place throughout the city, it is variable throughout the day depending on the environment in which it is placed. It would be a mistake to think of these news-stands as static stages with fixed displays or as consisting of any very uniform structure.

Finally, to put this point of sale into comparative perspective I made observations in three places in the United States: Washington, DC – the capital; Ann Arbor, Michigan – the campus of a major public university; and Oberlin, Ohio – the campus of a small, private college. Apart from the very much smaller selection of newspapers available, the most striking aspect of newspaper sales in these three very different American cities was the highly mechanized form it takes. With one exception in Washington, to which I will return, all of the newspapers sold on the public stage, as it were, were sold in coin-operated boxes chained to posts on street corners.[8]

These coin-operated boxes are set up so that the full upper half of the front page is visible for the potential buyer to read. The boxes are set next to each other, usually in a row – a separate box for each publisher's daily, so that competing versions of headlines, cover photographs, and lead stories can be seen and read *before* making the purchase.

The placement of these automated stages of discourse is, as I said, almost exclusively on street corners where papers can be easily purchased by both pedestrians and drivers of cars. While there is some apparent relationship between early morning activities – in Oberlin and Ann Arbor such stands were placed on corners near early-opening restaurants – the stage seems quite cut off from other social activities compared to Hong Kong's close association of news-stands with entrances of tea houses and markets. To compare with the Hong Kong routinization of this point of sale, where there is a minimal communication with the seller, it is clear that in this American pattern there is *no* human contact between the buyer of the paper and any person connected with constructing this stage of discourse. While this contrastive example may say more about North American social practices, it does call attention to the role of the human interpretative processes which are called into play in the transaction between buyer and news seller in most other places.

Finally, the one exception to this highly mechanized street corner point of sale I observed is a large 24-hour news-stand and reference book shop in Washington DC. This store displayed a very large selection of newspapers from around the world and from around the US, including the international edition of the *South China Morning Post* (but no other Hong Kong papers nor any papers in Chinese). Most significant, perhaps, is that these papers were all displayed so that the full upper half of the front cover was easily viewed by the potential purchaser. Though there were hundreds of them, none of them was obscured by another covering or partially covering material for sale. Furthermore, all of them were displayed for self-selection by the customer who would then take them to a separate counter for purchase.

The point to be drawn from this brief comparative view and which will be discussed in detail below is that all of the newspapers which I observed on sale in the US were displayed so that the upper half of the front page could be read before buying the newspaper. None of the newspapers I observed had any major material in this upper half other than the title of the paper and editorial (that is, news as opposed to advertising) content. Whether purchasers of newspapers in the US do or do not actually read and compare papers before buying cannot be established from these observations. It seems likely that they do not. Nevertheless, newspapers on the American stage present themselves *as if* they were in competition with each other and *as if* the upper halves of their front pages were their most telling and enticing material. The parallel to the display of *South China Morning Post* and *Standard* and the contrast with the Chinese-language papers in Hong Kong seems striking.

Player routines

The newspaper seller plays a major role in what is seen by all others as the 'front' of the newspaper, no matter what design efforts have been invested by the producers of the newspaper. In the case of the Chinese newspapers, the seller displays them so that they must be bought sight unseen. No advertising, or for that matter sensational headline, is likely to have much effect on purchasers until after the purchase has been transacted.

There are two common routines for the purchase of newspapers at news-stands observed throughout Hong Kong. The first is the 'Chinese paper' pattern of stepping up to the seller, saying the few syllables of the name of the desired paper while handing over payment. This is reciprocated by the seller handing over the paper and the change nearly simultaneously. In this routine there is often little or no exchange of glances between seller and buyer.

The 'English paper' routine is different in that there are two alternate routines. In one of these the buyer steps up to the stack of papers, picks up the paper (*South China Morning Post, Eastern Express* or *Hong Kong Standard*) and hands over the money and then waits while the seller looks up to establish the paper and price and to return the change. The second alternate is for the buyer to step up to the stack of papers, compare the English papers, and then to pick up one of them for purchase. This alternate[9] also has the sub-routine which is almost never seen in the purchase of Chinese papers of actually looking over the paper for a few moments or minutes before purchasing.[10] It also includes putting the paper back down and selecting the other for perusal or even putting the paper down and turning away without buying. These latter behaviours I have never observed in the purchase of Chinese-language papers. The purchase of foreign papers is like that of the English papers with even longer periods of perusal and apparently selection procedures.

Further evidence that these are the expectations of Hong Kongers comes from a number of stands which are intermediate in structure, especially those in convenience stores. In these both English and Chinese papers are arrayed on racks for the customer to select and take to a counter for purchase. While I have only observed two or three cases of potential buyers actually looking into the newspapers before purchase, I have observed that many of these stores have put up signs saying, 'Do not open before purchase'.

Finally, following purchase of English and foreign papers, the most common move is to fold the paper or put it into something and walk away for the paper to be read elsewhere. Following the purchase of Chinese papers there is a sub-routine which is often, though certainly not always, observed, that is the sub-selection among sections of the paper and refolding of certain sections to the front. Quite often sections of the paper are discarded before the purchaser walks away.

While much remains to be learned yet about player routines both at the point of sale and away from the point of sale, the question can now be raised about what kinds of knowledge are required to gain access to the various newspapers available for sale in Hong Kong and what kinds of assumptions, conventionalizations, are made by players. The two main patterns are distinguished by ease and speed. It should be clear that in some sense it is much easier to buy an English-language newspaper and much faster to buy a Chinese-language newspaper. The English-language paper only requires stepping up, self-selecting the paper and handing over an estimated amount of money. The Chinese-language paper requires knowing what paper one wants to buy in advance, unless one is conducting this sort of research and can try to get away with 'all of them', and saying the name of the paper in a way which is intelligible to the seller.

Disruptions and confusions occur when one steps out of the expected patterns of conventionalization. When, for example, I step up and ask for *Ming Pao* in accented Cantonese, the seller, rather than selecting my paper for me looks up. Then, seeing an expatriate, he points to the *South China Morning Post* which is much closer to me than to him and gestures that I should pick it up. In other words, he suggests I enter the English paper routine. When I repeat the syllables *Ming Pao* and point towards the bank of Chinese papers he has little interpretive room left and so finally and with some apparent difficulty searches among his papers until he comes up with a copy of *Ming Pao*. This he hands to me very tentatively, even though I hand the payment to him. When I accept the paper, he finally apparently decides that this is, in fact, the paper I have asked for, makes my change, and then looks at me again for a long time. Meanwhile several other buyers have spoken the names of their papers and have waited uncharacteristically long to have them handed over.[11]

The routines played out by players consist, then, of sets of broad expectations on who will enter the discourse in which languages and with which papers, depending on obvious racial[12] characteristics. These expectations feed into sub-routines for the transactions needed for purchase. While disruptions of expectations can be dealt with, it is clear when they happen that both parties must move from the level of the playing out of routines to the level of turn-by-turn negotiation.

It remains to be learned how and when these various routines are learned. Most central among them is: How does a purchaser know, when approaching a news-stand, which paper he or she wants to buy? It is clear, at least in the case of the English newspapers, that many buyers expect to make the decision at the time of purchase, or at least the stage of discourse is so constructed that if a player wants to make this decision, then it is easy to do so. This corresponds with the *as if* practices I described for the sale of American newspapers; the sale of a newspaper is constructed as if it is a competitive sale in each instance, whether or not most sales are actually routines which have been carried out for years. Chinese newspapers in Hong Kong, on the other hand, are sold *as if* every purchaser knew exactly which paper he or she would buy; it is as if the decision were made elsewhere or long before. For these papers, what comes easily is buying a paper upon which you have already decided; what is difficult is to make your decision on the spot at the point of sale.

Interviewing has led me to believe that, in fact, newspaper readers in Hong Kong do exercise long-standing commitments to particular newspapers. Interviewees who are asked what newspapers they read normally have little difficulty in answering. It is not as if they might read one one day and another another. There tends to be a clear-cut response to the question, and the answer is usually in the plural.

When asked why they read a particular paper, especially the first one mentioned, they frequently answer, 'Because that's the paper my father (or our family) subscribes to'. When asked why the father (or family) subscribes to that paper the answer is often, 'Because that was my grandfather's paper'. In other words, interviewees show a fairly high amount of familial and transgenerational loyalty to particular newspapers.

It would be a mistake, however, to equate this loyalty to purchase or reading as indicating either any form of acceptance of the ideological positions of the newspapers or any form of identity with any groups with which the newspaper might be associated. Interviewees when asked, 'Do you like X?' (the paper to which their father/family subscribes) often say that they do not. Therefore, they read another newspaper as well, one which is more to their liking.

While much remains to be studied on the question of player routines, especially routines carried out away from the point of sale, it does seem clear that the layout of the stage at the point of sale converges well with the routinized practices of the purchasers. One can generalize to say at the very least that buyers of English-language papers prefer to act as if their decision-making is spontaneous and done at the point of sale; buyers of Chinese-language papers prefer to act as if their purchase is a matter of custom, habit, or at least long-standing personal practice.

THE CONSTRUCTED 'ENGLISH' AND 'CHINESE' NEWSPAPER BUYER

The governing question in my overall research project is: How is the person socially constructed in the public discourse of newspapers. There are, of course, many kinds of 'person' to be considered from newsmakers, observers, and reporters of news agencies around the world to users of newspapers in Hong Kong, including both readers and those who use the paper to pack goods for shipment. These persons at the extreme ends of this communicative process first meet on the stage where the newspaper reaches the public, in most cases, that is the news-stand. Their meeting is mediated in most cases by the seller of the newspaper who has received it from the publisher, collated it, and displayed it for ease in the transaction of purchasing.

As I have suggested above, newspapers, are not, in fact, direct communications between writers and readers. Nor can we cover the very lengthy and socially complex distance between the original authors of news stories and their readers with either the mechanical concept of a channel or the shorthand notion of conventionalization. As I have argued, in this one stage of the much larger theatre of public discourse, the pivotal point at which we turn from the productive frame to the receptive frame, the news seller's transaction with the buying potential reader, there is a social process of construction of not only the transaction between the two, but also of the roles each can be presumed to take. As in any form of face-to-face interaction, these roles are simultaneously presented for ratification and further negotiation.

As a site of engagement, the principal concern of the news agency is indexing the attention of the reader so that he or she may enter into participation in the discourse, or begin reading, and that is where the front page takes on the pivotal role in mediating the productive and receptive aspects of this theatre of discourse. Where the competitive frame is dominant in the selling stage, the front page is what first captures the attention and interest of the reader. This is how he or she decides to engage in that particular framing of the public discourse; that is how those particular writers and that particular news organization captures that particular audience to put it from the point of view of the production of the discourse. To put it from the receptive point of view, the front page is the first index by which the potential reader makes his or her selection of a point of entry into the daily discourse. The front page of the newspaper is the analogy of the ring of the telephone (Schegloff 1972); it is the summons which calls for opening up a state of communication. The reader's answer is to scan this summons to determine whether or not he or she will respond.

On the Hong Kong stage of newspaper discourse, a Chinese newspaper is sold as if the summons has already been made, as if the state of communication is already presupposed, as if there is no need to first establish that this person will enter into discourse with that particular newspaper organization's texts. To continue the parallel with the telephone conversation, the Hong Kong newspaper is more closely analogous to the intercom than to the telephone with outside lines. On an intercom system one knows that a buzz on that particular line will be a call from a particular person or office, though one still does not know, of course, what topics will be introduced. That is to say, the channel and to some extent the relationship is taken as given or pre-established, not to be newly negotiated with each transaction.

This, then, is the greatest single contrast between the English newspaper and the Chinese newspaper on the news-stand stage of the theatre of public discourse in Hong Kong: in the English papers the discourse is presented as newly negotiable with each encounter of the participants (writers and readers, news organizations and public); in the Chinese papers the discourse is presented as conventionally established with each encounter continuing a socially and individually ratified pre-existing role or relationship. The discourse of English newspapers is formally treated like that among acquaintances or strangers; the discourse of Chinese newspapers is formally treated like that among established friends or kin. Using the metaphor of the stage of public discourse allows us to see that the person of the Hong Kong newspaper reader is constructed around different metaphors for English and Chinese readers. I believe that this distinction between kin and stranger metaphors could be shown to parallel distinctions more widely displayed throughout the speech community. I hope to have shown that the use of the metaphor of the theatre of discourse has provided the analytical light by which this distinction can be more clearly observed.

THE NEWS-STAND AS A SITE OF ENGAGEMENT

With this ethnographic background we can now enter into the discussion of how the news-stand can be seen as a site of engagement within the framework we are developing here. The primary heuristic question is: What sort of mediated action is going on? The most apparent answer is the buying and selling of a daily newspaper. While buying the paper on the news-stand is not the only way a reader can come into possession of a paper to read, in Hong Kong at least, it is the primary way in which this is done.

I have said above that a site of engagement is constructed through an interlocking set of social practices which produce a window within which a potential for mediated action becomes instantiated as discourse in real time. The social practices involved in this site of engagement are manifold. For many they include the practice of taking exercise, buying a newspaper, and then entering a teashop for morning tea, conversation and newspaper reading. These practices also include various practices for the exchange of money in service encounters (Pan 1996). As I have argued above, there are at least two recognized social practices for the display of newspapers depending on whether it is an English-language or a Chinese-language newspaper. These among many others work together to construct the site of engagement as a moment in which a potential reader can get a newspaper to read.

Most important for my purposes, however, is to see that each of these social practices carries an implicit and sometimes explicit set of identity claims and imputations. That is to say, if we move from the first maxim, attend to the situation, to the second maxim, attend to the positioning of relationships, we can see that there are imputed and claimed identities involved in the selling and buying of newspapers on the news-stand. I have suggested above that the social practices for layout and purchase of a Chinese newspaper imputes to the potential purchaser a kin-like identity. It implies that he or she is someone who knows just which paper he or she intends to buy and that no further discussion or deliberation is necessary at the point of sale, this site of engagement. In most cases this imputation of member of the group is accepted and ratified without challenge by the simple purchase of the newspaper.

At a broader level, the Chinese-language newspaper and its seller impute to the buyer the identity of 'reader of Chinese'. Again, this imputation is normally ratified through speaking a word or two of Chinese and taking the paper offered. But, as I have indicated above, in some cases where the imputation is made and then quickly withdrawn as I, a non-Chinese, try to buy the paper, it is taken as a contestation of that identity, even if momentarily. The seller withdraws his imputation to me of Chinese-reading identity and makes a second imputation of English-reading identity. I, in turn, contest that second imputation, make a counter claim to restore his original identity imputation and, taking the paper, walk away ratifying my claim to being able to read the paper.

This may seem like a lot of claiming and counter-claiming for a moment's transaction, but as I will argue below in discussing handbills, such rapid claims and counter-claims, contestations, negotiations and ratifications are the stuff of identity work in face-to-face social interactions. The site of engagement is the place where social practices converge in the production of real-time discourse and, from the point of view I am developing here, discourse is inherently an identity-making activity (Fairclough 1989, 1995b; Gee 1990; Wertsch 1991; Lave and Wenger 1991).

HANDBILLS

Another site of engagement which has been useful to study has been in busy pedestrian thoroughfares where people pass out handbills to pedestrians passing by. Again, like the news-stand, the situation may seem a rather minimalist one for the study of mediated discourse, but as I have argued elsewhere (R. Scollon 1997a), because it is a minimalist setting for mediated discourse the key elements can be seen in greater relief. A major problem in studying mediated discourse is simply the complexity of the phenomenon. The daily newspaper is a genre complex of normally hundreds of different types of text interdiscursively melded into an array of dozens or more pages. In a large city one finds a dozen or more such genre complexes and often a single reader will have access at some time or other in the same day to several of them. Thus, by focusing on a very minor form of mediated discourse such as the handbill, the social-interactive features of the sites of engagement can be analysed while at least temporarily setting aside the greater complexity of coming to understand how such texts are appropriated into mediated actions.

The common situation in Hong Kong, as well as other crowded Asian cities such as Tokyo, Nagoya, Shimonoseki or Seoul, is to find a person standing in the middle of a flow of pedestrians moving along a sidewalk and handing out leaflets or handbills to individuals as they pass by. The actions by which this transpires on the surface of it simply amount to the person glancing back and forth between the handbills and the crowd flowing towards him or her. A handbill is separated from the batch, grasped with one hand, handed into the path of an oncoming pedestrian and at the moment the pedestrian accepts it, the distributor releases it. Obviously some people take the handbill and some do not. In my data, virtually everyone who does take the handbill looks at it at least briefly and then does one of three things: (1) holds it as he or she walks along; (2) puts it away in a pocket or handbag; or (3) discards it at the next trash container.

As a text to be read, these handbills have a very brief moment in which to get their message to the person who accepted it. The determining message is not, of course, anything like the full content of the handbill or leaflet or brochure. It is whatever minimal amount of information the reader needs to decide whether or not to keep it or discard it. In Hong Kong as well as in the other Asian cities where I have studied this, but most decidedly not in Chicago nor in China where I have done comparative study, the pedestrian traffic is too dense for the person receiving the handbill to take any other options. In Chicago and in China, not only does the person receive the handbill, he or she most frequently stops then and there and reads it through, often while the person handing it waits for a reaction or begins to engage in a conversation. That is to say, in Chicago and in China,[13] handing the item to the pedestrian is the first move in opening up a dialogue much like the summons described by Schegloff (1972) as the telephone ring. In Hong Kong the entire transaction between the two people is, not unlike the purchase of the Chinese newspaper, brief, involves little or no verbal exchange, and is terminated immediately.

Most of the handbills in Hong Kong are printed in Chinese. My presence as an expatriate in the pedestrian flow produces an interruption in a steady flow of identity assignments and ratifications. The distributor generally glances up only enough to be able to hand the item to the pedestrian. In my case, she[14] stretches out her hand to hand me the handbill, then she notes my apparent racial characteristics, she begins to retract her hand and ready herself to hand it to the next person coming along on the basis of a different racial assignment. In this brief move we can see the assumption being made that as an expat I am not likely to be able to read Chinese, or conversely that apparently racially Chinese people are likely to be able to read Chinese. While both of these are reasonably warranted guesses, we should not lose sight of the imputation of identity taking place here. The distributor, in a momentary glance and slight set of hand movements has assigned to me an identity based on racial characteristics but with implications about my linguistic competence. In such hesitations and reconsiderations we see that in the untested case where she is handing one to each passerby she is not simply distributing them as fast as possible, she is making a set of social judgements, a set of identity imputations as an inherent aspect of doing the work of getting the handbills distributed.

But in this case I contest her identity imputation. Yes, I am an expat but, no, it is not true that I do not want the handbill. Of course she cannot know that I have two motives for wanting the handbill. I want it to read, in part because I can, in fact, read the Chinese, but I also want it because I am studying handbills as an interesting site of engagement. It would be stretching the credulity of the reader to suggest that by reaching out to take the handbill I am making such complex and broad claims about my own identity. In the momentary decision, all I can be said to be doing is contesting the distributor's identity imputation to me as someone who would not want the handbill. She hands it to me, but in evidence that some negotiation has gone on and that my contestation has called the situation into question, she briefly stops in her action and turns her head to watch me as I move on. I too am looking back at her and this brief exchange of glances ratifies for both of us that a micro-social interaction in which an identity has been imputed, contested, and a counter-claim made and, since I have the handbill, to some extent legitimated.

This momentary transaction opened a window of reception for this text. The window remained open while I worked out what to do with the handbill. As I have mentioned, I had at the time an interest in coming to understand how the handing was transacted, but also in collecting handbills for a study of the texts themselves. For me the window closed again almost immediately as I put the handbill away in my bag for later study. Thus this site of engagement was constructed and decomposed again in a matter of a few seconds. Of what was it constructed?

It would be pointless to try to determine just how many social practices had converged in this particular instance to produce this site of engagement. One can isolate at least three, as I have done elsewhere (R. Scollon 1997a). One social practice might be called 'taking a walk'. I believe it can be argued that this does, in fact, constitute a social practice as there are considerations about how to walk, how fast to walk without blocking those behind or stepping on the heels of those in front, how to pass – whether on the right or left side – what to do if one wants to stop for a moment. The social practice of taking a walk is clearly constructed differently from place to place. In Hong Kong passing is said to be on the left, an analogy with the road traffic. In practice one follows the flow which on any particular stretch of walkway might be on either the left or the right.

A second social practice which can be analysed here has to do with handing and receiving objects. In my own socialization in a North American city, I recall being carefully instructed to never take an object from a stranger. Thus the social practice of handing and receiving objects which I do understand is contextualized for use with intimates or at least people with whom I am familiar.

A third social practice might be called 'being a good citizen'. This social practice has a rather explicit instantiation in the signs posted nearby saying there is a fine for littering handbills.

These three social practices separately and taken together not only converge to produce the site of engagement, they are the basis for imputations and claims of identity. A knowledgeable (i.e., local) person knows to follow the flow, not to insist on right passing or left passing exclusively. A foreigner runs into people and in doing so claims his or her outsider identity. An urban North American does not accept handbills from strangers and in turning away from the distributor ratifies the distributor's imputation of expatriate identity. A good person does not litter handbills and so by carrying the handbill received to the next trash container to discard it accepts the imputation of that identity.

It will be obvious that all of these identity claims and imputations, contestations, and negotiations are open to reanalysis both within the situations by the participants and outside of them by the analyst. It will always remain somewhat indeterminate just which imputations are being made when multiple imputations are the most common case. What seems difficult to ignore, however, is that each of the social practices which are integrated into the mediated action produces some positioning of the actors both in respect to the social practice – member or non-member – and in respect to the other participants in the mediated action – ratification, negotiation, or contestation.

PHOTOGRAPHS

In Chapter 2 I outlined an analytical approach to photo-taking as a way of coming to understand the way social interaction is polarized into posing or spectacle roles on the one hand and watching or observing roles on the other. Now I would like to return for a moment to such photography sessions to look at them as sites of engagement. From this point of view the crucial question is no longer phrased as how is a with reconstituted as a watch as it was in that chapter. Here the relevant questions are: What is the mediated action taking place? How do the participants appropriate mediational means to accomplish their actions? How do those mediational means interpolate into the situation the social practice of the broader sociocultural lifeworld of the participants?

As mediated action, the photo-taking session (if we focus for now on the dating couple) is a date. The camera in the narrow sense and the photo shoot in the broader sense provide a mediational means of organizing the date by providing conventionalized social practices for the couple to enact. As I have said in Chapter 2, in Hong Kong the sociocultural practice which these events reproduce is, for most, fashion photography. Thus there are social practices governing the clothing styles which are appropriated for wear – particularly by the model to be posed. There are body postures and facial expressions to be taken on at the moment of the snap frame. Photographer and model alike construct their actions around the goal – clearly stated in ethnographic interviews as well as observed and documented – of producing 'professional-looking photographs'. This body of social practice provides a set of texts, movements, and conventionalized goals which guide the behaviour of the dating couple as each of them brings to the photo shoot their own competencies in these social practices gained from watching television, reading magazines, looking at light-box posters in the Mass Transit Railways and discussing such matters in conversations with friends. These social practices and their texts, which have been appropriated at prior sites of engagement, are called upon in the construction of the current, ongoing discursive event.

Thus, as I have argued above in respect to the news-stand and the handbill, these social practices also bring with them suggested ascribable identities. In one sense the model may pose as a known entertainer or fashion model identity. She (or on a very few occasions, he) may be trying to look like a particular person, or more to the point, like a particular photograph of that person. Thus the appropriated photograph is the identity the poser is claiming within the scope of the snap frame; it is a role taken on temporarily and enacted upon the stage of that snap and its consequent photograph.

In a slightly broader sense, it may be only the general style or form of presentation which is being claimed by the spectacle. She is not looking like Faye Wong or Björk[15] but more inclusively looking like a singing star. Thus the poser appropriates the colours, patterns, movements, postures, and facial expressions which claim entertainment provenience.

What is crucial to my analysis is that within this set of social practices are ascribable identities which the poser and photographer, spectator and watcher, jointly work to construct in the photograph thus produced. What is not a possibility within this set of social practices is failing to construct an identity. If one fails at the identity one is expected to claim, the result is not non-identity, it is failed or ruined identity. That is to say, it is not simply that the poser claims an identity which the photographer neutrally snaps. The photograph is jointly produced and in the subsequent session with the developed photograph in hand there is a discussion of the extent to which the claim was substantiated. As with the passing out of handbills where distributor and receiver together negotiate an identity for the receiver, one can succeed or fail, one can impute, claim, negotiate, or ratify, but what one cannot do is take a photograph or receive a handbill without some identity negotiation taking place. It is inherent in social practice that the identities of participants are constructed, sustained, or falsified in undertaking mediated actions.

LIVING ROOMS

While it is of great concern to the understanding of mediated discourse to have a fuller analysis of the social practices which converge in the ordinary living room where a television set is playing, that analysis is still at an early stage of development (Morley 1990; Livingstone 1992; Moores 1993; Ang 1996).[16] Our own research (R. Scollon and Yung, 1996; R. Scollon, Bhatia, Li, and Yung 1996) indicates that the situations in which television might be viewed or a newspaper might be read are highly complex intersections of social practices and mediated actions. In Hong Kong, for example, it is typical, not exceptional, for several people to be gathered in the same room, simultaneously engaged in several activities. Some may be eating a meal, some engaged in a conversation, some doing homework with significant overlapping among these separable activities. At the same time a television will be set to the evening news, a CD player will be playing music, and a computer will be engaged in a game. While Hong Kong might represent an extreme, a few less systematic observations in North America indicate that for a younger generation such polyfocal, multiparticipant activity is the norm, not the exception. It is clear that to elucidate the social practices which converge in such a situation is a descriptive headache and ultimately an explanatory nightmare.

It is important here, in drawing this chapter's analysis to a close, to reiterate a point made in Chapter 1. While the governing question is 'What mediated action is taking place in this concrete situation?', such a question has as its purpose to elucidate a point of view, not to objectify or reify mediated actions into countable entities. We could ask about the segment from the Doyle novel cited above in Chapter 3: What's the situation? What mediated actions are taking place? As an answer we would have to say that for the youngest son it is a language lesson in which the television programme, *The Virginian*, is appropriated only for its title. For Paddy it is a chance to appropriate Da's language and style at a moment when it is safe from Ma's censure. For Da it is a way to show non-involvement or disengagement with his family. The television programme is negatively appropriated as something he does not see, does not pay attention to; it is something he ignores. The crucial question is always to ask what analytical purpose can be served by a focus in one place rather than another.

All sites of engagement are convergences of multiple social practices which prepare ascribable identities for the participants. There is in analytical practice no means of untangling these practices into separable entities for discrete analysis, nor would it be desirable to do so. What is of primary concern is seeing each situation as a site for the struggle among conflicting discourses (Fairclough 1989, 1995b; Candlin 1996), only some of which are necessarily relevant in any particular analytical case.

SITES OF ENGAGEMENT OF NEWS DISCOURSE

The sites of engagement of news discourse which might be studied are concrete and manifold. In this chapter I have only sketched the outlines of four of them: the news-stand, the handbill, the photograph and the living room. What I hope to have successfully argued, however, is that all such sites of engagement are socially negotiated constructions of person within a converging set of social practices. One must expect each such site of engagement to manifest its own concrete conditions of production. A living room in which a television set is playing in one of Hong Kong's public housing estates might, in fact, approximate a living room in Roddy Doyle's 'Barrytown' of Northern Dublin as socioeconomic conditions might well produce a similar complex of social practices and technologies. At the same time our research tells us that only a few hundred metres away from one such living room in Hong Kong are other living rooms inhabited by expatriate university professors where the converging social practices and available technologies are so different as to constitute highly divergent mediated actions and social/discursive identities.

My goal in this section has been to argue two main points: (1) the communications in which news discourse or, more broadly, other forms of public discourse are significant for watchers and readers cannot be encompassed within a sender–receiver model of communication, that is, the communication cannot be construed as an interaction between news 'senders' and news 'receivers'; and (2) the sites of engagement in which the texts of news discourse may be appropriated within mediated actions are highly complex convergences of social practices and that the reception of news discourse cannot be usefully interpreted outside a theory of social interaction as social practice.

In the first case, I have suggested that the primary social interactions are among journalists as the producers of the spectacle which is observed by readers and viewers of the media. I have tried to develop this argument first by outlining the social practices by which spectacles and observers are formed, primarily by focusing on the social practices through which readers or watchers construct their social interactions. In the second case I have argued that the spectacles are not simply open and available for consumption but are, in fact, available only through windows or sites of engagement which themselves are constructed through various social practices which inherently ascribe identity to the participants.

In the section which follows I will then shift the focus from the social practices of reception to the social practices by which the participants in news discourse claim, ascribe and contest identities as they construct the spectacle of news discourse.

NOTES

1. To be sure there are persons who cannot resist a chat with the seller of the newspaper and there are places and times when such incidental conversational exchanges take place. Nevertheless, such social exchanges, which go beyond the immediate transaction of buying the paper, are relatively rare and become highlighted as exceptions to the practices I will describe here.
2. Mass Transit Railway (MTR) and Kowloon–Canton Railway (KCR) stations often have several news-stands as well as convenience stores selling newspapers and other periodicals.
3. There is, of course, a common third way in which a reader comes into possession of a newspaper and that is by reading a paper purchased by somebody else. Students of journalism generally assume that for every newspaper sold there are multiple readers. From the point of view of the theatre of discourse, I have not considered non-purchasing readers to be particularly significant. From the point of view of the participation framework, it also seems to make little difference to a reader opening the paper to find the financial news whether or not he or she has bought the paper or borrowed it from a friend.

4. As I will indicate below, news sellers make a number of assumptions about who their buyers will be and what these will take as normal behaviour.

5. While I have observed many women reading newspapers and women interviewees report that they and many other women read newspapers, I have observed many fewer woman actually purchasing a newspaper from one of these news-stands. It remains to be seen to what extent the behaviours and practices I describe here are gender-specific domains.

6. The *Eastern Express* has closed since this portion of the research was conducted.

7. Hotels which cater to foreign tourists and the airport, of course, do display foreign and locally published international newspapers.

8. While the whole box is chained and locked firmly in place, a small amount of money, usually in the neighbourhood of 50 cents, will open the door to the box and expose all of the stack of papers. Security of these boxes is focused on keeping the accumulated money safe; the newspapers themselves may be stolen for a very small investment. In a discussion among Hong Kong Chinese it was affirmed by some that it would be reasonable to pay for one paper, take them all, and resell them on the street elsewhere for a good profit.

9. Further study might allow us to categorize these behaviours as those of different types of customer. A tourist at the Star Ferry might well need to consider which paper to buy of several papers he or she did not know. On the other hand, other Hong Kong residents might leave their decision until they see which particular stories are covered by the various newspapers as they are frequently quite different. In either case the behaviour observed might appear to be the same.

10. As a caution against broad cultural generalization I should note here that in a number of cities in China in which I have made comparable observations (Guangzhou, Kunming, Xiamen, Wuzhou, Guilin, Beijing, Harbin, Qingdao) there is much discussion with the news seller as well as a considerable amount of examining of the papers before purchase.

11. A young woman colleague has reported that at least in one case a news seller has taken her to be a teenager and tried to hand her a comic book. Another news seller found it confusing to sell me a magazine in Chinese which is often reported to be the most popular among college-age students.

12. I do not know but can suppose that other characteristics such as class, gender or age enter in as typical characterizations. I would guess that newspaper sellers are likely to know approximately which customers are looking for racing sheets, which for upper-end dailies and which for more popular entertainment sheets.

13. From more recent observations in Kunming, Yunnan, it appears that the Chinese practice is changing in the direction of Hong Kong practice with many more handbills being distributed on the streets than were seen even just the year before. Whereas earlier handbills were almost all orientated towards medical treatments and handed out on the doorsteps of clinics and medicine shops, now there are many advertising restaurants and other shops and they are being distributed at some distance from the premises being advertised.

14. I use the pronoun 'she' in this case not generically, though the great majority of handbill distributors in Hong Kong are, in fact, women. Here and below I am citing specific, documented instances though, of course, without specifically identifying the person being referenced.

15. It was said in Hong Kong two or three years ago that the extremely popular Hong Kong and Chinese singer, Faye Wong, had come back from a European trip trying to look like the European singing star, Björk. Whether or not this is the case, what is crucial was that Hong Kongers in press and private conversation alike found it a significant topic of discussion to try to determine what identity was currently being enacted by a star whose identity many others appropriate in their private lives. It is a game of tracing back the chains of appropriation to original sources played by ordinary people in respect to entertainment stars, not just by literary critics in the Bakhtinian mould or critical discourse analysts.

16. Earlier studies by the Birmingham group (Hall 1980; Morley 1990) are certainly the major precursors in this, but only within the past decade has the interest in critical reading of popular culture begun to take an ethnographic focus.

INTERLUDE:

MEDIATED TRANSACTIONS

MODELS OF MEDIATED COMMUNICATION

The sender–receiver model has dominated thinking in communication for a long time, as I have said above. I have argued that a framework of mediated action within communities of practice is a more useful way of understanding mediated discourse. In this interlude, my purpose is to sketch four models that seem necessary at a minimum to account for the materials we have analysed so far. Also, I will suggest that it is not a simple matter of slotting any particular instance into *one* of these models as what seems to be going on is a highly active dynamics of playing one off against another.

For my analysis I think it is important to have two general concepts in mind, the *players* and the *transaction*. I actually want to downplay the *message* which is often a considerable distraction. This attitude reflects an interest in interactional sociolinguistics, which I am working to define as a concern to study the ways in which people in communication with each other mutually construct the situations they are in and their identities in those situations through discourse.

Players: These are the people who have and are recognized as having the right (perhaps obligation) to affect the development of the ongoing discourse. The normal model is the face-to-face conversation with primary speakers, responders, listeners and so forth who are all taken to have the right to take the floor, to issue backchannel responses, or to excuse themselves from the situation. I gave the business telephone call as the prototypical example or representative anecdote for this kind of social interaction where a hierarchical set of three practices were summarized with three Maxims of Stance: (1) attend to the definition of the situation; (2) attend to the positioning of the participants; (3) attend to the topic.

By this definition, someone watching a television show is not normally a player since he or she is not expected or allowed to chime in with a change of topic or even a comment which will be geared into the ongoing discourse. Notable exceptions are call-ins, of course. In television, the main players in the production community of practice are the actors, producers, directors, camera people, and the like on the production end who produce a 'spectacle' for broadcast. On the reception end there is a different community of practice, a different set of players; these are the people sitting around the television set carrying on their conversation about this and that, which might include what is on television, but their play is not geared into that of the television players in any kind of interactive social exchange. If the viewers introduce a topic, like Paddy Clarke's Da, it is not as players.

Transaction: Here I am not so concerned with the interactive discourse – what goes on among players. The concern is basically with who pays whom for what. I suppose I would not want to think only in terms of dollars exchanged, but to rough out a model that conceptually should keep the attention away from other forms of interaction.

I find in the media literature a concept frequently stated by enough different authors without the citation of anyone in particular that I think it is public domain. This thought is that the primary transaction that is going on in the daily newspaper or on television is the selling of an audience of readers and viewers to the buyers of advertising space. Broadcast television is free, except for the price of the set and the electricity to power it and the cover price of the daily newspaper is not enough to pay for the bulk newsprint, let alone the time of the news writers, editors, and the rest. The newspaper and television broadcast are paid for by advertisers. This is an old formula, going back to the advent of the modern newspaper in Europe, America and Tokugawa Japan in the seventeenth century and Hong Kong beginning in the nineteenth century. The 'consumer' who buys something is the product sponsor. The 'producers' are the advertisers together with the newspaper's advertising offices. The 'product' is the reader who is sold to the sponsor. Thus newspapers have a strong interest in building the size of their 'product' as well as making that 'product' to the specifications of the buyers, their advertisers.

This line of thought has been replicated here and there for all of the forms of the media, television, radio, and other media, now including the internet. I think it could be replicated as well for the developmental media in controlled states by simple alteration of the terms. Perhaps it could be argued that what the developmental media 'sell' is not a political message to the populace, but just the other way around: they sell the populace to the political leadership. It is their goal to manufacture a populace of certain specifications to the political leadership which supports their publication. Thus, like the commercial newspaper, it is in their best interests to create the concept of this readership, to exaggerate its size and loyalty, to hone its definition to those desired by the political leadership. It is to their own disadvantage to recognize the complexity of this 'reader-ship' in the same way that commercial readership surveys have little interest in the ethnographic complexities of their actual readers. This book will not sell advertising space. Saying that it is difficult or impossible to determine just who reads or watches what does not sell advertising space to those who are paying for it.

THE MESSAGE MODEL

This is the hoary sender–receiver model which assumes that the main players are the senders and the receivers of messages and that whatever transactions there might be are mutually negotiated (or at least negotiable) among the players. Perhaps the personal letter correspondence is the best example of the mediated version of the message model. I write to you; you write back. Each of us pays the postage; each responds to what the other has written.

There are some forms of public discourse which fit this pattern as well. Perhaps such things as street signs, traffic lights, maybe even laws fit this traditional model. The government has something rather specific to say: 'Stop', 'Do not turn left', 'This is Tat Chee Avenue'. Though it is a bit hard to see that there is much return conversation, at least it seems clear that the government is one player and the ordinary citizen is another, though with a rather restricted role.

THE SALES MODEL

In traditional advertising it seems the sales model is much like the message model. Together, the manufacturer (or service provider) and the advertiser create a message of the kind, 'If you want X, here is where you can get it'. This does not seem too much different from the traffic signal. And in Direct Advertising it is a good bit more interactional than government signage. 'The first 50 callers will get X', and a telephone number. One *can*, in fact, interact with the sender of the message. Here the receiver of this message is a player and there is a fairly overt, clearly outlined transaction. I leave aside the banks who mediate the credit card transactions in this, though that is in some ways a rather significant limitation on who may volunteer as a receiver of these direct advertising messages.

THE GAME MODEL

Above I have described this model as a 'watch'. That is, some set of people act as players in creating a spectacle for the observation of some other set of people. The simplest sort of watch is the ordinary photo-taking I described in Chapter 2. A with polarizes through a set of negotiated moves to create a spectacle, the posing model, and a watcher, the photographer. More complex watches are football games in which one set of players engages in a set of social interactions and that spectacle is sold to an audience of watchers who buy tickets for the privilege of being watchers.

In the football game, the spectacle is the main product which is jointly produced among the football players, the field judges, the owners of the teams, the government controllers of the stadiums, and so forth. This product is sold to the consumers, the fans who buy tickets. In such a spectacle, it seems to me to be stretching things to talk about messages being sent by the players to the fans or vice versa (except in rare cases such as when a football player leaps into the face of a fan shouting racialist slogans). Messages in the game model are largely sent back and forth among the players on the spectacle side (the football players, coaches, field judges) or back and forth among the players on the watch side (fans shouting at each other or with each other).

THE WALLPAPER MODEL

It is hard for me to see where public discourse in the sense of intending to send messages drops off and public discourse in the sense of what Eco (1995) calls 'anonymous design' takes over. I have in mind, in fact, wallpaper, room and building design, city layout, park design, pavements and other pathways for pedestrians or vehicles and all these other ways in which a discourse of at least suggested use is symbolized. One sees simply from the layout and landscaping the directive of the government to sit, stroll or relax in this place. It might be hard to call these communications in the message sense, but I would certainly want to include them in a broad picture of public discourse.

As to the problem of where wallpaper discourse shades into more purposive forms, in Hong Kong's Times Square food court, for example, there are plants along the sides (inedible) as decoration; there are rows of beans, rice and other grains in jars (edible, but uncooked; not available for sale in that food court); there are photographs on the wall behind the tables of unprepared fruits (edible, not available there), prepared fruits such as a watermelon cut open (edible, not available), steamed dim sum (edible, often available in such places, but not actually available), and cooked vegetable dishes (edible, and actually available in that place); there are photographs in the area behind the serving counters of dishes of food all of which are actually available for sale in that place.

These decorations form a continuum from purely decorative to promotional and I see no principled way of saying where to draw the line. The design aspect of the inedible plants fades further into the woodwork, the colour scheme in the floors and ceilings and so forth. The promotional aspect of the photos of the foods for sale fades further into the actual menu with prices of items behind the cashier. If I go to this food court with a particular food in mind to order, all of this may simply be wallpaper communication; I pay it no attention other than to know that I am in the familiar place. While in this case it is hard to imagine a customer who might want to buy the beans in jars along the room divider next to the tables, that scenario is not so absurd if one considers similar mistakes one has made in visiting foreign places. The tourist literature is full of anecdotes of people drinking the water meant to clean fingers or of people washing up in the Japanese green tea. My main point here is twofold: (1) there is a class of public discourse which, like the wallpaper, is meant to be minimally communicative – but that doesn't mean that it is not communicative; and (2) much public discourse, whatever the producers may intend, is treated as wallpaper, as unanalysed and unattended background decoration. The television news broadcast displayed on all the bank of television screens in an appliances store is not in most senses a new broadcast, it is closer to wallpaper. In the same way, as I have argued above, television in the homes we have observed and analysed is as often wallpaper to decorate a family chat as it is the object of focal, interpretive attention.

A COMPOSITE MODEL

This last example is not a composite so much as a case of variable treatment. That is, any of the models of discourse above might range from their prototypical use through to wallpaper. A direct advertising commercial on television which I leave on while I converse with somebody is no longer functioning in the sales (sender–receiver) model; it has been transformed to wallpaper. It is something decorating the room while other activities go on. A composite is somewhat different and the game model might be the easiest case to illustrate.

I said above that I thought we could think of a game as a kind of watch; that is, the players construct a spectacle for the observation of the watchers. The transaction is between the audience and the players (as well as the organizers and, in some unfortunate cases, the gamblers who have encouraged certain modes of play on the field) who put on the spectacle for tickets. But, of course, that whole entity – game plus watchers – can be spectacalized and broadcast on television (and photographed for the sport pages of the newspapers and magazines). In this case, however, it is a different sort of transaction. The observers, such as home viewers, are not paying to watch the game, that is, at least not on public broadcast television are they paying – I set aside cable and video versions as another framing. The primary transaction is one in which the broadcast of the game is the means of producing the product, the audience, to sell to the advertiser or other sponsor (corporate or otherwise).

It is a chained set of spectacles and watches in which the stadium viewers pay out good money to enjoy the spectacle and the home viewers get a free game in exchange for submitting to the process of being fashioned into a deliverable audience to the sponsors of the broadcast.

THE SOCIAL IDENTITY MODEL

The composite, then, seems to be the prototype for many advertisements by which the viewer is delivered by means of the spectacle
over to the sponsor for a price. What is the game being watched by
the viewers of advertising? One might call it Art, Social Discourse,
Contemporary Identity Symbolism and so forth. I am not ready yet
to say that the main game being watched is social identity, but it
seems that is a significant part of it. As adverts emerge from wallpaper status to fuller focal attention, that is, as we stand around
waiting for the Mass Transit Railway and notice a lightbox that had
just been an area of colour and design just a moment before, it
might not be stretching things too much to say that we move into
becoming observers of a game of social identity. These are the products, designs, colours, symbols, meanings of people of a certain
kind. This product or service are ways of identifying those people.

In the social identity model, a popular clothing store can be the
setting for the construction of social identity isomorphic with the
construction of audience for sale to the corporate owner as Giroux
(1994) has argued. A person who goes in and buys a pair of popular
jeans not only engages in an instance of the direct sale transaction,
he or she also marks himself or herself as the sort of person who
buys things there. Perhaps we can assume this person also wears
those things. A person who decides to walk out of the store and not
buy because a group of people not of his or her own self-claimed
group has walked in or purchased something has chosen to distance his or her own image from that of that store's other customers.
The same person seeing a lightbox advertisement or commercial on
television might treat it as wallpaper behind a conversation with a
friend or might treat it in the sales model as an indirect suggestion
to buy or might additionally treat it as a claim to common social
identity (if perhaps he or she is wearing an item of that brand of
clothes) or as an opportunity to claim distance from that brand's
wearers.

TENSION IN SOCIAL PRACTICE: COMPETING DISCOURSES

I have used the word model but could probably go back with very
few adjustments and use the word social practice without significantly changing the gist of this interlude. What is interesting in

looking at public discourse from this framework is not trying to decide which social practice is the dominant or hegemonic practice in any particular instance so much as seeing how one social practice is often being played off interdiscursively against another. In the composite model, for example, using the social practices of the game to give the home viewer a free game to watch without a ticket provides a pleasant distraction from the social identity social practice which is also being instantiated. One does not mind a discourse in which one is identified as someone who watches football games around the house if one is getting a good free game without the messes of travel and bad weather.

Certainly there is much interdiscursivity across these social practices in the course of an evening's television, a browse through a newspaper or magazine, or a walk along Nathan Road in Hong Kong or Madison Avenue in Chicago. What is wallpaper for one person is the game social practice for another; what is social identity for one is an ordinary sale for another. A commercial on television is a cry to call up and buy on one day ('Let's call up and get that'), social identity on another ('Hey look, there's that commercial for that junk out on the back porch we were dumb enough to buy'), and wallpaper on a third when it is not even noticed.

RECEPTIVE DISCOURSE IDENTITIES

I am rapidly retreating from any hope of establishing any more substantial concept of receptive discourse identity than something that is like a strobe light that flashes on and off in variegated colours. At one time I might have thought that research would lead to a few somewhat distinct receptive identities that could somehow be matched up to productive identities and therefore tell us something about how people learn to take on such roles as author or reader/viewer. Now it seems to me the puzzling questions are: Where does the notion of monomorphic, unifocal, consistent identities such as 'the reader' or 'the author' come from? Out of what have we constructed the idea that texts are written by authors and read by readers? How have we constructed the idea that a message is sent by one person and received by another?

The provisional answer of this interlude is that at least some people have a vested, ideological interest in fixing these notions.

We know historically that publishers, for example, fixed copyright law largely to produce the concept of ownership of text. They needed to create a commodity out of the flux of ordinary written discourse. It is clear enough that in order to enlist the producers of that discourse in their cause they had to restrict their freedom to produce similar texts for other publishers (R. Scollon 1994, 1995; Sherman and Strowel 1994; Pennycook 1996). That is the known history of copyright. So publishers have an interest in there being such things as single authors to be held responsible for signing over their polyvocal, highly intertexually constructed creations as distinctly bounded and unique textual commodities. In exchange publishers pay authors for their cooperation in producing these commodities.

On the other end (and a good deal more recently) the people who sell television and newspaper advertising space (not to mention lightboards on the Mass Transit Railway or the sides of buses and trams) need to be able to convince commercial sponsors that some definite (and usually large) number of people of a specific type exist and can be delivered to them. No room in market surveys for the vagaries of kaleidoscopic social identities that fade interdiscursively in and out of focal awareness.

Apparently the answer to the question 'What are the principal receptive discourse identities to be found in news and other forms of public discourse?' is 'Who cares?' If you are a market surveyer, you should want to ensure fixed, identifiable categories of buyers to be sold to corporate sponsors. But what if you are a teacher of academic writing? a speech writer? a publisher? an advertising copy-writer? In each case there is a rather different ideological need for there to be certain kinds of discourse identity.

WHAT DO JOURNALISTS DO?

The gist of this reflective interlude is that we now have a serious analytical problem to face in making our bridge between interactional sociolinguistic studies of media reception and studies of what journalists do. The first four chapters have worked to argue that in any useful sense of the word 'audience', the audience of news discourse is not really there. At best we can speak of communities of practice in which the spectacles of the media are appropriated. There is no simple, concrete, and identifiable audience to which any bit of news discourse is being sent. The sad news to journalists from the field of interactional sociolinguistics is that the audience is not there. They are broadcasting and writing into a highly interdiscursive, contested, and social space in many cases and in others they are being pasted up as wallpaper or used to wrap fish.

The question this leaves us with is: What is it journalists and the media are doing? They are certainly active in their work and it is the concern of the following chapters to work through how the work of journalists and newsmakers is carried out as a form of primary social interaction among themselves as a community of practice. For this analysis I will look directly at the texts of news discourse and their presentation as newspapers and television broadcasts. First I will argue that the identities of television journalists are constructed within the community of practice through a set of framing practices. Producers and editors provide the broadest frame through the use of station logos and other on-screen identifications by which they frame the presenters as the on-screen authorities. Presenters, in turn, delegate the floor and a portion of their power and position to the reporters. Reporters for their part ratify their identities through self-identifications and explicit relinquishing the floor back to presenters. Through these practices the community of practice of television journalists positions their identities primarily in relationship to each other, not in relationship to the viewer of the television broadcast.

Newspaper journalists, using the analogous practices of headlines, leads, bylines and source attributions show themselves to be taking up positions in relationship to others in their own community of practice. This becomes particularly clear when, in Chapter 7, I show that in both television and newspaper journalism the utterances of the newsmakers themselves are largely used as the discursive means by which journalists claim and position their own identities in relationship to other journalists while delegating only the most limited range of voice to the newsmakers.

PART III:

THE DISCURSIVE CONSTRUCTION OF THE PERSON IN THE NEWS MEDIA

FIVE

Television journalists

OPENING FRAMES

In the telephone call, as well as other social interactions, callers and answerers are identified in what Schegloff (1972, 1986) termed an identification sequence, as I have indicated in Chapter 2. Goffman (1963) refers to ritual practices by which members of a 'with' establish their rights to join into this primary social interaction. To begin to unpack the social interaction in which journalists are given identity and voice, in the television news broadcast, I will look first at reporters. I will begin by considering how a news report is framed within the broader framework of the television news programme. In television, in most cases, the reporter is introduced by the presenter.

The story which follows was recorded from TVB Pearl in Hong Kong on 13 January 1994.[1] As an example of a television news story, it displays the most common elements of such a story.

> [FEMALE PRESENTER (on screen)]: China has issued a
> strong warning to countries in the region which have
> received unofficial visits from leading Taiwanese politicians.
> The comments were aimed at Singapore and Malaysia
> and coincide with reports Taiwan's President Lee Tung
> Hui will be travelling to Indonesia next month. (PAUSE)
> *Annabel Roberts reports.*
> [FEMALE REPORTER (voice-over narration)]: Beijing has no
> time for Taiwan's pragmatic approach to its diplomatic
> isolation. The island has official contacts with only a
> handful of countries as most choose to recognize the
> mainland and not Taiwan as the legitimate government
> of all China. [*REPORTER IDENTIFIED WITH ON-SCREEN
> CHARACTERS*] Recently the island's senior politicians

have been paying private visits to countries in the region such as Singapore and Malaysia where unofficial meetings have taken place with national leaders. Beijing does not approve. Today the officials condemned the practice as diplomatic trickery, and warned the offending countries that such visits would not be tolerated.

[ACTUALITY (Wu Jianmin, China Foreign Ministry Spokesman)] (Voice of translator: actuality omitted)

[FEMALE REPORTER (voice-over narration)]: But the Foreign Ministry was happy to be able to authorize a Sino–French communiqué signalling a thaw in relations between the two countries. This has not gone down well across the Taiwan Straits. Relations between France and China deteriorated in 1992 when the French sold more than sixty fighter jets to Taipei. They've now pledged to ban future weapon sales to the island. The Taiwanese say they have to buy arms to protect themselves and this agreement threatens the security of the whole region. Officials claim the mainland defence budget is increasing all the time, and Taiwan should not be prevented from buying adequate protection. Germany, Britain, and the Netherlands have made similar promises not to sell arms to Taipei. The Taiwanese feel that losing the French market as well is the final straw. *Annabel Roberts, TVB News.*

[FEMALE PRESENTER (on screen)]: Authorities . . . (begins another story)

The story begins with the presenter's two-sentence summary or lead. As she speaks these lines directly into the camera, above her right shoulder is an inset with the insignia of the Mainland Chinese government superimposed upon an outline map of China which is, in turn, superimposed upon a flag of the People's Republic of China. As a regular element in such news stories, I suggest we could call this summary statement the *opening frame* (OF).

The third sentence follows a short pause and is said in a somewhat lowered voice register, *Annabel Roberts reports*. In this, the presenter indicates that responsibility for the story is now being passed over from her to another person, a reporter named Annabel Roberts. I suggest that we can call this the *delegation frame* (DF) in that its function appears to be to delegate the floor, at least temporarily to another speaker.

There are two aspects of the delegation frame which seem worth considering. The first of these is that the person to whom the floor is being delegated is identified by name by the presenter. It is worth noting it in this instance, even though it is the most common means of framing the report, because this is not always the case, as we shall see below. The second aspect is that the verb chosen here is 'reports'. Again, while this is by far the most common verb used in the delegation frame, it is not the only one. What seems significant is that it is a verb of speaking which highlights the reportorial frame. One does not find, for example, 'Annabel Roberts will be speaking next', nor 'the next voice is that of Annabel Roberts'. That is to say, the presenter, in delegating the floor to Annabel Roberts, does not delegate it to her in an open-ended way. We understand that while Annabel Roberts will have the floor, she will only have it for a specific purpose – that delegated by the presenter – reporting.

This should be compared with Schegloff's (1972; see also Chapter 2) early observation that in telephone calling, the answerer of the summons (or call) does not have rights to the introduction of the topic. The answerer replies in such a way as to turn the floor back to the caller after completing the identification sequence so that the caller may introduce his or her topic. In the case of the television news report we see that it is the presenter who asserts the right and power to define unilaterally the situation and to introduce the topic and only rather narrowly and temporarily delegates the floor to the named reporter. I say narrowly because the reporter is understood to be required to report within this already specified topical frame. I say temporarily because the reporter is understood to be required to return the floor to the presenter when the report is finished. Thus the reporter is positioned in a decidely secondary status in respect to the presenter.

Following on the delegation frame, then, the next voice one hears is that of the delegated reporter. Or one assumes so. The reporter, Annabel Roberts in this case, is not immediately identified. On screen is Wu Jianmin, China Foreign Ministry Spokesman, who is seen speaking. The voice, which we might presume to be a woman's voice, in juxtaposition with the on-screen face, a man's face, cues us that this voice is the voice of the named reporter. This inference is further warranted by the topical paralleling of the presenter's opening line. Notice that the presenter has begun by saying 'China has issued a strong warning'. The delegated reporter begins, 'Beijing has no time for Taiwan's pragmatic approach'.

Finally, as the phrase 'legitimate government' begins there is a cut to a shot of news cameras shooting the scene of Wu Jianmin speaking. There we see on the screen the characters 'ANNABEL ROBERTS [underlined] TVB News' as the picture returns directly to the Foreign Ministry Spokesman. That is to say, the reporter is directly labelled by on-screen characters and indirectly suggested by the shot of the news cameras.

This latter point is of some significance as well. The press conference is being held in Beijing in this case where the TVB News camera crew has recorded it. The reporter, Annabel Roberts, may or may not be there in Beijing. Normally at that time she covered only Hong Kong stories. She does not appear in the shot of the cameramen and reporters. In other words, her reliability as an on-the-scene reporter is implied in this manner when, in fact, she most likely has introduced the narration in a Hong Kong studio.

THE CLOSING FRAME

I will not yet move down into the further re-delegation of the floor which occurs when the reporter turns the floor over to the Foreign Ministry Spokesman, Wu Jianmin, in what is usually called an actuality – the recorded speech of a newsmaker. That is an issue I will take up in Chapter 7. Instead, I will move on to the closing frame.

As Goffman has argued (1963, 1974), social interactions require formal closings as well as openings. In business telephone calls I have studied above in Chapter 2, for example, callers go through a hierarchical sequence of closing out the topic before closing out the relationship and then finally closing the channel – 'OK. Thanks. Bye.' Similarly, in television news broadcasts, the delegation of the floor to the reporter requires a parallel closing which turns the floor back to the presenter. This is normally accomplished, as it is in this case, with a statement of the form NAME + NEWS AGENCY: *Annabel Roberts, TVB News*. As I will indicate below, where this reporter is assumed to be in the same location as the presenter, this is the entire frame. When the reporter is presented as being in another location the frame is NAME + NEWS AGENCY + LOCATION. For example, there is *Julie Mapleston, TVB News, London* in the seventeenth story of this same news broadcast.

The next shot is that of the presenter who is re-established at the news desk where we saw her in the opening frame. While this is the opening frame of the next news story, it should be borne in mind that this also serves to ratify the reporter's closing framing statement. This particular story, then, has the following framing structure:

Female Presenter <China criticizes Taiwan visits>
  Opening Frame (Summary introduction)
    Delegation Frame *Annabel Roberts reports*
      FR {IDNO;IDCE}
    Closing Frame *Annabel Roberts, TVB News* {IDNS}

In angle brackets <> is a mnemonic phrase indicating the content of the story. The codes in brackets {} indicate the form of identification: IDNO means 'identified; named by other'; IDCE means 'identified; characters in English'; IDNS means 'identified; named by self'. There is also here at least one other type of identification which should not be missed, that is, 'identified through voice'. In some cases this is, in fact, the only form of identification available.

In this story, in fact, it is only an assumption of continuity added to this voice identification which tells us that after the actuality with Wu Jianmin it is the same reporter, Annabel Roberts, who retakes the floor. It is an assumption we make easily enough; it does after all represent the maxim covering identification and relationship that once identity has been established it is assumed to be maintained until further notice, but in a fair number of instances, this is the only means by which the delegated reporter is identified.

Taken together, we see that the reporter to whom the television news story is delegated is multiply identified. She is named by the presenter. She names herself in closing. Characters on the screen identify her. We know her name and her news agency and, in this case, her voice (but not her face). As I will argue in Chapter 6 below, this is a good bit more than we know about the corresponding reporters in newspaper stories. Finally, we have also seen that the reporter's activities are rather closely constrained by the delegation of the presenter to the activity of reporting on a particular topic.

DELEGATION FRAMES (TELEVISION)

The delegation frame is the statement which says to whom the following responsibility for authorship is delegated and the delegation is further constrained topically by the lead statement of the presenter. This delegation frame is the discoursal means of formal turn exchange or passing of the floor to another. At the other end is the closing frame. This is where the person to whom the floor and the responsibility for authorship have been delegated signals that he or she is returning the floor and its accompanying responsibility for authorship to the designator, the presenter. The news story takes place within this frame.

Of course, within the story the reporter further delegates responsibility and authorship to the newsmakers, but that is another issue somewhat differently managed in actual cases which I take up in Chapter 7. For the moment I am interested in seeing what can be said about the discoursal means by which the person of the reporter is constructed, established, and sustained in a number of actual cases.

In most cases in my data the delegation frame is spoken as in the example I have given above. The formula is as follows:

NAME + *reports* (English)
NAME + *boudouh* ('reports', Cantonese)[2]

Where the reporter is located away from the city of the presenter, the formula is as follows:

NAME + *reports* + LOCATION (English)
NAME + LOCATION + *boudouh* (Cantonese)

The difference in the order of elements in the two languages reflects syntactic differences between these languages. Thus we have the following instances of these delegation frames in the news reports I have studied:

NAME boudouh
NAME reports
    (32 instances)

NAME haih bakging boudouh ('NAME reports from Beijing')
NAME haih gwongjau boudouh ('NAME reports from Guangzhou')
    (6 instances)

NAME reports from London
    (1 instance)

There are variations on this delegation frame which add further identifying elements. For example, there is

Correspondent NAME reports

in which the named person is further labelled 'correspondent'. It is likely that the word 'correspondent' carries further significance regarding the degree of relationship or the position that reporter has with the sponsoring news agency. For example, a CBS reporter is labelled 'White House Correspondent NAME' which is, presumably, a higher ranked position than 'correspondent'. This same frame may occur with or without a designated location as in the following story:

Correspondent NAME reports from Little Rock (CBS)

The location may also be embedded in the organizational description:

CNN's Detroit Bureau Chief, NAME reports (CNN)

In many cases, however, the delegation frame is even more varied than we have seen in these 'standardized' frames. Following the Annabel Roberts story above is a second story in which she is given the floor as follows:

Here's Annabel Roberts again (TVB)

We are left to presume that she is back to do the same thing she did in the preceding report, that is report on the introduced topic. What is different in this case is that there is no verb indicating the role the reporter is expected to play. Of course, within the continuation context of the preceding news report, this reporter was clearly identified and clearly delegated to the same or very similar topic.

In other cases a reporter is not identified as a reporter, but is said to 'have that story'. For example, there are the following:

Correspondent NAME has that part of the story (CBS)
CNN's NAME has the story (CNN)

In the second case we are to assume that the designation as belonging to the CNN organization implies a reportorial function. We would be surprised to have a CNN accountant, for example, appear to discuss CNN's internal financial matters.

One of the more elaborate identification sequences found in a delegation frame indicates the cultural importance medical doctors are presumed to have within the audience of CBS News.

CBS News health correspondent Dr NAME has the story (CBS)

The reporter is quadruply elevated above the status of the ordinary reporter by being labelled a 'correspondent', a 'CBS correspondent', a 'health correspondent' and a doctor.

In other cases 'has the story' is modified to 'having the details' of the story already established by the presenter as in:

NAME has the details of the rescue package (CNN)

This neutral frame of 'getting' or 'having' rather than 'reporting' is used most often in cases where the story is not attributed to a particular reporter but to an agency. Thus we have the following:

We get that story from CBS News (TVB Pearl)
We have details from ABC News (TVB Pearl)
ITN has more details (TVB Pearl)
We have this report from ABC News (TVB Pearl)
This report from WTN (TVB Pearl)

I have said above that within the delegation frame two discoursal moves are made: the identification of the following voice (or source) and the restriction of the topic. In some cases a somewhat fuller view of the activities of a particular reporter is given. For example, as a story was developing the presenter delegated the floor with the following frame:

We have been receiving late updates from Moscow and NAME has been monitoring them. (TVB Pearl)

In this case we picture the named reporter sitting elsewhere in the studio all day watching these news feeds. Further, we can gather that the presenter himself does not know what will be found in the report to follow. That is to say, he is unable to restrict the topical relevance of what will follow more than to say that it will be a continuation story on the theme he has mentioned.

Another type of continuation story is the series of reports on a special topic which might run for a few days consecutively. One of these called 'Eye on America' occurs in this data. The reporter, who is called a correspondent in this case, is said to be investigating.

Correspondent NAME investigates for tonight's 'Eye on America' (CBS)

A similar situation is when the presenter is framing a sequence of related stories. For example, in covering a series of stories concerning the US President, the first story contained the following delegation frame:

White House correspondent NAME begins our (re)coverage (CBS)

In transcribing this delegation frame I have chosen to retain the apparent slip of the tongue in '(re)coverage'. While one could never be sure to have established the source of this 're', I suggest that the source is the word 'report'. This is not quite the same as 'coverage', of course, and as subsequent items in this broadcast indicate, this was, in fact, coverage in the sense that there were a series of reports from different points of view, one of which was live. Although I would not want to make too much of this, I suggest that 'report' implies a fixed, finalized, edited news story but 'coverage' allows, even if it does not fully imply, a more spontaneous and even live presentation. I think we can further presume that 'coverage' is restricted to institutionally well-established figures as the news organization must risk putting them on the international networks without editing. There may be in the slipped word 're' a mistaken positioning of lower status for the 'White House correspondent NAME' than is institutionally allowable and this is at least one reason for the immediate correction.[3] The story which follows is, in fact, a fixed, edited report.

Whatever the situation might have been in the first instance, when the presenter continues in the second story with another correspondent, the delegation frame indicates the 'coverage' is now 'live'.

Chief Washington correspondent NAME live on Capitol Hill tonight with the latest, Bill? (CBS)

In this case the frame is strikingly different from any of the others considered so far. There is no verb at all to indicate what activities are to be expected of this correspondent. The floor is delegated to him in two ways, by formal title with full name on the one hand and by the vocative 'Bill'. While his 'story' is framed within the topic set by the presenter, it is clear that of all the stories considered so far, this correspondent has the greatest topical or discoursal freedom.

I suggest that both the status of this correspondent as Chief Washington correspondent for CBS News and his live reportage are factors in this more open-ended delegation frame. As I have suggested above, it is likely that status and live coverage are linked; the risk involved in opening an international network to the activities of a report must carry with it a weight of responsibility which is only delegated to reporters (correspondents) of significant status within the news organization. One might go so far as to suggest that 'live' status is, in fact, close to passing over into becoming a presenter, a kind of shift of role within the overall framework of the news reporter.

The double identification in this delegation frame has another interesting feature. The first identification is rather formal identification of status; the second switches to the quite informal first-name basis. This places the viewer in the position of viewing the presenter and the correspondent as they engage in quasi-informal conversation. The delegation frames we have considered above contrast with this one in presenting us with a neutral, formal and omniscient narrator who tells us the facts of the case. Here we see two news people, a studio presenter and an on-the-scene correspondent (he is standing in front of Mr Clinton's house – the White House) talking back and forth, addressing each other, not the viewers about what is happening in Washington.

Another type of delegation frame occurs when sometimes the delegation frame is embedded within a longer summarizing statement as it is in the following cases:

> But as NAME reports, some lawmakers believe the increase in
>   public expenditure doesn't go far enough (ATV World)
> As correspondent NAME reports, the violence of recent days has
>   not slowed the campaigning. A caution: Some of the scenes in
>   this report are quite graphic (CBS)
> As CNN's NAME reports, the two discussed a wide range of issues,
>   including Russia's evolving relationship with the US (CNN)
> As CNN's NAME reports, the Rabin government has had enough
>   of anti-Arab lawlessness (CNN)
> But as Bill Dorman reports from Tokyo the two sides are still far
>   from reaching a connection on other economic matters (CNN)

These longer summarizing delegations, however, are rather rare. There are only these five instances in the six full news shows I have closely analysed. They do, however, present the reporter in a somewhat different light from that of the standard delegation frame. They suggest, whether it is actually true or not, that the presenter is in the position of quoting or of giving information gleaned from the reporter's story. Rather than suggesting that the presenter is restricting the reporter to the designated topic, these summarizing delegations suggest that the shoe is on the other foot, that it is the presenter who is limited to what the reporter has originally prepared.

In all of the delegation frames I have presented so far there has been some explicit linguistic form of delegation. Nevertheless, there are also cases where the delegation frame is accomplished through gesture without speech. This occurs when there are two (or more) presenters and one of them provides the opening frame for a story reported by the other. At the slot where one of the delegation frames above would normally be found, the presenter turns his or her head in the direction of the other presenter. The picture then switches to the other presenter who begins the story on camera. While there are only two of these within the materials I have closely studied (ATV Home), I have frequently observed this pattern in other news broadcasts, especially at points of transition between major segments of the news broadcast such as between the spot news and sports broadcasts or sports and the weather.

Finally, there are a number of cases (10 instances) where the presenter reports his or her own story. In such cases there is no linguistic delegation frame. In many, but not all cases, the presenter delegates himself or herself by looking down, presumably at a television monitor, at the point where the camera switches from the presenters' desk to the film clips of the news story and at which time we go from hearing the presenter's voice in the studio to the same person's recorded voice on tape. In none of the cases I have recorded is the reporter/presenter further identified by screen characters.

CLOSING FRAMES

Once a reporter (or correspondent) finishes with his or her delegated turn at the floor, in most cases he or she returns the floor to the person who originally delegated it. The linguistic frames which are used are more regular and simpler overall than the delegation frames, as is appropriate for a participant in a discourse who is positioned in a secondary status (Scollon and Scollon 1995a). The basic closing frame is this:

NAME + NEWS AGENCY (LOCATION) [English]
NEWS AGENCY, ROLE + NAME (LOCATION) *boudouh*
  [Cantonese]

There are two differences here between the English and the Cantonese frames on which comment may be necessary. The first of these differences is in word order, the Cantonese giving organization first, before the reporter's name and the English inverting this order. This is most easily understood as a difference in intrinsic ordering of such elements within the syntax of the two languages (Li et al. 1993). The second difference, however, may not be directly under the influence of syntactical requirements. The Cantonese news reports on television specifically mention both the reporter's role *geije* ('reporter') and the verb for reporting *boudouh* ('reports'). Otherwise these closing frames may be taken to be quite regular in both languages considered. As in the delegation frames, where the location is not given it may be assumed that the reporter is located in the same city as the presenting organization. The following are examples which I have recorded in English:

NAME, TVB News
NAME, ABC News
    (7 instances)

NAME, TVB News, London
NAME, CBS News, Detroit
NAME, CBS News, Denver
NAME, CBS News, Little Rock
NAME, CBS News, Tambiza
NAME, CBS News, Charlotte
NAME, CNN News, Jerusalem
NAME, CNN Business News, London
NAME, CNN Business News, Tokyo
NAME, CNN, Detroit
    (10 instances)

The following are examples of Cantonese closing frames which show the analogous patterns in that language:

ajau dihnsih geije NAME boudouh ('ATV reporter NAME reporting')
mouhsin dihnsih geije NAME boudouh ('TVB reporter NAME reporting')
    (24 instances)

mouhsin dihnsih geije NAME haih bakghing boudouh ('TVB reporter NAME reporting from Beijing')

ajau dihnsih geije NAME haih bakging boudouh ('ATV reporter
  NAME reporting from Beijing')
ajau dihnsih geije NAME haih gwongjau boudouh ('ATV reporter
  NAME reporting from Guangzhou')
    (6 instances)

There are not many closing frames which depart from this no-
nonsense, secondary positioning approach and very few in English
in which any indication of the reporter's roles or statuses are
considered. In one case, however, there is the following:

Dr NAME, CBS News, New York (CBS)

This is the 'CBS Health Correspondent Dr NAME' which I have
discussed above as quadruply identified in the delegation frame.
In the closing frame, while he does not go to the extreme of the
delegation identification, he does make sure to identify himself
as 'DR NAME'. Furthermore, this is the one case in all of these
delegation or closing frames in which I find an exception to the rule
that a reporter does not identify his or her location when in the
same city as the news desk from which the news is emanating. This
Dr NAME claims that he is in New York. CBS News originates
from New York as well. I will leave it to the reader to consider
whether this departure is for one or the other of two reasons; either
it is to borrow on the North American prestige associated with
New York or it is to distance himself from the rest of the news
staff there in New York, who no doubt work at editing consoles
within a few feet of this 'health correspondent' within the studios
of CBS News.

Other exceptional cases suggest that where there are exceptions
in the closing frame there are special circumstances in either the
nature of the report or of the reporter. In the frame given above the
slot LOCATION is almost always filled with the name of a city.
There are a few exceptions, however. In one case in a delegation
frame, for example, the Chief Washington Correspondent is said to
be 'on Capitol Hill'. Most Americans, indeed most viewers of this
broadcast elsewhere, would understand this to mean in Washington, DC either at the US Congress or the White House. This latter
would itself be known to be the President's residence much as
international viewers would also know that '10 Downing Street' is
where we would find the British Prime Minister and 'the Kremlin'
where we would find the Russian President.

In the continuation report given over several days, this day's report was on airport security. While no mention was made of the location in the delegation frame, in the closing frame we have the following:

At Washington's International Airport, NAME for 'Eye on America' (CBS)

This is the only case in which a specific place within a city is given other than Capitol Hill, but in this case it appears that the significance of the mention of the International Airport is not associated with prestige so much as to differentiate the locations of the sites of this series of reports.

Another closing frame which is found in these materials is the following:

NAME, CNN, with the Secretary of State, Vladivostok, Russia (CNN)

This is the only case where a reporter tells us with whom he is travelling or indeed makes any mention of anyone else. There are two points to be considered. The first is that we understand this reporter is not stationed in Vladivostock. For that we would have the frame NAME + NEWS AGENCY, LOCATION. We understand him to be travelling with the US Secretary of State who in this case was returning to the US from a visit to China by way of the Russian city.

While we might want to understand this identification as focusing on the prestige of association with the US Secretary of State, and there is certainly reason to think that is an important aspect of this identification, there is the second factor – the mention of where in the world the city Vladivostock is, that is, Russia. This clarification seems to imply that the reporter expects that the viewer may not so easily locate Vladivostok as other cities mentioned in these broadcasts such as Detroit, London, Denver, Charlotte, Tokyo, or Jerusalem. The point to be drawn from this is that whether one looks from the point of view of prestige or simply of orientation for the viewer, the location of the report must be understood as at least potentially reflecting an aspect of the identity of the reporter.

Not all closing frames are made explicit through linguistic identifiers, however. As in the case of delegation frames, there are instances of closing frames in which the story just ends with a fall in the pitch of the narrator's voice and a return to the main news desk. Two of these, those in which there was a gestural delegation frame, are closed with a corresponding turn of the head towards the other presenter. The camera then switches to the other presenter who introduces the next story.

Correspondingly, when the presenter frames his or her own news story, there is in some cases (but not all) a gestural retaking of the floor when the camera comes back on the presenter. He or she is found looking down or off camera, presumably at a monitor, and then returns his or her gaze directly to the camera to signal a return to presenter status. I have not analysed these separately from another and somewhat larger group of stories in which there is no closing frame at all but simply a return to the news desk for the opening frame of the following story. Most of these are, in fact, international news stories, not locally produced ones, but I am not prepared to surmise further about the circumstances in which there is such a minimal closing frame other than to say that overall this is a rather small number of the total number of stories and mostly from one news organization.[4]

There remains one exceptional case to be accounted for. As I have indicated above there was one story on CBS News in which the Chief Washington Correspondent was delegated the floor with minimal topical restrictions and with the rather informal first-name tag, 'Bill'. When that quasi-conversational exchange was completed, it came time for 'Bill' to relinquish the floor and return it to the CBS News presenter in New York. He does this with the rather casual,

> *Connie?*

At the news desk in New York, the presenter hesitates and then says,

> *(Co-)NAME on Capitol Hill, thank you* (CBS)

The syllable in parentheses 'Co-' represents a false start which is self-corrected. Of course we do not know what might have been intended by this interrupted word; it seems likely that it would be 'correspondent'. This person is the one identified as 'Chief Washington Correspondent NAME.' What is important is that the presenter jumps in to supply the missing closing frame in this report by identifying the correspondent by name and by location. She then reiterates the conversational frame by saying, 'thank you' before taking up the opening frame of the following story. This line is said in a quick, lowered voice, much like the voice usually assumed by reporters in ending their own reports. I would suggest that both in terms of content and prosody, the presenter sees herself as filling a necessary closing frame; a task which must be accomplished before moving on to the following story.

POWER AND POSITIONING

Television news stories, then, can be seen to work within the same set of social practices I have outlined in Chapter 2 for social interaction. The Maxims of Stance provide a framework for understanding how and why the floor is rather formally handed over to the reporter, the reporter is quite clearly identified, and then in closing, the reporter quite clearly turns the floor back to the presenter. Even where the pattern appears to falter as in the last example considered, the presenter works together with the reporter to accomplish jointly the closure on his behalf.

The question of identity in such discourses needs to be understood as not just a matter of naming reporters; more importantly, it consists in accounting for their authority to be taking over the floor as well. That is to say, there is a question of authorship, principalship, and animation as Goffman (1974, 1981) has suggested. We have seen in the examples above that not only are reporters identified, they are positioned as participants according to their place within an organizational framework of the news agency. Thus we have seen 'reporter', 'correspondent', 'Chief Washington correspondent', 'CBS Health Correspondent', 'Dr', 'with the Secretary of State', 'White House correspondent' and the like. Furthermore, they are given roles varying from off-camera voice-over narration on one extreme to quasi-conversational live chatting with the presenter on the other. Each of these indicates some difference in the degree of responsibility for the words spoken which is being assigned by the news organization to the reporter in his or her role as a reporter.

In most of the cases I have observed there are only the smallest of mistakes made, which, while they provide a glimpse into the workings of these identity-making aspects of the discourse, are at best suggestive. One radio news story which I have recorded, however, indicates that delegating the floor and the reportorial role as well as accepting this role are not always accomplished without glitches.

The following news report is a radio broadcast on the morning of 1 January 1993 (Metro News, Hong Kong). At midnight there had been a tragic crowd panic which resulted in 21 young people being crushed to death in the New Year celebration. This recording was made at 8:30 the next morning at a time when the reporters can be assumed to have been working most of the night without sleep.

[NARRATOR, CHARLIE CHARTERS] 20 die in New Year tragedy./ With Brian Curtis I'm Charlie Charters this is the Metro News World Report./

Twenty people have died after New Year's celebrations in Lan Kwai Fong went out of control as crowds stampeded over fallen party goers./ The government has promised to hold an enquiry and police have sealed off the area as they collect what evidence remains of the nighttime tragedy./ Most of the injured and dead were rushed to Queen Mary Hospital and it's from there that Metro's Francis Moriarty joins us live with the latest details.

[FRANCIS MORIARTY] Yes

(long silence)

[NARRATOR, CHARLIE CHARTERS] Francis!

[FRANCIS MORIARTY] I'm here.

[NARRATOR, CHARLIE CHARTERS] Can you give us the latest details?

[FRANCIS MORIARTY] The latest details?

[NARRATOR, CHARLIE CHARTERS] Yeah, the latest details on the injuries.

[FRANCIS MORIARTY] Um, I can only give you the figures that I've been given. I don't know if you have anything further or more comprehensive than that.

[NARRATOR, BRIAN CURTIS] Francis, we're live on the radio – AM 1044 in Hong Kong./

[FRANCIS MORIARTY] Live, live on the radio, sorry, em (shift to 'radio narrator voice') The latest figures that I have up HE::re are that, eh, there were eighty-six casualties. Eh, that includes the twenty people so far who are dead./ There are also a number of critically injured, eh, ten at this hospital./ I think all of the critically injured should be here. There are other injured who were taken to Ten Shu Kin Hospital and also to, eh, Queen Elizabeth Hospital. Eh, that, that rounds out the total number of eighty-six. (report continues)

The delegation frames in radio are quite like those in television. In this case the presenter, Charlie Charters, uses a summary delegation frame which includes the location (Queen Mary Hospital), the news organization (Metro News), the name of the reporter (Francis Moriarty), and his status (live). Note that the verb given is consistent with the live status; it is 'joins' and it suggests the quasi-conversational status which we saw above in the live CBS News report from Capitol Hill.

The reporter's answer, however, is quite surprising for a reporter's utterance following a delegation frame. He says only, 'Yes'. This, plus the long silence which follows, suggests that something has gone quite wrong, as do the next few lines. From these lines it seems clear that the reporter has taken this as, in fact, a telephone call, not as a live radio report. Note, in fact, that Moriarty is following the sequence typical for a telephone call. He has been called (apparently) by Charlie Charters and answers in the most open-ended way (Schegloff 1972). When Charters attempts to solicit information, that is, when he introduces the topic of the injuries ('the latest figures'), the reporter seems puzzled by what is being required of him. He behaves as if he is expecting Charters to exercise his caller's right to introduce the topic.

It is the second presenter in the studio (the station's news director) who sees what is happening and brings into explicit awareness the nature of the problem when he directly tells Moriarty that they are speaking live on the radio. He further takes this as an opportunity to insert a Metro News identification sequence.

I have argued in Chapter 2 that channel, relationship (identification), and topic are hierarchically ordered so that a breakdown at a higher level disrupts the lower levels. This interaction has broken down at the highest level – on one side it is assumed to be a live news report, on the other it is assumed to be a telephone call, presumably for information. Thus, Curtis enters into the situation at the highest level, accomplishing in one move the re-identification of the radio station (and thereby defining the interaction as not a telephone call but a radio report) and the re-identification of the reporter, 'Francis'.

Moriarty immediately picks up his mistake and quite explicitly directs his next utterance to the channel frame 'live, live on the radio'. Then he turns to the second level, his identification as a radio reporter (not a casual conversant), first saying 'sorry' – that is apologizing for his breach of social expectations – and then putting on his 'radio narrator voice'. This sequence of channel attention ('live on the radio'), relationship attention ('sorry' + voice/role identity), and then, finally, topical attention ('The latest figures that . . .') shows once again that these three aspects of communication are in a hierarchical order of precedence, even when such a normally tightly framed instance of social interaction as a radio broadcast is at issue.

I would argue that we should not be misled by the very high levels of professional accomplishment we normally see in radio and television broadcasting into thinking that no such implicational interactional hierarchy of social practices is in operation. It is just that these social practices so seldom break down that we have very few instances of departures from expectation against which to test them.[5]

THE CONSTRUCTION OF THE TELEVISION REPORTER

I can now discuss the ways in which the person of the television reporter is constructed within the television news broadcast. First of all, the reporter is multiply identified by naming, both by the presenter and in his or her own final signature, and normally with on-screen character identification as well as in many cases video identification.

This person may also be titled with varying degrees of authority and social prestige. That is, he or she is clearly positioned both in respect to the presenter as his/her subordinate and is positioned within the news organization's power structure overall. Identification as a member of a particular organization is also part of this labelling, as is location in some cases ('CNN Detroit Bureau Chief'). Names may also be used as part of this status differentiation with 'live' reporters being placed on a first-name basis with the presenters. Generally, as with presenters as well, first names only appear to signal higher status than full names.

Topical limitations provide varying degrees of status ranging from 'live', the highest status, to a single-topic, low-interest local report. This range of topical control also varies from the normal report in which the reporter appears to be delegated his or her topic to the summarizing report in which the presenter leads in with a statement of what the reporter will shortly be telling us.

Finally, a reporter's relationship with either the news organization or someone else may be used to signal status. A reporter may be said to be 'specially engaged' on the one hand or an 'intern' on the other. One may be on assignment in a particular place or stationed there. Also, one may be assigned 'with' status; that is, he or she is travelling with some important personage and have, therefore, exclusive rights to reportage on the activities of that person.

These are the principal means by which television reporters are identified in the materials I have studied. The combination of these various subtle ranges of statuses and identities forms within itself a discourse of identification by which the status, power, and authority of a particular reporter are constituted.

PRESENTERS

I have made reference to presenters and editors as those who perform the delegation frames within which reporting journalists are identified. These 'higher level' journalists must themselves also be identified and positioned and that is the question to which I turn now.

Before going on, however, I want to call attention to the reasons I have put 'higher level' in quotation marks before 'journalists' above. I want to leave open the question of whether or not these journalists themselves actually occupy positions of greater authority in the organizations within which they operate. Reported salaries for American presenters, for example, indicate a significantly higher institutional commendation. On the other hand, in the television news emanating from the People's Republic of China or from other government-controlled news sources, one assumes that the presenter occupies a significantly lower position of authority than the party or governmental agencies which produce the text which is read. That is to say, one should not assume that an analogous position within the structure of a news broadcast or a newspaper indicates everywhere the same structure of social authority.

My interest here, however, is neither political nor ideological analysis in the broad sense. Here my focus is on the somewhat more mundane discursive and linguistic issues of the actual means by which presenters and editors are identified and positioned for viewers and readers. Obviously, however, that broader ideological analysis would rely upon the sort of analysis I present here.

The ATV Home main news bulletin of 25 February 1994 at 6:00 pm begins as follows:

1. ATV Logo
2. LEADS (with male voice-over narration)
   \<HK budget\>
   \<Hang Seng Index falls\>
   \<Hebron attack\>
3. ID SEQUENCE (Theme music)
4. Male Presenter [fuhng siuh nihng]

The first three items in this sequence present the three levels for which I have argued in Chapter 2 – channel, the identification and positioning sequence, and topic introduction – but it could be argued that they are not in the expected order. First is the ATV Logo with an anonymous voice identifying the channel as ATV. This is followed by three quick video clips with a voice-over narration.

The voice-over in this leader series, as it turns out, is that of the first presenter who is later identified as *fuhng siuh nihngh*. As Schegloff (1986) and others (Houtkoop-Steenstra 1991) have pointed out, the identification sequence in telephone calls is often accomplished indirectly through voice recognition. From this point of view, one might argue that the person of the presenter is identified here. I would find that a weak argument since we have already heard the voice of ATV in the opening logo sequence and not been tempted to consider that a voice identification.

It seems more plausible to say that television intentionally violates the Maxims of Stance in presenting topics before the participant(s) have been identified. The concept of maxims does not mean that there are never violations, but that violations signal altered circumstances, however conventionally and repeatedly those alterations take place. According to the maxim I have given in Chapter 2, if one violates the maxim of attending to person identification (relationship) before introducing the first topic, one must set about remedying this situation before successful communication can proceed.

There are two things to note in this 'hooker' opening. First, not one topic but three topics have been signalled. Thus it does not constitute a normal opening move of introducing the first topic at the anchor position, the position after the identification of the participants. Secondly, just after this violation of the maxim on attending to relationship, there is a recycling back to the highest level. The programme (ATV main news) is formally identified through item #3, the identification sequence (with theme music) and then the presenter appears on the screen, fully identified with characters on the screen under his image, and he begins to introduce the first topic of the event.

His first utterance in this case is *gok wai* which is literally something like 'each and every respectable person' but more conventionally 'ladies and gentlemen'. This is a standard Chinese form used at the outset of virtually all addresses to a gathering of people. It is functionally comparable to the English 'good evening' or 'good morning' which seem to be the preferred presenter openings in English-language television news broadcasts.

To summarize, this television news broadcast, like all of those I have studied, begins with an affirmation of the Maxims of Stance. The channel is addressed through some form of on-screen logo as well as theme music. The person of the presenter is identified by placement in first position as a talking head and this person is identified through on-screen character naming. This presenter uses a formula of address such as *gok wai* or 'good evening', and then proceeds to introduce the first topic of the news broadcast. This opening frame is terminated with the delegation frame in which the presenter delegates responsibility to a second reporter.

One of the powerful tools television has seized upon to engage the potential watcher is to precede this rather conventional application of the Maxims of Stance with a direct flouting of these maxims by quickly introducing several topics before attending to the person identification sequence. This, then, 'requires' a return to 'repair' the violations of the person and channel maxims and thereby legitimates a double announcement of the channel identification sequence.

While the other news broadcasts I have studied follow this pattern fairly closely, there are some differences among them. For example, the CBS Evening News of 15 March 1994 broadcast in Hong Kong at 7:30 am began as follows:

1. CBS Logo: CBS Evening News (music)
   NARRATOR: *This is the CBS Evening News with Dan Rather and Connie Chung*
   (on-screen character identification of both)
2. FEMALE PRESENTER: (Connie Chung)
   Good evening, Dan is on assignment
   Opening Frame: <Webster Hubbell resignation>

In this and other CBS broadcasts the maxims are followed much more closely than in the other broadcasts. First, there is clear channel identification in the CBS Logo stating that this is the evening news. Within that channel identification is included the person identification in both on-screen characters and with voice-over narration. Nevertheless, there is a problem with the identification sequence; it is in error. We have been told that we will see two presenters and their order of precedence. When we are given our first view of the television news desk, however, it is Connie Chung who is seen there; or not to prejudice the analysis, we see a woman whom we only presume is Connie Chung.

Her first move then is first to open the relationship frame with 'Good evening' and then immediately to repair the false identification by saying that Dan is on assignment. She is, by implication, the Connie Chung announced and she then proceeds with the introduction of the first topic. In this instance we can again see the operation of the Maxims of Stance as social practices which call for repair work to be done when violated.

COMMERCIAL REFRAMING

The maxim of relationship states that one attends to relationship positioning before going on to topic. A higher level maxim holds until further notice, but if there is a breakdown or a change of status, repair work must be done. One instance of this repair work occurs when stations shift frames for commercials.

Commercials are framed as not occurring within the news broadcasts in two main discursive ways (other than in different production techniques, messages, and the like): news topics which will occur after the shift in frame are foreshadowed, and upon returning from the commercial(s) the channel and the presenter are re-identified, albeit in a somewhat abbreviated fashion. In all of the programmes studied, the commercial shift in frame is followed by a truncated version of the originating station's logo, a short few bars of the theme music, and by placing the name of the presenter on the screen again.

This latter point is what I take as evidence of the operation of the maxims on identification of persons. The total time lapse between the first identification and the end of a series of stories is normally quite a bit longer than the lapse of time taken for commercials (though it may seem very much the other way around). In some cases a particular news story may produce gaps between on-screen views of the presenter which are longer than the gaps in commercial frames. Nevertheless, presenters are not re-identified when there has been no break in the news frame. This re-identification only occurs following the frame shifts of the commercial.

CLOSING TELEVISION PRESENTER FRAMES

The close of the television news given by ATV Home on 25 February 1994 is as follows:

27. Male Sports Presenter {IDT} <olympics>
    Opening Frame
      Male Reporter (MSP) {IDV}
        Closing Frame (MSP turns to MP, FP) *boudouh yuhn*
        ('end of the report')
28. Male Presenter <departure to MSP>
29. Female Presenter <departure to MSP>
30. Male Presenter, Female Presenter <Departures to camera>
31. ATV Theme, lights down on presenter set
    Editor: [*leuih wahn sang*]
    Director: [*cheuih yuhng gwok*]
    ATV News Production (c) MCMXCIV

Item #27 is the last item in the sports news given by the male sports presenter (MSP). He ends his report by explicitly saying that that is the end of the report and turns his head towards the other two main news presenters, male and female (MP and FP). They in turn bid the MSP good night and then turn to the camera and say good night to the camera or viewers. The lights then go down as the characters indicating the editor and director come on to the screen. This is followed by the ATV copyright notice and date.

Here again, we see the careful closing out of the three frames, the topical frame (#27), the person frame(s) (#28–#30) and the channel frame in the reverse order from their opening which we observed above. This parallels the bracketed openings and closings of frames which I have observed in telephone calls (Chapter 2).

There is in this case, however, the appearance of two personae who have not been mentioned up to this point – the editor and the director. Their appearance here at the end of the broadcast is a kind of signature (as opposed to byline). That is to say, by appearing here at the end as a signature, but not at the beginning as a byline, the editor and director show themselves to be claiming responsibility for all that has preceded. This final signature lends them a superordinate authority (or an ultimate responsibility) as the nearly invisible hands which have crafted what we have seen to this point, including, presumably, the actions and words of both categories of journalists, the reporters and the presenters.

No doubt the actual relative positions and power of the editor and director on the one hand and the presenters on the other is hotly debated behind the scenes of the news broadcasts which we view. My purpose is not to enter into the actual workings and professional status negotiations of journalists. What I am concerned with is the frames as they are presented to the public as aspects of public discourse. From this point of view, I would argue that by taking up this final position and affixing their signatures, the editor and director are claiming for themselves a superordinate position in the overall framing of persons in the typical television news broadcast.

Finally, to close out this summary of television closings I would like to look back at the ending of the CBS Evening News story above in which one identified presenter, Connie Chung, was obliged to repair the identification sequence of the channel frame. It will be recalled that she said, at the beginning of the broadcast and before introducing the main topic:

Good evening, Dan is on assignment

At the close of this broadcast we find the following (. . . indicate that I have deleted extraneous material)

30. FP *And that's our news . . . coming up tomorrow < . . . > I'm Connie Chung in New York. Dan will be back tomorrow . . . Good night.*
31. Credits

In this sequence the presenter first closes out the current topical frame with 'And that's our news'. She includes a foreshadowing of the news which will be seen in the next encounter. Here we should bear in mind that Goffman (1974) has argued that departure formulas do much more than close out the current social encounter. They also establish the state of the current relationship. One of the ways in which this is done is by foreshadowing how the participants can be expected to meet again in the future. They are, in Goffman's concept, forward-looking to the next encounter as much as they are backward-looking to the just-finished encounter. From this point of view, then, it is not surprising to find the presenter foreshadowing the topics of the next event. This is one way of signalling that there is every expectation that whoever has been engaged in this encounter will have found it satisfactory enough to be willing to seek future and similar engagements.

Her second move is to close out the identity frame which she does with a signature-closing statement of self-identity. More than that, she also refers back to the opening frame repair in which she has accounted for the absence of 'Dan'. She promises that the misstatement made at the beginning will be rectified upon the next encounter, and in doing so, finished the repair work on this frame which she began in her opening utterance.

Finally she signals the closure of the channel frame with 'Good night'. It is with this utterance that she produces a mirror image of her opening utterance 'Good evening'.

> *This is the CBS Evening News with Dan Rather and Connie Chung*
> > *Good evening*
> > > *Dan is on assignment*
>
> > > *Dan will be back tomorrow*
> > *Good night*
> *Credits*

It is this mirror-imaging of utterances across so many intervening sub-events which leads me to argue that there is an implicational hierarchy of social practices framing of channel, relationship (or person identity) and topic. We see it not only in business telephone conversations, but also in such relatively fixed, edited and formally structured forms of social interaction as television news broadcasts.

THE TELEVISION NEWS BROADCAST AS
SOCIAL INTERACTION

In my study of telephone calls in Chapter 2 I took the position that the main participants are engaged in a kind of social interaction in which there was a hierarchy of considerations to be dealt with, channel or situational definition, relationship positioning (or at a minimum, identification), and topic. There I argued that a disruption at any higher level must be repaired before continuing at any lower level.

In coming to consider television broadcast news, I have argued that such arrangements could be seen to be operating in television (and, by implication, radio) news broadcasts. I have shown that attention was directed first towards the channel, which in the case of television or radio includes not only the actual broadcast band, but the definition of the situation as a news broadcast. Immediately following upon the establishment of the channel comes the identification positioning of the presenter(s), and that is followed by the introduction of the first topic. This sequence of embedded frames is then reciprocally closed out at the end with first, the closing of the topical frame, secondly, the closing of the relationship positioning frame, and finally, the closing of the channel/situational frame in the final credits.

Within this set of enclosing frames of broadcast, presenter identification, and topic introductions is a further embedded set of frames within which news reporters are delegated temporary responsibility for taking over the topical floor and presenting stories. Further embedded within those stories are the actualities, the statements of the newsmakers, which I take up in Chapter 7.

I believe it can be argued that television (and radio) news broadcasts form a type of social interaction within a community of practice which is of a kind with the business telephone calls I studied above, and by extension, many other forms of social interaction. This social interaction is not between the journalist (presenter or reporter) and the viewer or watcher as one might have supposed; it is social interaction among the journalists. The proto-typical case, though perhaps actually rare, is the 'live' presenter–journalist quasi-conversation I discussed above. The viewer is positioned as a watcher of the journalists' conversational game.

I argued that in the telephone call the frames which are set must be mutually ratified between or among the participants; that is, one does not go on unilaterally to topic from the identification sequence unless or until the identification is ratified by the other participants. In the television broadcast, however, it appears that the channel identification moves rather swiftly into presenter identification and from there equally swiftly into the introduction of the topic. It is only when this fails to happen that we see that, in fact, there is a ratification response from another participant in the interaction. In the case of the 'live' quasi-conversation these ratifications are carried out between the presenter and the 'live' news reporter. The example of the major glitch in the radio broadcast highlights how directly the whole frame breaks down when one of the participants fails to make his ratification.

The same occurred in the CBS News report when the person identified as 'Chief Washington Correspondent' failed to signal the close of his segment with the closing frame, but simply turned the conversation back over to the presenter with a first-name tag, 'Connie?' In both of these cases, we see that the role of the viewer is not that of a ratified speaking participant in this social interaction; the role of the viewer is as a kind of by-play to the main interaction.[6] The viewers are ratified as legitimate listeners or overhearers of this social interaction among the primary interactants who are the journalists and others involved in producing the news broadcast.

It is the genius of television that it presents these 'in-house' or at least in-group social interactions for us to observe in such a way that we may rather easily forget that we are, in fact, only observers of a primary social interaction which takes place outside of our socially interactive frame. We are not able to intervene in the ratification of channel, relationship or topic. Our only choice is to switch among the similar socially constructed interactions available to us for monitoring. In some cases, of course, the non-ratified and perhaps non-ratifiable side-play of television observers becomes an object of interest in itself as we saw in the excerpt from the Doyle novel in Chapter 3.

Only in the rarest of cases is the framing of this primary social interaction among the journalists and the production staff broken through and the viewing audience directly addressed. In the broadcasts covering the New Year tragedy reported in Li et al. (1993) there is such an instance. At the end of the news report, the presenter then directly addresses the viewing audience in their homes:

ATV World, 12:30 pm special news bulletin, 1 January 1993
[MALE NARRATOR] A hotline has been set up for relatives
    needing more information. / The numbers are 8,6,0,2,3,1,0 /
    and 8,6,0,2,3,1,8. / Repeat, 8,6,0,2,3,1,0 and 8,6,0,2,3,1,8. /
    Join us again at four o'clock for another special update
    bulletin into the Lan Kwai Fong tragedy / when we'll
    bring you the latest developments as they happen. / Until
    then / Good afternoon.

(Li et al. 1993: 89)

This telephone hotline number is provided for anyone watching to call the police for further information. This segment is set off from the rest of the news broadcast prosodically by a long pause preceding these sentences. Further, the presenter ratifies the primary 'in-house' frame by saying 'join us', though maintaining the temporary focus on the viewing audience with the pronoun 'you'. The cross-play found in this frame departure is normally found, however, only in such special, non-scheduled emergency coverages, not in standard spot news slots.

We find a similar framing of the social interaction in the radio broadcast covering the same event:

Metro News, 12:00 pm special news bulletin, 1 January 1993
[MALE NARRATOR] And police have issued a special
   number, a bilingual hotline for anyone wanting information
   on family and friends they believe may have been in Lan
   Kwai Fong last night. / That number is 8,6,0 / 2,3,1,0. /
   That's 8,6,0,2,3,1,0 //The governor Chris Patten we have
   just heard has confirmed the government is holding / a
   judicial enquiry into last night's tragedy at New Year.
[NARRATOR, JERRY KAY] *Metro News* time is twelve o six.
                                                    (Li et al. 1993: 86)

The double stroke (//) following the second iteration of the telephone number represents a prosodic terminal phrasing. One hears a major juncture between this telephone number and the news concerning the governor's judicial enquiry. In other words, the presenter makes this departure into directly speaking to the listening audience and then sets it apart prosodically as he recovers the 'in-house' framing for the mention of the newest news item which has just then come in.

AUDIENCE DESIGN

Bell (1991) has pointed out that it is not at all unproblematical to understand who is the audience implied in news stories. While journalists will often say that they have in mind some ordinary person within the community to whom they are speaking or writing, Bell argues that there is little evidence that a journalist has any clear conception of who this person is or what his or her characteristics might be. He further points out that even though news organizations engage in major marketing studies to determine the audiences they wish to target, the results of these surveys rarely enter into the working consciousness of the journalist in his or her day-to-day work.[7] Bell's point is that, in his analysis, the primary audience to which journalists address themselves is, in fact, other journalists. Journalists write their stories for the critical eye of other journalists, whether that might be in the form of the overseeing editor, other actual colleagues who might see their work, or an imaginary critical editor journalist who will judge their work according to the standards of journalistic practice.

There is some further support for this idea in the comments made by Murray Fromson, formerly a foreign correspondent for CBS News and Associated Press and now Dean of the Journalism School at the University of Southern California. In a lecture at the Hong Kong Baptist University Department of Journalism, 23 February 1994, 'The role of the international reporter,' he frequently presented a polar opposition between what he referred to as 'authority' or 'the government' and 'journalists'. In one case he disparaged 'representing government rather than independent reporting', going on to say that there is 'an inherent conflict between government and journalism'. He further pointed out from time to time that '[t]he journalist's major obligation is to be a voice to the voiceless'. In this latter case his meaning was clearly understood within the context to mean a voice *for* the voiceless; that is, the journalist's responsibility in his view is to speak on behalf of those who do not have a voice. As the government, in Fromson's view has its own voice, it is the duty of journalists to speak against the government and by doing so to represent 'the people'.

Coming from an American journalist who elsewhere made comments on the American system of representative government, one begins to see that 'the people' are seen by this journalist at least to have two voices speaking on their behalf: one is the voice of political representation through the electoral process, the second is a journalistic voice of political opposition to that same government. That this should not be seen simply as an odd view of a single American journalist, I also draw attention to the British editor quoted on the BBC, 3 March 1994 as saying, 'It's the job of the British press, of any free press, to hold politicians responsible'.[8]

While it might be excessive to draw many conclusions about the nature of journalistic discourse from just these two instances, I believe that they indicate a widely held view among journalists that they

are, in fact, speaking on behalf of 'the people'. The logical implication of this, of course, is that they, therefore, are not speaking to
'the people'. As these two journalists I have quoted have suggested,
they see themselves speaking either to each other about 'the government' or, in some cases, directly to 'the government'. What these
journalists do not ever mention is speaking (or writing) to their
audience of readers and viewers.

While this point in Bell's study is well supported by his own
research and also his own considerable experience as a practising
journalist, and although it is also supported to some extent by the
comments of practising journalists, he does not present evidence
from the actual discourse to support this primary interactive focus
upon other journalists. The cases I have analysed above, however,
do provide such evidence. The analysis of television news broadcasts shows that the primary social interaction(s) take place among
journalists (and production staff), not between journalists and the
viewing audience, except in the rare and clearly marked cases of
cross-play in which journalists depart from this taken-for-granted
situation and address the viewing audience directly.

THE CONSTITUTION OF THE JOURNALIST

This analysis of several television news broadcasts supports the
argument that in the first place, television news can be seen as a
kind of social interaction. It is not a social interaction between journalists and viewers, however, but one among journalists which is
carried on as a spectacle on behalf of the watchers. That social
interaction is carried on with the same fundamental ritual practices
for establishing the grounds for interaction (the channel), establishing the identities and social positioning of the participants, and
establishing topics as found in other forms of social interaction such
as telephone calls and face-to-face withs (Goffman 1963, 1974, 1981).
Within that social interaction, identities are not simply taken for
granted; they are established through discursive means which delegate not only identity, voice, and rights to topic, but also status and
position within the general journalistic discourse. This analysis argues
that such phenomena as the evening news on television display
the same underlying principles governing social interaction as we
have studied above in respect to face-to-face social encounters.

NOTES

1. I have studied the following broadcasts with full transcriptions:
    ATV Home, 25 February 1994; 6:00 pm, Main News; Chinese
    (Cantonese)
    ATV World, 25 February 1994; 8:00 pm, Main News; English
    TVB Jade, 13 January 1994; 6:30 pm, Main News; Chinese
    (Cantonese)
    TVB Pearl, 13 January 1994; 8:00 pm, Main News; English
    CBS News, 15 March 1994: 7:30 am, Evening News; English
    CNN, 15 March 1994; 6:30 am, Breakfast Selections; English
    Each of these was recorded and studied in Hong Kong. Nevertheless,
    two of them, CBS News and CNN are international English language
    services. The CBS Evening News is broadcast as it is in the US without
    internal modification, or so it is presented. The CNN news consists of
    a series of 'selections' from their 24-hour news service. In addition to
    these primary six news broadcasts, I have used the corpus collected in
    the Public Discourse Research Group's archive, Department of English,
    City University of Hong Kong for a much broader survey of Hong
    Kong news discourse, print and broadcast, in searches for counter-
    examples to the conclusions I draw here.

2. I use the Yale system romanization to represent in this English text
    words or characters which were presented either in Chinese written
    form (as in this case) or which were spoken in Cantonese. For words
    spoken in Putonghua (Mandarin) I use pinyin. I also use pinyin repres-
    entations where these are direct quotations of what appears on the
    screen. See Li et al. (1993) for a fuller discussion of the complexities
    involved in transcribing Hong Kong Chinese into English.

3. In support of this argument that there was some slippage in calculating
    the status of the 'White House correspondent' especially in respect to
    the presenter, this is not the normal lead presenter of this news broad-
    cast. The broadcast begins with this presenter saying that the usual
    first presenter is 'away on assignment'. To complicate matters, the White
    House Correspondent's first name is 'Rita', another possible source of
    what I have transcribed as 're'.

4. While I have not been able to verify the truth of the accusation, when-
    ever this point is raised regarding this news organization in Hong
    Kong, I am told an anecdote, widely believed, that this station was
    sued by their single local competitor for running one of their stories
    without attribution. While this story may have the status of folklore, it
    does point up the expectation that stories will be run with attributions
    and where this station has departed from practice it is noted by the
    public which uses this as evidence of devious dealings.

5. Nevertheless, this professional competence does break down in many
    instances other than this one I have reported. Goffman's (1981) chapter

on 'Radio Talk' is a highly insightful as well as entertaining treatment of these departures from professional competence and their social-interactive consequences.

6. Goffman (1981) defines three types of non-central social interaction. That is, he defines three ways in which participants other than the main speakers and addressed participants may engage in talk, by-play, side-play and cross-play. By-play is 'subordinated communication of a subset of ratified participants'; cross-play is 'communication between ratified participants and bystanders across the boundaries of the dominant encounter', and side-play is 'respectfully hushed words exchanged entirely among bystanders' (1981: 134). At a meeting of an official government committee, for example, the dominant encounter would be among members of the committee who currently held the floor. By-play would be comments back and forth among committee members not currently considered to have the floor. Side-play would be comments among journalists or other observers who are not official members of the committee. Cross-play would be interactions between members of the committee and, say, a journalist standing nearby.

7. This point has been borne out in ethnographic interviews with both journalists and with advertisers who regularly ignore marketing surveys in favour of the judgements of their peers about what will be a successful campaign strategy.

8. Unfortunately, I 'joined' this broadcast just following the identification sequences and therefore am unable to name the quoted journalist. He was thereafter referred to as an editor of a significant British newspaper. The topic in reference was the row over Malaysian–British trade agreements.

SIX

Newspaper journalists

BYLINING AND ATTRIBUTION IN NEWSPAPERS

Newspapers differ from broadcast news reports in many ways. In fact, there is a systematic error brought into our considerations by the naming of the two media. Newspapers have the concept of 'news' structured into their naming, and so one tends to think of the news as the primary case of their reason for existence as well as for their day-to-day use. However wrong this may be, the name leads us to think in this direction. Television news broadcasts, on the other hand, like radio news broadcasts select out of the much fuller stream of programming just those portions of their broadcasting thought of as news. It would be better in this study (and others) to keep in mind that here we are studying just the news portions of both print and broadcast theatres of public discourse. With these cautions in mind, then, I will turn to look at the framing of the person of the reporter in newspaper news stories.

There are four basic elements in a printed news story, as Bell (1991) indicates:

1. Headline.
2. Byline or source attribution.
3. Lead.
4. Story.

Each of these elements has a characteristic placement and a characteristic 'author'. The headline and byline or attribution (as well as photograph placement if there is one) are normally prepared by a sub-editor charged with these tasks (Zhang 1988; Bell 1991). The story is understood to be the work of the bylined writer or to be taken from another news agency. The lead is apparently somewhat variable; while it is normally written by the bylined writer, it may also be rewritten or heavily re-written by the sub-editor as, indeed, the story itself may be rewritten.

THREE STORIES

Before looking at the many variations in these conventional practices, we should look more closely at three actual instances. The following three stories appeared in the *South China Morning Post* on 17 March 1994, all on page 36 of the *Sports Post*.

1. LEAD STORY <headline>
   By **JEREMY WALKER**
   THE Asian Football Confederation are prepared to launch their own investigation into allegations of match-fixing by mainland teams if they are unhappy with the findings of the Chinese Football Association . . . etc.

2. SECOND STORY <headline>
   By **JEREMY WALKER**
   THERE will be no Mercedes cars and no cash jackpots, only pride and prestige, for Saudi Arabia's Al-Qadisiyah players if they beat Hong Kong's South China in the Asian Cup Winners' Cup final . . . etc.

3. THIRD STORY <headline>
   THE 24 countries competing in the World Cup finals in the United States this summer are under orders from world governing body FIFA – entertain the fans or pay the price through the turnstiles, *writes Jeremy Walker*.
   The General Secretary of the Asian Football Confederation, Peter Velappan, is also the chief co-ordinator of the nine World Cup venues and will be based in Los Angeles during the month-long tournament from June 17 to July 17 . . . etc.

These three stories are very similar in style in having (1) a lead, (2) an introduction to the personae, (3) an introduction of the person to be quoted, and (4) a quotation from the person introduced in (3). In stories one and two, JEREMY WALKER is the bylined writer of the stories. Nevertheless in the third story, the writer, Jeremy Walker, is not bylined; he is referenced as in the television delegation frame (Chapter 6).

The delegation frame in the Jeremy Walker story above leads one to believe that not only the headline in this case is written by another writer but the lead as well. From just the evidence presented in the newspaper there is no way of knowing if this is a slip or if it is intended to signal a different situation. One possibility is simply that the editor, having three large stories by the same writer on the same page, set this one up with a different format to avoid the third repetition. This is the pattern used in a similar case in *The Times*, 1 April 1994, where there are two stories by the same reporter on a single page.

DELEGATION FRAME OR SIGNATURE

What we can see, however, in all three of these is that we should take the byline as a form of delegation frame, not as an author signature. That is to say, the third case, that of a summary introduction which is not unlike the summary delegation frames in television, shows clearly that the name we see functions to convey a message from the editor about the writer and his or her position, not a message from the writer. Bylining is, by this argument, taken to be projecting the voice of the editor (sub-editor, actually), not the voice of the author. The function of bylining may be argued to be that of delegation of the following space and (apparently) of the sentiments and ideas expressed there to the author thus named. It is a way of setting this space apart from the generalized editorial space otherwise assumed to be the territory of, and to express the voice of the editor of, the newspaper. It not only sets apart, it also positions the author of what appears in that space as secondary to the editors who set the frame. With this in mind, then, we can look at the various ways in which the author receives this delegation from the normally anonymous editors and sub-editors.

The *South China Morning Post*

I will begin by looking closely at Hong Kong's most widely circulated English-language newspaper. Bylining practices in the *South China Morning Post* show one of the standard patterns for English-language newspapers in the UK, the US and Australia. I have said 'one of the standard patterns' to caution the reader that there are a number of variations on these patterns, even within the English newspapers of Hong Kong, and the discussion which follows is intended to outline the various means of bylining and attribution, not to serve as either a normative standard nor as a set of exotic exceptions.

One person bylines

Bylines in the *South China Morning Post* are usually set out below the headline but above the text of the story in boldface capital letters as indicated in the first two of the stories quoted above. In the majority of cases these bylines are for single reporters. On 25 February 1994 the first two sections of the newspaper produced 47 instances, 31 instances in the first section and 16 instances in the *FOCUS* section. These two sections together make up the main news section of this newspaper and are on some days combined as a single first section of the paper.

More complex bylines

In some cases two reporters are named in the byline (3 instances) and in others a place is indicated as well (4 instances). In still other instances, the NAME is associated with a news organization. For example, the following occurs three times:

NAME *of the New York Times* (3 instances)

One writer is given a special, perhaps elevated designation as follows:

(Racing Editor) NAME (2 instances)

While most of the bylines in the *South China Morning Post* are of this fairly unvaried standard format, some of them are written much like the summarizing delegation frames in some television reports (Chapter 5). In these cases, similar to the third news story shown above, the NAME appears as part of an opening frame. In these cases, however, the whole statement is set apart from the text of the story in a different typeface and with a space following, indicating the shift from the editorial voice to the author's voice. All three of the following occurred in the *FOCUS* section of the newspaper, that is, in the second non-spot news section.

> But, as NAME *reports from Auckland, when the Hong Kong immigrants moved into New Zealand, the triads weren't far behind.*

> *NAME argues that far from being a masterpiece of Western diplomacy, the withdrawal of the big guns from Sarajevo is a victory for the Russians and Serbs.*
> *NAME talks to the Merseysider who is singing here again.*

Feature writers, the delegation of space

A number of stories or sections of short pieces are the work of a regular feature writer. In these cases, rather than bylining there is a regular column header with the name of the writer, in some cases the name of the column, and often a photograph of the writer as well. The *South China Morning Post* of 25 February 1994 credited a feature writer in 10 cases.

The conventionalization of their byline, column title and photograph indicates a more permanent and open-ended form of delegation. In the case of the feature writer, it is not only this story on this day for which authority is delegated. It is this space every day. Within that space the feature writer is understood to have considerably greater topical and other liberties than a writer bylined in the normal manner. This is somewhat similar, in fact, to the 'live' designation in the framing of television reporters with the difference that the 'live' reports are generally of the most current spot news topics whereas features in newspapers are virtually all non-spot news. It is clear that the delegation of greater topical latitude is consonant with a somewhat elevated positioning in the community of practice.

Opened but not closed

In each of these cases there is a clear opening frame, normally the headline or, in the case of the feature writer, the column header and/or photograph of the writer. This opening frame includes the delegation frame of the byline. There may or may not be a certain degree of penetration of this opening and delegation framing done by the sub-editor into the lead paragraph itself. Bell (1991) points out that editorial penetration is a good bit deeper than that, in fact. Editors may alter textual matters at every point in the story written by another author.[1] Nevertheless, as a matter of framing, the third story of the first set we considered is really the only case in which the voice of the sub-editor is clearly heard as far into the story as the end of the first paragraph. Normally this voice is replaced by the authorial voice in the space between the byline and the first sentence of the lead.

There are two points which should be brought out now by comparison with television news stories. The first is that in newspapers news stories there is no internal identification of the writer. Feature writers, of course, write features, not news stories, and their voice is often heard throughout the story in the form of the first-person identifications ('I', 'we') or quasi-third person identifications ('this writer', 'the writer'). I know of no instances, however, even in feature columns, of the self-identifications found in television and radio (*'Annabel Roberts'*, *TVB News*). One does not find the frame: 'This is NAME writing'.

That is the first point – there is an absence of any form of internal identification in written news reports. The second point is that there is no closing frame with or without writer identification. Of course, it is journalistic practice to use the 'inverted pyramid' in writing (Zhang 1988; Bell 1991). This story structure places the most important details at the beginning and then subsequently introduces details of perceived lesser importance in successive paragraphs. It is understood that the story may be cut from the tail by the editor in making it fit the procrustean bed of the space allotted for any particular story. The structuring of a news story is itself a tacit recognition of the super/subordination positioning of the editor and journalist as it is the editor who can cut and the journalist who must anticipate this. Of course journalism textbooks legitimate the hegemonic position of editors in making this necessity into a virtue by arguing that the best stories put the punch into the first lines. It is interesting in this regard, as Bell (1991) has observed, that when writers have the freedom of space in writing features, they rather quickly depart from this self-evident maxim of good journalistic writing.

While there is, in fact, virtually never any closing frame,[2] in some cases there is a 'turning', that is, an indication to go on to another page for a continuation of the story. One might be able to argue for a closing frame of sorts by the absence of a continuation reference or a turn-to statement. When the story *does not* say where to go to find the rest, it may be assumed to be concluded. In contrast with the very explicitly marked closing frames in television news (as well as in business telephone calls) it seems clear that newspaper stories are operating within a very different social-interactive framework. I will return to this point below.

AGENCY ATTRIBUTIONS

In saying that newspaper news stories do not normally have a closing frame, I should make clear that I am speaking specifically of *bylined* news stories in the *South China Morning Post* as well as in most other papers surveyed. In that same newspaper there is another class of stories, those received from one of the international or other news agencies from which that corporation buys its news. Those stories, while not bylined at the beginning, do have a closing frame – the name of the agency from which the news was purchased.

Thus we have the following pattern of delegations and closings when stories are attributed to bylined authors and agencies:

	Delegation Frame	*Closing Frame*
Author	byline	—
Agency	—	attribution

These closing agency attributions are found in 18 cases in the first section and seven cases in the *FOCUS* section.[3]

LETTERS TO THE EDITOR, SIGNATURES

Only in the case of letters to the editor do NAMEs appear at the end of items in the *South China Morning Post*. One might want to say that the reason is that while news stories follow the cut-from-the-end or inverted pyramid structure, letters do not. Nevertheless, newspapers regularly reserve the right to edit letters to the editor as well as other materials they print and any letter appearing there cannot be assumed to have been printed unedited. The reasons for adopting a closing frame including a NAME or 'NAME withheld' must be sought elsewhere than in editing practices.

Perhaps the only thing one might be certain of regarding the person of the writers of letters to the editor is that this person *is not* to be regarded as a journalist.[4] These letters must not be taken to have the status of the editorial reportage found elsewhere in the paper. Nor should they be taken to be advertisements or what Evans (1976) refers to as 'bought space'. Thus, the page layout clearly marks out these portions of text within a separate space. Their different status is further marked by using a pattern of identification not found elsewhere in the newspaper and, of course, corresponding most closely to that found in normal business correspondence, with the NAME found at the slot at the end.[5] That is to say, these names are signatures, not bylines. They are self-identifications taken to be made by the author who is also principal of the text which is printed there. In this they depart clearly from bylines which are delegations of principalship and social status positionings made by the sub-editor and which carry with them specific restrictions on topical relevance. That is, the bylines are in the voice of the sub-editor who is delegating the space temporarily to the author of the text to follow. The difference between bylining and signature may be indicated within the Goffman (1974, 1981) framework of production format as follows:

Production format role	News story	Letter to the editor
animator	news staff	news staff
author	reporter	reader
principal	editor	reader

While principalship (the responsibility for what appears in the text) is delegated to the reporter, it ultimately resides with the news organization which has sponsored that text to appear within its editorial spaces. In contrast, the writers of letters to the editor retain principalship and, therefore, may be held responsible for what is printed within the spaces allocated to them. What is at stake is responsibility for the contents; the byline indicates that responsibility is at least partly shared with the reporter by the newspaper's editorial staff, but the signature indicates that the newspaper's editorial staff relinquishes such responsibility to the author whose name appears at the end.

PHOTO CREDITS

Photographs are framed somewhat differently. In the *South China Morning Post* one finds both bylined and agency-attributed photographs. Here there is no variation in pattern; the photograph carries its attribution just below the bottom right corner, above the caption. This attribution may be either the name of a photographer or the name of a news agency, but the position is the same in either case. The photographs of this date were as follows:

NAMEs (15 instances)
Agencies (9 instances)

UNATTRIBUTED STORIES

When attributions are made, there are no exceptions to the pattern I have given above in which there is either a delegation frame with a bylined writer or a closing frame with the name of a news agency. That is to say, the positioning of these elements, bylined writer and agency, are never altered. Nevertheless, there are cases in which no attributions are made at all, either in the opening frame or closing frame. There were 11 items in the first section and 24 items in the *FOCUS* section in the *South China Morning Post* of this date which ran without attributions.

One is inclined to say that items without attribution are those with the least significance. These are mostly small, one-paragraph pieces of news grouped together under such headings as 'IN BRIEF'. There is no telling where these items come from. There are also the weather bulletins, television and radio schedules, announcements of events about town, and that large set of bits of information carried in most daily newspapers. Most of the unattributed items are of this kind.

Nevertheless, there is another small but significant set of items which appear unattributed either for author or agency; these are the editorial columns and commentaries. There are not many of these, but in the *South China Morning Post* they run without any identification of author except for their significant placement in a different typeface below the title of the *South China Morning Post* on the editorial page. In this they follow a pattern found widely in other newspapers. What is notable about the *South China Morning Post* (and other Hong Kong newspapers) is that the editorial board and publishers are not identified within the pages of the daily newspaper. In this the Hong Kong papers follow what may well be a British pattern – *The Times, The Daily Telegraph* and *The Guardian* also do not identify the newspaper publishers and editors – but not most of the other newspapers which I have studied. Outside the group of Hong Kong and British newspapers, it is the customary practice to identify clearly both publishers and editors.

Finally there is the last group of items, the advertisements. While these are not normally attributed to authors, they are always clearly identified for the agency which is being promoted and in being so identified can be assumed to represent those agencies.

THREE HONG KONG CHINESE NEWSPAPERS: *MING PAO, DONG FONG YAT PO, WEN WEI PO*

Chinese newspapers in Hong Kong are multiple and highly varied (Zhang 1988; Li Jiayuan 1989; R. Scollon 1997b). In this study I have chosen to look at just three of them as these three represent a fair sampling of the spectrum of papers available for sale. They range from the somewhat elegant linguistic style of *Ming Pao*[6] through the most popular *Dong Fong Yat Po* (*Oriental Daily News*) to the Beijing-supported *Wen Wei Po*. Attribution practices in these papers are much more uniform than one might expect from papers so different in other ways.

BYLINING

The most common frame for a named reporter is:

NAME (LOCATION) (cable/report)

This is as follows in Cantonese:

> *bun bou geije NAME* ('This paper's reporter named NAME')
> *bun bou geije NAME (LOCATION) jyun dihn* ('This paper's reporter named NAME cable/report from (LOCATION)')

In this case the understanding is that the newspaper's reporter is only reporting from the place named. That is to say, the reporter is not normally stationed there. For a reporter stationed in another place there is the following frame:

> *bun bou jue (LOCATION) geije NAME jyun dihn* ('This paper's (LOCATION-stationed) reporter named NAME cable/report')

A third status attributed to a reporter is that of being 'specially engaged'. This may, perhaps, refer to a stringer who reports to other news agencies as well, though I have not established under just what special circumstances a reporter might be considered specially engaged. What seems clear is that the status of such a report differs significantly enough from *bun bou geije* (i.e., 'this newspaper's reporter') to bear special mention. The form is as follows:

> *bun bou dahkyeuk geije NAME (LOCATION) boudouh* ('This
> paper's specially engaged reporter named NAME's report')

Another special status which may be conferred upon a reporter
is indicated in the following delegation format:

> *bun bou saht jaahp geije NAME (LOCATION) dihn* ('This paper's
> intern reporter named NAME's cable from (LOCATION)')

In this formulation the status seems to be even more provisional
than that indicated by 'specially engaged' and to signal a distinct
junior or even trainee status. Again, I choose not to speculate
on why a newspaper would care to indicate this minority of status
to its readers other than to point out that in all of the cases of this
delegation frame I have observed the person so designated was
located in a potentially difficult place such as Beijing. One might
surmise that this would provide a useful cover for the newspaper
should anything go awry in the reception of the report. One might
see this as a fairly extreme form of the delegation of principalship
and positioning of the reporter, suggesting that the newspaper will
bear minimal responsibility for anything found in these reports.

UNATTRIBUTED STORIES

Having given these forms of bylining, I can indicate now that
they are used relatively rarely in the Chinese newspapers of Hong
Kong. As I will indicate below, most of the stories found in these
newspapers are either not attributed at all, attributed simply to
'agencies', or rather vaguely attributed to something like 'this
paper's synthesis', as indicated below.
    The most common forms are these:

> *bun bou (jyun) seun* ('This paper's own (special) report (from
>   LOCATION)')
> *(bun bou) juhn hahp (boudouh)* ('This paper's synthesis' =
>   English 'agencies')

The first of these indicates a synthesis made by the newspaper's
personnel somewhere other than in Hong Kong, presumably at the
place where the news story is being covered. The second of these
is used for a story compiled from other news agency reports. Zhang

(1988) points out that because most of the stories received in Hong Kong newspapers from other agencies are received in a language other than Chinese, most of what appears in Chinese newspapers on international news is, in fact, translated. It is his point that using this vague designation allows the newspaper to cover itself against claims of poor, inaccurate or inappropriate translation. Zhang believes that much of what is presented as 'synthesis' is better interpreted as simply 'hastily translated'. At the same time, this explanation should be accepted with caution as many of the news stories, particularly those concerning Chinese affairs, are received in Chinese, printed verbatim, but still reported as 'this newspaper's synthesis' (Scollon and Scollon 1997).[7]

OTHER FORMS OF ATTRIBUTION

What should be noted is that, like the *South China Morning Post* stories, the writers of stories are not identified within their stories either directly through self-reference nor indirectly through first-person or even third-person pronominal reference. The writers of these stories are, if anything, more transparent or less visible than the corresponding writers in the *South China Morning Post*.

Furthermore, there are in these newspapers I have studied very few cases of attribution, either to person or agency in any position but the story-initial position. The attributions I have indicated above normally appear as the first words of a story and set apart in brackets, sometimes also in darker typefaces.

The exception to the statement that attributions do not occur other than in initial position is in the few attributions to named persons in editorials and other commentaries or feature columns. Normally the lead editorial, like the *South China Morning Post* lead editorial, runs unattributed.

DELEGATION, BYLINING AND ATTRIBUTION (REPORTERS)

I have already noted various differences both between the Hong Kong English paper (*South China Morning Post*) and three of the Chinese-language papers, and between these newspapers and several television news broadcasts. Now I would like to summarize some of these differences to draw attention to some major differences in patterns of delegation of reportage roles. To do this I compared the 10 sources that I have studied in greatest detail.

In Table 6.1 'Bylined' means that the author of the story was identified by name in print. In the newspaper this means in print, normally at the head of the column; in Chinese newspapers this byline is sometimes placed together with a central headline or at the end in the case of editorials. In television broadcasts this identification is done either with characters placed on the screen or orally by a narrator or presenter. In most cases on television both forms of identification were used. I have counted the author as identified by continuation from a preceding story in the case of presenters but not reporters. That is to say, I considered the presenter identified even if the name was not repeated for consecutive stories.

One further complication of which the reader should be aware: in Table 6.1 I have counted all items which have appeared – I have counted not just spot news stories and features, but also advertisements, weather reports, title blocks, bar codes, and the like. I did so in the absence of a principled way to decide which items should be most relevant to the question of the sociocultural construction of the person in these forms of public discourse. I would suggest now that subsequent study might see what are vague outlines here in greater relief if such an analysis were to be made.

These 10 news sources show a fair similarity among those of the same medium as well as striking differences across the media. Of course, there is a very large difference in the total number of items, with television broadcasts having only between 17 (CNN News) and 31 (ATV Home and CBS News) items but newspapers having between 129 (*Ming Pao*) and 258 (*South China Morning Post*) items in their first sections. Nevertheless, the column which indicates percentages rather than raw numbers gives some indication of the differences in these media.

Most striking is that most of the items in the television news shows were bylined; that is, they had clear delegation frames or the reporter was designated by on-screen characters. In contrast to these relatively few of the newspaper items bore bylines; *South China Morning Post* had the most at 38.8 per cent, *Dong Fong Yat Po* had the fewest at 7.5 per cent of the items identified for an author.

I have used 'items' rather than 'stories' to remind the reader that in these figures I am including all items from news stories and features to weather reports, obituaries and advertisements. It should

Table 6.1: Source attributions

News organization	Number of items	Number of items bylined	Percentage of items bylined	Items attributed to an agency only	Percentage of items attributed to an agency only	Items in which no source is given	Percentage of items in which no source is given
ATV Home	31	24	77.4	0	0.0	7	22.6
ATV World	23	13	56.5	0	0.0	10	43.5
TVB Jade	24	20	83.3	0	0.0	4	16.7
TVB Pearl	24	19	79.2	1	4.6	4	12.9
CBS News	31	23	74.2	3	9.7	5	16.1
CNN News	17	15	88.2	0	0.0	2	6.5
Ming Pao	129	22	17.1	20	15.5	85	65.9
Dong Fong Yat Po	146	11	7.5	39	26.7	96	65.8
Wen Wei Po	171	29	17.0	73	42.7	69	40.4
South China Morning Post	258	100	38.8	32	12.4	126	48.8

be no surprise that there are many more of these unattributed items in a newspaper than on television which generally does not programme such material – at least not within the 'news' broadcast frame.

One might argue that a better comparison would be to focus only upon 'news' stories in the newspapers and to exclude all of the other items, especially advertisements. One could, of course, do this; but one could not do it prior to a careful analysis of genres to determine what is or is not within the 'news' genre in the newspaper. Evans (1976) has argued that a newspaper should clearly mark the difference between 'bought space' and 'editorial space', that is, between advertising and the rest. In contemporary newspapers (and in television as well) this distinction is becoming more difficult to make as advertisers use the news format to present their products and as news organizations present more and more press releases from what are essentially marketing, not information campaigns.

One aspect of comparison between television news discourse and that carried on in daily newspapers is that they are not, in fact, strictly comparable. Television news broadcasts present a much clearer 'news' frame around the items and stories presented there than is found in any of the newspapers in Hong Kong where items of many different sorts are mixed together on a single page.[8] One finds between the international spot news and the follow-up stories, but within the same visual field, advertisements for women's underwear in a way that is never matched on television where commercials are packaged tidily within short commercial breaks and so may be seen as separately framed. That, then, is one reason why in Table 6.1 there are so many more items in the newspaper columns than in the television columns. It is also why there is such a high percentage of unattributed material in the newspapers by comparison with the television broadcasts.

On the other hand, the newspapers had many more of their stories attributed to agencies than the television broadcasts. That is to say, in these cases which are largely news stories, there is still a difference between television and newspaper practices: in television the attributions are largely to people, but in newspapers the attributions are often just to agencies.

This contrast between reporter-attributed stories on television and agency-only or non-attributed stories in the newspapers may actually be a greater contrast than appears here at first. As I have said above, in the television attributions there are usually multiple attributions within a single story. The reporter is usually named within the delegation frame, again identified with on-screen characters giving the name and news organization, yet again identified in many cases with direct on-camera shots, and then finally self-identified in the closing frame. While I have not counted these multiple identifications, it is fair to estimate that where I have counted one identification in each case, the average might well be closer to three. Newspapers, in contrast, almost never identify the writer of their stories more than once, if the writer is identified at all. A commentary in *Il Messagero* with both a byline and a final signature is the rare single exception within these data I have studied. Note that the signature in this case is the reproduction of a handwritten signature which, in itself, sets it off as a departure from the typesetting of the rest of the page and newspaper.

POSITIONING OF THE JOURNALIST

One can summarize these figures for attribution to reporters by saying that the person of the reporter is much more strongly identified in television news than in these Hong Kong newspapers (both English and Chinese), though the English Hong Kong newspaper, the *South China Morning Post*, has a higher rate of writer identification than any of the three Chinese-language newspapers. Taken overall, television presents a framework around the news broadcast which highlights the person of the reporter (as well as other persons as we will see below). In newspapers, on the other hand, the person of the writer is a much less salient figure, appearing only occasionally in the byline of a small percentage of the items which appear on their pages.

NEWSPAPER EDITORS

The identity of journalists is framed through the delegation sequences in television news and through bylining in newspaper news. Presenters in television news broadcasts are framed and identified, in turn, by initial on-screen character identification and this framing is seen to be the work of the editor and director of the broadcast whose signatures appear in the channel closing credits (Chapter 5). The question to which I now turn is: How are editors in newspapers identified?

The answer to this is relatively straightforward, or apparently so, in a number of newspapers, but not in all of them. For example, *The Washington Post* carries a block statement of publisher, editorial and management responsibility which includes Vice Presidents for production, advertising, counsel and the like. This statement appears on the leader or editorial page, though in a lower corner, away from editorially highly valued space. Blocks carrying similar statements of responsibility do not appear in all newspapers, however. Another very important newspaper, *The Times* carries only a short statement of the address and telephone to which letters to the editor should be directed. While it is clear that the potential writer of a letter to the editor should contact him or her at this address, there is no indication here or elsewhere who this editor is of the more explicit kind printed in *The Washington Post*.

Within the sample I have collected, the following newspapers use a block similar to that in *The Washington Post* to identify publisher, editorial and management responsibility:

The New York Times (New York); English
USA Today (International); English
Frankfurter Allgemeine (Frankfurt); German
The Washington Post (Washington); English
The Washington Times (Washington); English
The Detroit News (Detroit); English
The Detroit Free Press (Detroit); English
Il Messagero (Rome); Italian
Aftenposten (Oslo); Norwegian

On the other hand, the following papers do not give any indication of such responsibility:

South China Morning Post (Hong Kong); English
Ming Pao (Hong Kong); Chinese
Oriental Daily News (Hong Kong); Chinese
Wen Wei Po (Hong Kong); Chinese
Renmin Ribao (Beijing); Chinese
Lianhe Zaobao (Singapore); Chinese

To this list might be added all of the rest of the Hong Kong daily newspapers in our corpus.

While one might be tempted to see in the first list, which includes a number of American newspapers, a great love of freedom of the press, and in the second list of papers either repression of press freedom or some form of self-censorship or dodging of responsibility, the following three British papers, which also do not have any such statement of ownership or editors, tends to preclude that line of argument:

The Times (London); English
The Daily Telegraph (London); English
The Guardian (London and Manchester); English

Such British papers have been well known to be as strongly in support of a free press as any of the papers listed above with clear editorial self-disclosures.

While it goes beyond the scope of this study, I suggest that the answer to the question of why some newspapers explicitly identify the key figures in their structures and others do not lies more in whether or not it is assumed that these will be known by the general reader. I would argue that whether it is *The Times* or *Renmin Ribao* (*The People's Daily*), potential readers would be equally aware of the bases of editorial authority. This is certainly true for virtually all of the newspapers published in Hong Kong (Zhang 1988; Li Jiayuan 1989). In contrast, I suggest that the explicit statements in the American (and other newspapers) may well reflect the highly mobile and less conservative populations of readers in their audiences. Of course it might also indicate that they see themselves as public corporations whose executives are accustomed normally to being formally published.

If we return now to the question of how the editors (sub-editors, actually) who delegate identity and authority to the reporters of news stories are identified, the answer is that they are not identified. The blocks of publisher, editorial and management responsibility list only editors at the highest organizational levels. The lowest of these levels of responsibility indicated is usually that of editorial page editor or deputy editorial page editor – that is to say, the person who can be assumed to take responsibility for the editorials written on that page.

Somewhere below the editorial levels indicated in the identification block and above the level of the reporters, correspondents and other journalists who write the articles which appear in the newspaper are the sub-editors and copy editors who work with the texts of journalists and who lay out the pages of the newspaper. This layer of responsibility, as significant as it may be, remains unidentified in the great majority of newspapers which one sees from day to day. That is to say, these sub-editors work under the delegated authority and policies of the named editors and they, in turn, are the personae who create the voice found in the headlines, the bylines, and even the leads, but they never step forward on to the stage of discourse to be identified themselves.

If we return to those editors who are identified, these are the voices which we find, normally anonymously presented at the location of the text, on the editorial page in those statements of editorial opinion found under the title block of the newspaper.

RESOURCES FOR PRESENTING THE PERSON

In the preceding discussion I have indicated that the identification of journalists goes considerably beyond the simple question of naming. We are now in the position to summarize the general resources available within the discourses of broadcast and print journalism for identifying and socially positioning journalists ranging from reporters and feature writers to presenters and editors. First, I will list them in general categories and then present them in comparative tabular form.

Delegated naming: A person is directly named by another; normally this is done by a presenter in television or by a sub-editor in newspapers

On-screen characters: The name is placed upon the screen; television only

Title/status gradation: This includes the range of titles including 'Correspondent', 'White House Correspondent', 'Chief Washington Correspondent', 'Specially Engaged', 'Intern Reporter'

First name: Most often seen in quasi-conversations between a presenter and a television reporter

Initials: Most often at the end of a newspaper article

Assumed name: Editorial pseudonyms are the most common form

'With' status: A reporter or feature writer is identified as being 'with' some important personage; status by association

Location: Statement of the place from which the story originates

Verb categorization: Describes the activities ('reports', 'has been monitoring', 'covers', 'is live') and by doing so suggests different statuses

Self-naming (signature): Usually in the frame 'this is' on television; found at the end of articles in newspapers

Voice identification: One recognizes a person through the voice; broadcast only, of course

Quoted at higher level: In the frame 'as X X reports', a journalist at a higher level makes reference to the language of a journalist at a lower level

Topical restriction: The story topic is delimited within the delegation frame; 'X X will report on Y'

Topical freedom: The journalist exercises freedom to frame his or her own topic; often it is not immediately clear what the topic will be

Exo-textual reference: The journalist makes reference to other stories found within the same broadcast or newspaper pages

Live/spontaneous: The journalist speaks or writes spontaneously without apparent knowledge beforehand of what will be said except, perhaps, for loose topical relevance.

Unframed: A stretch of speech or a text is not framed by any other journalist

Privileged position: Either a dedicated position (everyday in the same place) or a reserved position such as that for the editorials on the leader page.

Table 6.2 summarizes these resources for identifying the five journalist roles of presenter (P), television reporter (TVR), newspaper

Table 6.2: Resources for attribution

Identification	P	TVR	Ed	NPR	FW
Delegated naming	+	+	−	+	+
On-screen characters	+	+	−	−	−
Title/status gradation	−	+	R	+	−
First name	+	+	+	−	+
Initials	−	−	+	R	−
Assumed name	−	−	+	−	+
'With' status	−	+	−	+	+
Location	R	+	−	+	−
Verb categorization	−	+	−	−	−
Self-naming (signature)	R	+	−	−	+
Voice identification	+	+	−	−	−
Quoted at higher level	−	+	−	+	−
Topical restriction	−	+	−	+	−
Topical freedom	R	−	+	−	+
Exo-textual reference	+	−	+	−	+
Live/spontaneous	+	R	+	−	+
Unframed	−	−	+	−	−
Priviledged position	+	−	+	−	+

editor (Ed), newspaper reporter (NPR), and newspaper feature writer (FW). A plus (+) indicates that this feature is quite regularly found in my data; a minus (–) indicates that I have not found the feature. The letter 'R' indicates that the feature is quite rare.

SOCIAL INTERACTION

I am arguing that there might be some advantage to considering news reporting, both broadcast and print news, to be a kind of social interaction. Now it is time to return to this issue to see what might be gleaned out of the preceding discussion on this question.

In my study of telephone calls in Chapter 2, I took the position that the main participants are engaged in a kind of social interaction in which there was a hierarchy of considerations to be dealt with – channel, relationship (or at a minimum, identification) and topic. There I argued that a disruption at any higher level must be repaired before continuing at any lower level. I referred to these implications as a set of Maxims of Stance. While the case for television news broadcasts has been presented in Chapter 5, the case for the newspaper being a form of social interaction is somewhat more difficult to establish with direct evidence. It is the analysis of television which opens a window on this problem.

In the now tired sender–receiver model of news communication, if newspaper news is looked at as a kind of social interaction between the writer of the news story and the reader of that same story, it is very difficult to establish most of the necessary elements for this analysis. On the production side it is very difficult in many, perhaps in most cases to determine who is the actual writer. As is well understood in studies of journalism (Zhang 1988 and Bell 1991 are only the most accessible sources), most stories go through a highly complex process of writing and re-writing, including primary authors, editors, translators, further editors, further writers, and the like, that makes it very difficult to establish responsibility for the text as it finally appears within the pages of the newspaper. The word 'authorship' seems unreasonably stretched to cover this process of the creation of a text.[9]

On the receptive end, as I have argued elsewhere (R. Scollon 1996b) and in Chapter 3, it is very difficult to identify any single hypothetical 'reader' of any particular newspaper or even more generally a participant in the newspaper discourse. Any particular reader picks and chooses among stories and other items of one or, most often, several newspapers. He or she reads all of this story, a bit of that, skimming headlines here and ignoring internal structure of the story there. There is little or no evidence that any particular story can be taken to have a reader who starts reading at the beginning and reads straight through to the end and who, thereby, fulfills the characteristics of some implied reader (Booth 1975; Chatman 1978), though, of course, some readers may also choose to read the newspaper in this way.

As I have argued in Chapter 3, as a form of social interaction on the receptive end, the newspaper is more likely to form an element of an interaction between two people at breakfast, on a city park bench, or in an office where the production participant framework is far from both their awareness and from their socially interactive purview. It is really stretching a point to try to think of the authors of newspaper stories being in any direct, socially interactive way engaged with the readers of these stories. Certainly, if there is an engagement, it is far from the conscious awareness of the participants and it is also rather distant from any possibility of socially interactive repairwork when there are breakdowns.

If we only ask the fundamental questions, we can see how distant this possibility really is: How is the channel opened and the opening ratified? How is it closed and the closing ratified? How are the identities of the participants established and ratified and how is this frame closed? How are topic frames opened and closed?

If we try to use these questions with the assumption that the interaction is between writers and readers, the answer can only be that channel, identification and topical frames are all opened and closed unilaterally on the production end. The reader is almost completely restricted as a social interactor to letters to the editor (or perhaps in some rare cases, a telephone call). In any case, these letters and phone calls are all after the fact from the point of view of the primary interaction as they cannot have any effect on the primary channel, identity and topical frames.

The interactive framework of television shows us more clearly that the primary social interaction in the case of newspapers as well is not between 'writer' and 'reader' if by that we mean the journalists and the purchaser of the newspaper, it is an interaction among journalists. Quite analogously to the situation described for television, the reader is in the role of a ratified but non-interacting overhearer. It is a spectator role. The reader of the newspaper is in a role analogous to that of the spectator at a football match; while you could not say that he or she was a player in the game, it is not likely that the game would continue to be played for long without such spectators. One could say that both television and newspaper news reports are a kind of spectacle which is staged for the amusement, edification, information or entertainment of the spectators – perhaps all within a single span of broadcast or a single day's newspaper. The primary forms of social interaction, the ones which correspond to the structures of the business telephone calls, are carried out among the players, but with the understanding that at least some of the play will be made available to paying spectators.[10]

From this point of view, the primary social interactions are those in which the editorial staff lays out the daily newspaper, taking into account both advertising and editorial concerns. In doing so, they delegate position and significance to the persons whose writing appears in the newspaper. Through processes of bylining and headlining, sub-editors further delegate the rights to take voice and to introduce topics to reporters. Thus, within this pattern of social interaction, the person of the reporter is constructed, constrained, and finally displayed as a spectacle for the interpretation of the consuming reader.

NOTES

1. This earlier text, of course, is likely to be based upon texts even prior to Bell (1991).
2. That is to say, there is virtually never any linguistically realized closing frame. Page layout corresponds in space to some extent to sequencing in time and so should not be entirely ignored when considering the framing of printed news stories.
3. While this is the general pattern and is invariable within the papers I have included in my study, I have since noted a very few cases in which there has been both an initial bylined author and a concluding attribution to an agency. I have not formally studied changes in the *South China Morning Post*'s formatting and bylining practices since the change of ownership which has taken place since the first collection of data.
4. While the writer of the letter to the editor is normally not considered as a journalist, that does not preclude a journalist writing such a letter. Hutcheon (1983) comments that Henry Ching, who was the editor of

the *South China Morning Post* for many years, was often found to have written a letter to the editor (himself). He writes,

> Ching, the editor, was himself an occasional correspondent to his own newspaper under a variety of pseudonyms, and he was not averse to taking issue with points he had made in his own leaders.
>
> (Hutcheon 1983: 63)

5. Hutcheon (1983) notes that letters to the editor of the *SCMP* normally did not bear names until after the 1920s, though he gives no reason for this practice nor for its change at that time.

6. Fong (1992) points out that *Ming Pao* is widely recognized for the elegant quality of its written style. Li Tsze Sun (1993) chose *Dong Fong Yat Po* (*Oriental Daily News*) for his study on the basis of its very wide and popular circulation.

7. Interestingly, stories which may be verbatim reproductions with only the typefaces changed from simplified characters to traditional characters have been observed to be thought to represent very different sociopolitical positions (Scollon and Scollon 1997).

8. A possible exception to this statement are the infotainment shows which have become popular in Hong Kong during the period of this study. While these are not framed as news programmes, interviewing indicates that many people fail to perceive the distinction between the main news programmes and these shows featuring well-known movie and entertainment stars who go about Hong Kong 'investigating' the hottest new news items. What is clear from our research is that most Hong Kongers very much prefer the infotainment shows to the main news (R. Scollon, Bhatia, Li and Yung 1996; R. Scollon and Yung 1996; Yung 1996).

9. Kress (1993) gives an interesting example of a news text of considerable, though not unusual, authorial complexity showing that even within a single news story there may be represented a wide range of social institutions and their representatives, all contesting each other for position and voice.

10. As to the question of to whom the spectators make payment, there are further complications. The payment made to the newspaper is a fraction of the cost of their production as is the case when television broadcasts are paid for. The main costs are supported by the advertising companies (or governments in the case of non-commercial broadcasting and newspapers). In those cases it is the potential spectator who is sold to the advertiser by the company (or organization) which is staging the spectacle.

SEVEN

Newsmakers in newspaper and television

JOURNALISTS AND THE NEWSMAKER

While practising journalists like to think of themselves as speaking to a public, or even speaking for a public (Fromson 1994), I argue that the public discourse of news journalism in newspapers and in the broadcast media can be seen as primarily a discourse of and among journalists. They form the relevant community of practice. It is they who speak to each other; it is they who open and sustain channel, relationship and topical frames in the ongoing social inter-action. It is they who position each other in super and subordinate social roles. The viewers and readers of this discourse engage in it as a kind of by-play (Goffman 1974, 1981), that is, as spectators to an event staged at least partly on their behalf. Or they even engage in this discourse as a kind of side-play, that is, as kibitzers who comment on the spectacle among each other.

The question with which I begin is: What is this discourse about? That is, what do these journalists purport to be talking about? The simplist answer to this is: the newsmakers.

Newsmakers are the people from heads of state to local football players who figure as the central characters in news stories. The topical focus of the majority of news stories is what these news-makers say. While in some cases where there is a major event such as an earthquake, it might seem that the focus is on actions and events, nevertheless, we often see little of the actual event and much of what various eyewitnesses and officials have to say about the event. As Bell has said, 'News is what an authoritative source tells a journalist' (1991: 191).

In print news such tellings are called quotations and, where the quotation is word for word, or at least purports to be word for word, quotation marks are used.[1] In broadcast news such direct quotations are played directly as recordings made of the newsmaker speaking the words. Thus the quotation marks of print journalism correspond in some rough way with the cut to the words (and usually the face) of the newsmaker who is speaking his or her own words in broadcast journalism. These latter playings of a news-maker's own speech are referred to as 'actualities'.[2]

While one's impression from reading a newspaper or seeing a television news broadcast might be that one has heard from a news-maker directly, there is often little actual direct quotation of these newsmakers. Bell notes, for example: 'The principal difference between speech presentation in news and in fiction is the dimension of faithful reproduction. . . . The main method by which all media handle newsmakers' speech is to turn it into indirect speech or to run it unattributed' (1991: 205). As Bell later points out, 'Direct quotation is the exception not the rule in news stories' (1991: 209).

I will take up later the question of whether quotations and actu-alities should be considered to be delegations of the floor to the news-makers by the reporters in these stories (Goffman 1981). Fairclough (1992, 1995a, 1995b) has argued cogently that such discourse rep-resentations are the crucial discursive means by which newsmakers are positioned *vis-à-vis* the journalist.

First, I want to take up the more routine issue of just how and where these quotations and actualities occur. I will start by suggest-ing that, on the whole, television uses more actualities than print news uses the corresponding quotations. Then I will present evid-ence that a significant difference in the ways that the voices of reporters and those of newsmakers enter the discourse is that re-porters are simply and directly delegated the right to speak (write) whereas newsmakers are evaluated or characterized in the process of giving them voice.

Following on Goffman's (1981) analysis of production format roles, I then argue that while reporters take on both the roles of pro-ducing text (authorship) and of taking responsibility for things thus said (principalship), newsmakers are rarely delegated the right to authorship. On the other hand, reporters rather commonly delegate principalship, that is, the responsibility for the text, to newsmakers. Thus, quotation is used by reporters to delegate responsibility for their stories while retaining the power to craft the wordings. The role of newsmakers in this discourse, then, is constructed to be that of providing fodder for the reporters' construction of news stories. In two cases in which the right to introduce topics is

contested by the newsmakers I will argue that ultimately they cap-
itulate to the journalists who retain not only control over authorship
and the power to delegate responsibility, but also retain control over
the topics of the discourse.

DISCOURSE REPRESENTATION: QUOTATIONS
AND ACTUALITIES

Discourse representation has been analysed by Fairclough (1992,
1995a, 1995b) as a major site in which social positionings are constructed in discursive practice. Ranging from nominalizations to
direct quotation, these representations are the discursive means
by which one text is positioned within another text and through
that positioning the authors of the texts are also positioned both in
relationship to the author and in relationship to broader sociocultural practice.

Bell (1991) says that broadcast news and print news differ in
their quotation formats in that in the former the formula X *said 'Y'*
is used whereas in the latter the formula is *'Y', said X.* In other
words, according to Bell, it is customary in print to quote first and
attribute later. This difference has not actually been found in the
newspapers I studied. The difference in formats relates not to
medium but to whether or not the quotation is indirect or direct.
I found that the so-called broadcast format, X *said 'Y'*, was used for
indirect quotation – that is, X *said (that) Y* – and the print format
was used only for direct quotation. Further, I found a pattern which
was often used in which a quotation was divided into two paragraphs with the attribution placed at the end of the first paragraph
before the paragraph break between the two. That pattern could be
shown as *'Y', said X (P) 'Z'.* The second quotation was attributed
only through the assumption of continuation.

In order to establish at a general level just to what extent direct
quotation and actualities are used, I have made the following comparison among six news sources, two television broadcasts and four
newspapers, all of them in Hong Kong and representing both English and Chinese news broadcasts. The total number of items is, of
course, very different for the much shorter television broadcasts
and for the newspapers. The column labelled 'Q/A' gives the total
number of quotations or actualities. The next column of percentages is a simple division of those Q/As by the total number of

Table 7.1: Quotations and actualities

Source	Total	Q/A	Q/A(%)	A WQ(%)	WQ
ATV Home (Ch)	31	21	67.7	16	51.6
ATV World (Eng)	23	19	82.6	10	42.6
South China Morning Post (Eng)	227	129	54.6	79	34.8
Wen Wei Pao (Ch)	163	60	37.8	28	17.2
Ming Pao (Ch)	121	35	28.9	14	11.6
Dong Fong Yat Po (Ch)	137	24	17.5	13	9.5

items. This is not a very useful percentage, however, as many items which have quotations or actualities have several of them while others have none at all. Therefore, I counted the number of items with actualities or quotations as a subset of items (A WQ: 'articles with quotations') and show the percentage of quotations or actualities which appear in those articles alone. Table 7.1 gives those figures.

Two points can be drawn from this comparison: (1) the television broadcasts appear to use more actualities than the newspapers use quotations either overall or within just those items which contain quoted speech, and (2) the number of items with quoted speech in newspapers is rather small. *Dong Fong Yat Po* (*Oriental Daily News*) has the lowest percentage (9.5 per cent).[3] These two points suggest that Bell's claim that news writers prefer to use indirect quotation to direct quotation holds more for print media than for broadcast media. This is a difference between the media which further study might show would help to account for the greater sense of presence between the two media as Li et al. (1993) have suggested.

THE LANGUAGE OF ATTRIBUTION

In order to make this analysis more concrete, I will now turn my focus to a single news story which appeared on 25 February 1994 in the *South China Morning Post* (*SCMP*). There are three aspects which I will consider in turn: (1) the ways in which speech (or its contents) are attributed to the speakers or agents; (2) the characterization of those agents of speaking; and (3) the voicing of what is in the end a rather complex, polyvocal (Uspensky 1973) or heteroglossic (Bakhtin 1981a) story.

In the months preceding this story China and Great Britain held a series of negotiations regarding the future of Hong Kong following the transfer of the British territory to Chinese sovereignty. Those talks had broken down and the British side published a White Paper[4] summarizing the contents of the previously secret talks. The story concerned the publication of this White Paper and the Governor of Hong Kong Chris Patten's comments to the Legislative Council concerning this event.

In the story which follows I have used **boldface** to indicate the verbs and other forms used to give voice to the newsmakers and others found in the story. The story appeared as follows:

Lead Story, Page One: *South China Morning Post*, 25 February 1994.

'I think it was an extremely important mature moment in Hong Kong's history. Nobody can wipe it out' (Above headline)

TELL ALL, PATTEN **URGED**
'Distilled' version **conceals** nothing, **says** Government

By FANNY WONG

THE Government was last night under intense pressure to **disclose** more details of the 17 rounds of secret talks on Hong Kong's future political reforms, only hours after **publishing** what it **admitted** was a 'distilled' version of the negotiations.

Government sources **insisted** there had been no attempt to hide anything by not **printing** a fuller account and **suggested** instead that the administration did not want to **bombard** legislators and the community with 'a barrage of papers.'

But liberal legislators from the United Democrats of Hong Kong and Meeting Point last night **demanded** the Government **reveal** more than what was contained in the 36-page White Paper on the talks.

They **said** the White Paper was insufficient for people to make a proper judgment of the handling of the negotiations, which had led to an almost total breakdown in Sino–British relations with serious ramifications for the territory in the run-up to 1997.

Confusion mounted last night after the Chinese side **rejected** the British accounts of the talks.

Chief Chinese negotiator Jiang Enzhu **briefed** a group of Hong Kong members of the Preliminary Working Committee (PWC) with a different version of events.

There already **had been a warning from** Beijing that the British move might affect co-operation in other areas, including the crucial talks needed to get the new airport fully under way.

The Chinese side **rejected** the British **suggestion** that Beijing had changed its stance on issues such as the abolition of appointed seats to the district boards and municipal councils elections.

While **announcing** the **publication** of the White Paper yesterday and the **gazetting** today of the remaining parts of his controversial electoral package on the 1995 Legislative Council elections, the Governor, Chris Patten, **stressed** that the White Papers was 'a thorough factual account.'

Noting that China had already **disclosed** some details of the talks in the People's Daily on January 7, Mr Patten **said** the British side had decided to **publish** its version to fulfil a **promise to reveal** details of the talks when pressing ahead with the remaining legislation without the Chinese Government's agreement.

Mr Patten **said** the White Paper **set out** the background to the present position and the approach which Britain took in the negotiations with China, as well as the modifications Britain was prepared to make to his 1992 proposals as part of an overall agreement including the through-train arrangement.

He **said** he regretted no agreement could be reached, but **commended** legislators for approving the first-stage bill early yesterday morning on the three simple issues.

The council approved the lowering of the voting age from 21 to 18, the adoption of the single-seat, single-vote system for the three-tier elections and the abolition of appointed seats on the district boards and municipal councils.

'I think it was an extremely important day for Hong Kong. I think it was an extremely important mature moment in Hong Kong's history,' he **said**.

'Nobody can wipe it out. Nobody can pretend it didn't happen. Nobody can turn back the clock on what happened,' Mr Patten **said**.

Defending the decision to publish only an abridged account, government sources **said** if a blow-by-blow account of the talks was included, the document would be as big as a phone book.

'It's not sensible and it's not helpful to bombard the Legislative Council, the Parliament and the Hong Kong community with a great barrage of papers. It is sensible to summarise it in this way, there's nothing missing from here,' **said** a government source.

'It is a distillation, but everything that is important, everything that happens in the talks that is important is there.'

THE FORMS OF ATTRIBUTION

The first observation which can be made is that this story is very definitely a story about what authoritative sources have to say, though with the caution that there is much intertextuality here of things said to journalists and things said to the Legislative Council and other authorities. That is to say, while Bell has been quoted above as saying that news consists of things said *to* journalists, in this case that is only a portion of what is said. Much of this has been *said in the presence of* journalists; their position (not unlike that of the reader in reference to journalistic discourse) is that of by-play – they are ratified as present within the social interaction (a legislative council meeting) but not as speaking participants. They get a chance to have their word later in print.

The second observation is that the language by which attributions are made goes considerably beyond the use of the verbs of saying (Fairclough 1992, 1995a, 1995b; Caldas-Coulthard 1993, 1994). The list of verbs used is given below in alphabetical order:

admitted	disclose(d)2
announcing	gazetting
bombard	insisted
briefed	noting
commended	printing
conceals	publish (publishing) 2
defending	rejected 2
demanded	reveal

said 9	suggested
set out	tell
stressed	urged

While we see the verb 'said' appears nine times, it is certainly not the most striking of the verbs used here. What we see, in fact, is that the voices of the various participants are set out in a rather complex array of characterizations which range from the neutral 'said' to the stronger verbs such as 'demanded', 'insisted', and 'stressed'. One finds as well various forms of innuendo ('conceals', 'disclose', 'admitted') as well as verbs indicating performative status ('announcing', 'publishing', 'gazetting').

The ways in which attribution is carried out go beyond the use of verbs as well. The passive clause with a noun 'had been a warning from Beijing' might have been stated more directly as 'Beijing warned' if the choice had been to make a bigger issue of this warning. What is said to be a matter of 'announcing' on the one hand is said not to have been to 'bombard . . . with a barrage of papers' on the other.

The point I want to draw from looking at these forms of attribution is a point elucidated by Fairclough (1992, 1995a, 1995b). Even though newsmakers are given a voice in this news story, that voice is not given neutrally. We are told by the reporter not only *that* someone has said something, but *how* we are expected to respond. To put it within the framework I now want to use, we are shown how the journalist is positioning herself in respect to both the newsmakers and the reader.

If we compare this with the delegation of the floor which occurs in the interactions between a television presenter and a reporter (Chapter 5) or a newspaper editor and a reporter (Chapter 6), we see that those delegations are rather neutral in form. We are not told how we are expected to evaluate the story; we are just told who will be telling it. The difference we see is that the floor is delegated to the journalist by the news organization through the voice of the editor or presenter. Here, however, we do not see the delegation of the floor so much as characterization through quotation and attribution. The reporter is telling a story and a significant part of that story is evaluation of the newsmaker. As the story is being told, the utterances of the newsmakers are given a dose of character development as well as part of the overall construction of the reporter's point of view. While the newsmakers themselves may also engage in this characterization – it was one of the newsmakers who used the phrase 'bombard . . . with a great barrage' – the overwhelming number of characterizations are given by the reporter. It would be a subtle distinction to try to draw between delegation of the floor and characterization. As Fairclough (1992, 1995a, 1995b) has pointed out, both are forms of discourse representation by which writers position themselves in relationship to the texts they appropriate as well as to their authors. On the extreme end of delegation we would find the common verb 'reports' or 'says'; on the other extreme end of characterization we would find verbs such as 'slammed' (Li et al. 1993). I suggest these forms of attribution are on a cline which runs from delegation to characterization and that on this cline, on the whole, reporters are delegated the floor while newsmakers are characterized with their turn at the floor being restricted to the merest statements.

THE AGENTS OF SPEAKING

Perhaps the biggest contrast between the delegation of the floor to the reporter on the one hand and the use of quotations and actualities on the other is in the proliferation of speaking agents. A news story is, on the whole, told by a single bylined reporter; at least, that is how the story is presented to the reader/viewer. The newsmakers which appear in those stories, however, appear in a chorus of voices mixed together from a variety of sources.

To give a view of these different agents of speaking in this one story I have reformatted this same story, but in this case with the agents to which stretches of the discourse are attributed highlighted in **boldface**.

Lead Story, Page One: *South China Morning Post*, 25 February 1994.

'I think it was an extremely important mature moment in Hong Kong's history. Nobody can wipe it out' (Above headline)

TELL ALL, **PATTEN** URGED

'Distilled' version conceals nothing, says **Government**

By **FANNY WONG**

THE **Government** was last night under intense pressure to disclose more details of the 17 rounds of secret talks on Hong

Kong's future political reforms, only hours after publishing what **it** admitted was a 'distilled' version of the negotiations.

Government sources insisted there had been no attempt to hide anything by not printing a fuller account and suggested instead that **the administration** did not want to bombard legislators and the community with 'a barrage of papers.'

But **liberal legislators from the United Democrats of Hong Kong and Meeting Point** last night demanded the **Government** reveal more than what was contained in the 36-page White Paper on the talks.

They said the White Paper was insufficient for people to make a proper judgment of the handling of the negotiations, which had led to an almost total breakdown in Sino–British relations with serious ramifications for the territory in the run-up to 1997.

Confusion mounted last night after the **Chinese side** rejected the British accounts of the talks.

Chief Chinese negotiator Jiang Enzhu briefed a group of Hong Kong members of the Preliminary Working Committee (PWC) with a different version of events.

There already had been a warning from **Beijing** that the British move might affect co-operation in other areas, including the crucial talks needed to get the new airport fully under way.

The **Chinese side** rejected the **British** suggestion that Beijing had changed its stance on issues such as the abolition of appointed seats to the district boards and municipal councils elections.

While announcing the publication of the White Paper yesterday and the gazetting today of the remaining parts of his controversial electoral package on the 1995 Legislative Council elections, the **Governor, Chris Patten**, stressed that the White Papers was 'a thorough factual account.'

Noting that China had already disclosed some details of the talks in the People's Daily on January 7, **Mr Patten** said the **British side** had decided to publish its version to fulfil a promise to reveal details of the talks when pressing ahead with the remaining legislation without the Chinese Government's agreement.

Mr Patten said the **White Paper** set out the background to the present position and the approach which Britain took in the negotiations with China, as well as the modifications Britain was prepared to make to his 1992 proposals as part of an overall agreement including the through-train arrangement.

He said he regretted no agreement could be reached, but commended legislators for approving the first-stage bill early yesterday morning on the three simple issues.

The council approved the lowering of the voting age from 21 to 18, the adoption of the single-seat, single-vote system for the three-tier elections and the abolition of appointed seats on the district boards and municipal councils.

'I think it was an extremely important day for Hong Kong. I think it was an extremely important mature moment in Hong Kong's history,' **he** said.

'Nobody can wipe it out. Nobody can pretend it didn't happen. Nobody can turn back the clock on what happened,' **Mr Patten** said.

Defending the decision to publish only an abridged account, **government sources** said if a blow-by-blow account of the talks was included, the document would be as big as a phone book.

'It's not sensible and it's not helpful to bombard the Legislative Council, the Parliament and the Hong Kong community with a great barrage of papers. It is sensible to summarise it in this way, there's nothing missing from here,' said a **government source**.

'It is a distillation, but everything that is important, everything that happens in the talks that is important is there.'

The speaking agents found in this lead story are many. First there are the agents which appear in the editor's frame (Chapter 6), that is, the headline and byline. There we find the following:

I
Patten
Government
Fanny Wong

The story is opened, even above the headline, with a line set in direct quotation, but without direct attribution. The only agent indicated is the 'I' which we are to surmise is the Governor, Mr Patten. Later on in the story we find this same stretch of quoted speech, there attributed directly to Mr Patten.

While it goes beyond the scope of this study, the ways in which particular newsmakers are named is a significant aspect of the point of view taken towards them by the news agency (Caldas-Coulthard 1993, 1994). In an earlier portion of this study, I found that in the naming of Boris Yeltsin there were a range of forms from 'the Russian President Boris Nikolayevitch Yeltsin' to the Chinese *Lao Ye*, a rather colloquial characterization. One might in this case carry out further studies to determine the sociolinguistic valences of the range of terms 'Patten', 'Mr Patten', 'Governor', and 'Chris Patten'.

What one does see within the editor's frame, however, is that we are to expect to hear the voices of Mr Patten and the Government, that Mr Patten will speak directly, 'I', and that it will be Fanny Wong who will be delegated the story along with its rights of characterization.

The list of agents who are said to speak in this story indicates a range of considerable complexity. Some of these, of course, are references to the same person as the grouping below shows:

Governor of Hong Kong (8)
   Governor
   Chris Patten
   Patten (3)
   He
   I (2)
Government (7)
   Sources (5)
   it
   administration
British side (2)
White Paper
Chinese side (4)
   Beijing
   Chief Chinese negotiator Jiang Enzhu
liberal legislators from the United Democrats of Hong Kong and Meeting Point (2)
   they

Altogether there is a preponderance of voices on the 'British side' if you include the Hong Kong government and the Governor as well as the one inanimate agent, the White Paper, on that side. There are 18 of these in total. The 'Chinese side' comes up with only four references. The liberal legislators seem to be in an inter-mediate no-man's ground between the two sides.

As to actual people represented here, it is more difficult to know how to keep score. The Governor is named and the Chief Chinese negotiator, Jiang Enzhu, is named. The others are alluded to as members of a side or as 'sources'. Of course, it is well understood in journalistic circles that attribution to 'sources' may be used to protect the confidentiality of the person presumed to speak the words.

For my purposes the question of confidentiality is a secondary issue. What is primary is that within this story about talk, this discourse on the topic of the China–British discourse, no single voice is heard; what we hear is the chorus of voices assembled by the reporter in the process of telling this story. Even figures as significant as the Governor of Hong Kong, who is headlined as a main speaker, is played down against the background chorus of other voices.

Furthermore, in this chorus of voices we hear in this story, we see that only the reporter is positioned to present a consistent view of the discourse being described. While we have brief statements and evaluative comments by the Governor and others, in this story we do not have his view of what a coherent presentation of the facts of the case may be. The Governor's statements are part of the raw materials out of which this story is constructed, not the story itself.

VOICING

Before I can come to a conclusion about the voices we hear in this lead story regarding the White Paper, it will be important to con-sider the various ways in which these voices are presented. That is to say, there is a range of voicings presented, including the direct voice of the reporter, indirect quotation of sources, direct quotation of sources, and, finally, somewhat ambiguously voiced sections. These four kinds of voicing are indicated in the transcript below: **direct quotation**, *indirect quotation*, <u>ambiguously voiced</u>, voice of the bylined writer.

Lead Story, Page One: *South China Morning Post*,
25 February 1994.
   'I think it was an extremely important mature moment in Hong Kong's history. Nobody can wipe it out'
(Above headline)

TELL ALL, PATTEN URGED
'Distilled' version conceals nothing, says Government

By FANNY WONG

THE Government was last night under intense pressure
to disclose more details of the 17 rounds of secret talks on
Hong Kong's future political reforms, only hours after
publishing what it admitted was *a 'distilled' version of the
negotiations.*

Government sources insisted *there had been no attempt to hide
anything by not printing a fuller account* and suggested instead
that *the administration did not want to bombard legislators and the
community with* '**a barrage of papers**.'

But liberal legislators from the United Democrats of Hong
Kong and Meeting Point last night demanded <u>the Government
reveal more than what was contained in the 36-page White
Paper on the talks</u>.

They said *the White Paper was insufficient for people to make
a proper judgement of the handling of the negotiations*, <u>which had
led to an almost total breakdown in Sino-British relations with
serious ramifications for the territory in the run-up to 1997</u>.

Confusion mounted last night after the Chinese side rejected
the British accounts of the talks.

Chief Chinese negotiator Jiang Enzhu briefed a group of
Hong Kong members of the Preliminary Working Committee
(PWC) with a different version of events.

There already had been a warning from Beijing that
<u>the British move might affect co-operation in other areas,
including the crucial talks needed to get the new airport
fully under way</u>.

The Chinese side rejected the British suggestion that Beijing
had changed its stance on issues such as the abolition of
appointed seats to the district boards and municipal councils
elections.

While announcing <u>the publication of the White Paper
yesterday and the gazetting today of the remaining parts</u>
<u>of his controversial electoral package on the 1995 Legislative
Council elections</u>, the Governor, Chris Patten, stressed that
the White Papers was '**a thorough factual account**.'

Noting that *China had already disclosed some details of the talks
in the People's Daily on January 7*, Mr Patten said *the British side*

had decided to publish its version to fulfil a promise to reveal details of the talks when pressing ahead with the remaining legislation without the Chinese Government's agreement.

Mr Patten said *the White Paper set out the background to the present position and the approach which Britain took in the negotiations with China, as well as the modifications Britain was prepared to make to his 1992 proposals as part of an overall agreement including the through-train arrangement.*

He said *he regretted no agreement could be reached, but commended legislators for approving the first-stage bill early yesterday morning on the three simple issues.*

The council approved the lowering of the voting age from 21 to 18, the adoption of the single-seat, single-vote system for the three-tier elections and the abolition of appointed seats on the district boards and municipal councils.

'I think it was an extremely important day for Hong Kong. I think it was an extremely important mature moment in Hong Kong's history,' he said.

'Nobody can wipe it out. Nobody can pretend it didn't happen. Nobody can turn back the clock on what happened,' Mr Patten said.

Defending the decision to publish only an abridged account, government sources said *if a blow-by-blow account of the talks was included, the document would be as big as a phone book.*

'It's not sensible and it's not helpful to bombard the Legislative Council, the Parliament and the Hong Kong community with a great barrage of papers. It is sensible to summarise it in this way, there's nothing missing from here,' said a government source.

'It is a distillation, but everything that is important, everything that happens in the talks that is important is there.'

The story opens in the clear voice of the reporter; it ends with direct quotation of a government source. Mr Patten, in fact, is given very little direct voice. Later we see his words 'a thoroughly factual account'. Still later we see the words quoted in the statement above the headline about the historicity of the moment. As to the details, the facts of the case as it were, those are presented by others. In other words, while Mr Patten and the government are cited over a dozen times as speakers in this discourse, Mr Patten himself is only allowed to speak in his own words these two times. In the rest of it what he says is either indirectly quoted or paraphrased by the reporter or, even less directly, it is a government spokesperson who is only indirectly paraphrased.

One further note on the placement of direct quotation in this story is that it occurs in greatest measure towards the end of the story. As we have seen above, the news story is framed as a cut-from-the-end structure, the 'inverted pyramid'. As Bell has put it 'The news story consists of instalments of information of perceived decreasing importance' (1991: 154). Given this scale of decreasing importance it is clear that the actual wordings, the authorship, of newsmakers is of a relatively low priority in this case.

POSITIONING THROUGH THE DELEGATION OF PRODUCTION FORMAT ROLES

I have said above that in this story, as in many like it, the reporter does not, in fact, delegate the floor to the newsmaker(s). The news-maker is given no rights to the structure of the story nor to make claims for its evaluation. The reporter retains the right to structure this chorus of voices into a narrative of her own making. Her right to do this, of course, has been delegated to her by the sub-editor through the bylining we found at the head of the story. In this we see that while others may speak, they do not take the floor.

In social interaction, however, more than floor may be delegated. Goffman (1981) argued that it is useful to distinguish among at least three production format roles – animator, author and prin-cipal. In the story we are considering here we can see instances of how these roles may be separated and, therefore, that the reporter makes a partial delegation to one of the participants in her story.

The story begins with the claim that Fanny Wong is the author and principal of the story we are to read. That is, we understand her to have crafted the words (author) as well as to take respons-ibility for them (principal). She is the bylined writer. We know, nevertheless, that within the frame of the newspaper discourse animation, putting the words into physical form is a function taken over by the host of workers ranging from printers through to the person who sells the newspaper to the reader. One might, in fact, claim that the reader also shares in this animation by being the person who finally gives voice (even though only mental in many cases) to the words found there. That is to say, the process by which these words of whatever provenance, whether they are those of Governor Patten, of Fanny Wong, of Jiang Enzhu, or of an anonymous government source, are brought into physical existence is quite out of the hands of any of these participants in the discourse.

What is at stake are the roles of authorship and principalship. The first of these, authorship, is, according to Goffman, the role of giving the actual wordings to the thoughts thus expressed. The second of these, principalship, is taking responsibility for what is conveyed in those words. Thus, when I say above that the Governor is allowed to speak in his own words only twice in this text, what I am saying is that he is only delegated the right to authorship in two cases. Otherwise, with the other exception of the government source, authorship remains with the bylined reporter Fanny Wong. I can go back and rephrase Bell's (1991) comment on direct and indirect quotation by saying that in newspaper discourse, authorship is rarely delegated to newsmakers, even newsmakers of considerable importance within the community.

Now we have seen that the floor is not delegated to newsmakers (animation is performed by the newspaper organization's staff of printers and the like), authorship is also not delegated to newsmakers. What is delegated to them is principalship. While the reporter retains the right to find the wordings for the ideas (and thereby the power to characterize the evaluative valence of those ideas), the reporter rather willingly delegates responsibility for what is said to others through the delegation of principalship.

If we look at the opening paragraph, we can see the extent to which responsibility, that is principalship, can be delegated in what is otherwise an apparently straightforward statement. We are told the Government was under pressure. The pressure was caused by its publication of a document, the White Paper. What is in dispute is the degree to which this White Paper represents the contents of 17 rounds of negotiations between Britain and China.

The crucial phrase is 'what it admitted'. This phrase does a double task of delegation of responsibility. In the first place someone must have accused the Government of publishing a version which was less than a full, verbatim transcript. We are not told who has made this accusation; the accuser is, in fact, never mentioned, although indirectly it is suggested that 'liberal legislators' have 'demanded' a fuller version. The word 'admit' implies that the Government has come to take responsibility for the accusation made against it. Thus, in this one phrase the reporter delegates responsibility for the accusation to one unidentified party and delegates acknowledgement that the report is a brief one to the Government. This leaves the reporter in the position of never having to take responsibility for either suggesting that it was an excessively short report or suggesting that it was sufficiently long. The reporter, by delegating the responsibility for both of these positions in one phrase, stands aside from the argument, taking responsibility only for the words used. That is to say, the reporter takes responsibility for all of the words but 'distilled'. This two-syllable moment of authorship is attributed to the Government in a skillfully managed delegation of wording to make sure that no taint of principalship for this debate will fall upon the reporter of this story.

In like manner the reporter in most cases successfully delegates responsibility for the ideas or concepts by using either indirect or direct quotation. But what motivates the choice of indirect over direct quotation? I believe the preference for indirect quotation noted by Bell (1991) and studied in fuller detail by Fairclough (1992, 1995a, 1995b) reflects a concern for delegating principalship to newsmakers to the greatest extent possible. Nevertheless, in some cases direct quotation is required to achieve full distance. The danger involved with direct quotation is that without using caution the reporter may find control of his or her story wrested away by the newsmakers themselves. Indirect quotation keeps authorship in the hands of the reporter and as animation also is kept in-house by the printers, only principalship is handed out carefully crafted and evaluated to the newsmakers.

But what about the numerous cases of ambiguous voice in this story? These are the cases where there is little of direct linguistic force to show the writer's hand. Take, for example, the phrase summarizing the history of the Sino–British talks 'which had led to an almost total breakdown . . .'. This bit of journalistic summarization is included to bring the reader who is not familiar with the history of this particular story up to speed. In a sense it could be included anywhere as it is not narratively related to any particular moment in the story.

This line is not tagged on just anywhere, however. The facts are that the talks had ended without resolution in a breakdown and that that breakdown would certainly be consequential for the future of Hong Kong. These facts are tagged on as a 'which-clause' following an indirect quotation of the 'liberal legislators'. It seems rather likely that these legislators did say something like what is in the first (italicized) part of that sentence about the White Paper being insufficient information; it seems rather unlikely that they went on to say the part about handling of the negotiations and their effect on the territory. This latter part, while it might be taken to be understood by some readers and not by others, is attached here and carries with it a resonance with the voice of the 'liberal legislators', whether or not they said it. In other words, even in such cases where the principalship does not require being delegated by the reporter, it is rather easily passed off to one of the newsmakers. Like the hot potato, principalship seems to be something which is safest when passed on quickly to another.

EVENT REPORTING

The story of the Government White Paper which I selected to open my analysis may exemplify much about the framing of newsmakers and tends to support much of what appears in journalistic views of how news is written. Nevertheless, it is not a common story in any sense. It is a story about a discussion about the publication of a report concerning political talks; writing about talk about writing about talk. Not all news events are based upon such convoluted strands of intertextuality as this story.

In order to place this highly interdiscursive story within a context of what might be more common news reporting, I have chosen to look at a shorter and more mundane news story from the second page of the same newspaper.

> Story, Page Two: *South China Morning Post*, 25 February 1994.
> Customs swoop in on $20m shipment

> By SCOTT MCKENZIE
> MORE than $20 million worth of luxury electrical goods falsely manifested as air-conditioning parts have been seized in a waterfront customs raid.
> The operation, which began at 10 pm on Wednesday, was the result of a tip-off.
> Customs Senior Superintendent Ronny Tsang Hing-kam **said** an 883-tonne container vessel was stopped and searched

by an interception crew shortly after it left the Cha Kwo Ling docks bound for Zhuhai.

He **said** the vessel had 31 containers on board but officers were only able to inspect four because of the way they were stacked.

'The manifests for the cargo said the containers were loaded with air-conditioning parts, but when we checked it was electricals such as televisions and karaoke machines,' Mr Tsang **said**.

The vessel was subsequently detained for a complete search and was found to have 10 falsely manifested containers all shipped by the same Hong Kong exporter – a woman who was not identified.

Mr Tsang **said** the law only allowed the vessel to be held for 12 hours and because of difficulties in checking all of the cargo, **special consent** had to be sought from Chief Secretary Anson Chan Fang On-sang to hold the vessel for a further 12 hours.

He **said** the goods had been valued by the woman at $20 million but he considered this to be 'a conservative estimate'.

The goods would have been sold in China with at least a 50 per cent markup on the purchase price in Hong Kong, he **said**.

'The maximum penalty for this sort of offence is a $50,000 fine and two years in jail.'

He **said** it was a growing trend for smugglers to use container vessels to transport goods.

This story is a good bit simpler in terms of the language of attribution. We find only the verb 'said' which is used seven times. I have also included 'special consent' as a kind of performative which would be required from the Chief Secretary though I regard this as a rather marginal instance of attribution. I have also not included the 'said' found in 'The manifest . . . said', nor have I included later on the manifest as an agent.

Although it is much simpler in structure, this story shows us nevertheless that what is being described by the reporter is not the 'customs swoop' itself but the description of that seizure by Mr Tsang, Customs Senior Superintendent. That is, this is again a report about what someone has said as much as it is a report about what someone has done. The saying itself is treated very neutrally here with little evaluation on the part of the story writer. We should not allow the apparent transparency of this story to suggest that it is not a story about what someone in authority has said. It is very much that.

If we go back through the story to see who is saying what, we find that within the editor's frame there is only the person of the reporter identified, Scott McKenzie. Within the reporter's frame there are two participants who are given a voice and a third who, while a major party in the event 'was not identified'. Of course, since it is suggested that she is the owner of an exporting company which is being accused of smuggling, there is good reason why she might prefer to remain anonymous. For reasons of liability the newspapers concur in granting this anonymity.

The two identified participants are Customs Senior Superintendent Ronny Tsang Hing-kam and Chief Secretary Anson Chan Fang On-sang. The former is also the referent for the pronoun 'he' five times and in another two cases referred to as Mr Tsang. The Chief Secretary is actually only rather indirectly a participant. It is said that her 'special consent had to be sought'. This implies the Customs Office contacting the Chief Secretary's office and some response from the Chief Secretary in the nature of a performative ('I hereby authorize X').

VOICING

This story is similarly less complex in its voicing. In particular, while we find three levels of voicing – the reporter's voice, indirect quotation and direct quotation – there are no cases in which the voicing is ambiguous: **direct quotation**, *indirect quotation*, voice of the bylined writer

> Story, Page Two: *South China Morning Post*, 25 February 1994.
>   Customs swoop in on $20m shipment

> By SCOTT MCKENZIE
> MORE than $20 million worth of luxury electrical goods falsely manifested as air-conditioning parts have been seized in a waterfront customs raid.
>   The operation, which began at 10 pm on Wednesday, was the result of a tip-off.

Customs Senior Superintendent Ronny Tsang Hing-kam said *an 883-tonne container vessel was stopped and searched by an interception crew shortly after it left the Cha Kwo Ling docks bound for Zhuhai.*

He said *the vessel had 31 containers on board but officers were only able to inspect four because of the way they were stacked.*

'The manifests for the cargo said the containers were loaded with air-conditioning parts, but when we checked it was electricals such as televisions and karaoke machines,' Mr Tsang said.

The vessel was subsequently detained for a complete search and was found to have 10 falsely manifested containers all shipped by the same Hong Kong exporter – a woman who was not identified.

Mr Tsang said *the law only allowed the vessel to be held for 12 hours and because of difficulties in checking all of the cargo, special consent had to be sought from chief Secretary Anson Chan Fang On-sang to hold the vessel for a further 12 hours.*

He said *the goods had been valued by the woman at $20 million but he considered this to be* 'a conservative estimate'.

The goods would have been sold in China with at least a 50 per cent markup on the purchase price in Hong Kong, he said.

'The maximum penalty for this sort of offence is a $50,000 fine and two years in jail.'

He said *it was a growing trend for smugglers to use container vessels to transport goods.*

Like the White Paper story with which I started, this story also begins with the unambiguous voice of the reporter in the first and second paragraphs. The third and fourth paragraphs bring in the voice of the Customs Superintendent, albeit through indirect quotation. That is to say, the reporter retains control of authorship, but in those two paragraphs delegates principalship to Mr Tsang, the Customs Superintendent.

Note that in the fifth paragraph authorship is delegated to Mr Tsang. That is, the reporter makes no claim over what is said in this paragraph either as author or as principal. If we ask why this should be, the answer appears to lie in the contents of this paragraph. Unlike the preceding paragraphs where the details were largely factual and narrative, in this paragraph we have the discrepancy between the statements of the manifests and the inspection results of the Customs Officers. It is for this controversial moment in the narrative frame that the reporter temporarily relinquishes his control of the discourse in favour of the Customs Superintendent, making no claim beyond that implied of simple animation.

Near the end, in the fourth and third paragraphs from the end, there is an odd stretch of indirect quotation which is presented as if it were direct quotation, complete with 'he said' but without putting the indirectly quoted speech within quotation marks. Here again there is a point of doubt. What we are being told is not, in fact, what Mr Tsang said directly, but what Mr Tsang has told the reporter that the unidentified woman has said. In this case what we see is that principalship is doubly delegated, first by the reporter to Mr Tsang and by Mr Tsang to the unidentified woman exporter. To put this another way, not only the reporter but the Customs Superintendent as well are standing clear of taking any responsibility for these statements of the value of these goods. Linguistically this is accomplished by the form of discourse representation which is intermediate between indirect and direct quotation. That is, while principalship is clearly attributed to the woman, authorship is neither claimed by the reporter nor entirely relinquished to either Mr Tsang or the woman.

Finally, we have a somewhat odd direct quotation in the penultimate paragraph. Leading into this are three paragraphs of indirect quotation, though within the 'he said' frame of semi-direct quotation. The story is concluded as well with this somewhat less than direct quotation. Only this statement about the penalty for the offence is placed within direct quotations. This, of course, is the crucial legal point of the story and the reporter marks this clearly as not his words but those of Mr Tsang. In other words, the reporter delegates both principalship and authorship to Mr Tsang at just this point where there is the potential of legal misstatement. Otherwise, he retains control over authorship.

While this story is of somewhat lesser general and political interest than the Patten–White Paper story, we can see the same general principles apply even if somewhat less colourfully. On the whole it remains a story of the reporter, not of the newsmakers. Their role is to provide materials for the story constructed by the reporter. Only in a few cases does the reporter delegate authorship to one of the newsmakers, and this only where doing so directs potentially problematical responsibility for the contents away from the reporter and on to the newsmaker. In the rest of the narrative the reporter retains principalship only for the barest facts of the story and for the story frame. He retains responsibility for saying who said what and otherwise lets the newsmakers stew in their own juices of principalship.

Finally, like in the Patten story, much of the direct quotation comes from the middle towards the end of the story where it can be seen to be less crucial to the structure of the news narrative. That is, the statements in the newsmakers' own words are taken to be valuable only when they can be used as anchors for the responsibility of otherwise potentially difficult points in the narrative.

NEWSMAKERS ON TELEVISION

What are called quotations in print are called actualities in sound or picture. The actuality is the representation of the actual words of the person 'quoted' being spoken by that person as filmed by the television crew or recorded by the radio sound recordists. Of course, while they are called 'actualities', we should not lose sight of the fact that these slices of apparent reality may be highly edited into forms that may well be unrecognizable to the original speaker, much as quoted speech may be distorted or taken out of context (S. Scollon and Yung 1997).

In Table 7.1 above I presented some rough numbers in which I suggested that actualities may well be more frequently found in television news broadcasting than quotations are found in newspaper news. Now I would like to examine more closely just how these actualities are presented, especially in light of the preceding discussion of the voices of newsmakers in newspaper stories.

The first set of actualities are found in a CBS Evening News story recorded on 15 March 1994. The main personage treated in these actualities is Hillary Clinton. At stake in this story and the one to follow are various claims made regarding her and her husband's financial affairs in what has come to be called the 'Whitewater' affair. The full text of the story follows. I have presented it here in the format used above representing the several voices: regular print is the voice of the presenter or the reporter, *italics* represent indirect quotation, and **boldface** represents the actual words of the newsmaker.

CBS News, 15 March 1994, 7:30 am, Evening news.

[PRESENTER: Photo; Clinton] For her part, First Lady Hillary Clinton's Whitewater strategy was a lot like the President's today. Mrs Clinton got out of Washington and tried to change the subject to health care reform, with a campaign stop in Colorado. Correspondent Linda Douglass has that part of the story.

[REPORTER] As she arrived at a University of Colorado rally, Hillary Clinton seemed determined to let nothing shake her focus on health care. But the Whitewater controversy was never far away. Overhead there were airborne questions about profits from savings and loans, while a few in the crowd taunted her with questions about the suicide of her friend, Deputy White House Counsel, Vincent Foster. The First Lady suggested that *in the White House, it is sometimes hard to stay focused on public policy.*

[ACTUALITY] **You know it is really easy, once you do get to Washington to forget that politics and government should be about you (two-handed gesture to student audience); it should be about your (gesture) needs, about your (gesture) interests, and about your (gesture) futures**.

[REPORTER] (Scenes of military review) For weeks Mrs Clinton has resisted discussing her role in the Whitewater controversy, which many believe is more central than the President's. Finally today she took a few questions from local reporters in Denver. She said *she did nothing wrong but make a bad business deal.*

[ACTUALITY] **We lost money. Goodness knows what you all would be saying if we had made any money. I'm glad we did, eh, lose money. Eh, and we're just gonna, do whatever is appropriate to do and, that's what we've always, eh, done over the last, eh, fifteen years or so as we have dealt with this.**

[REPORTER] She responded to critics who accused her *of stonewalling.*

[ACTUALITY] **I've admitted that I've made mistakes in how I have perceived this and handled it. You know, you live and learn and you go on, and that's what I'm doing.**

[REPORTER: on camera; on-screen identification] This was a difficult day for Mrs Clinton, as she watched another close friend, Webster Hubbell forced from public life. She had urged him and other friends to join her to serve in Washington, yet despite her power she's had to watch some of them fall, and has been unable to protect them. Linda Douglass, CBS News, Denver.

As in the newspaper story, the presenter's frame includes the names of the key figures, 'First Lady Hillary Clinton' and 'Correspondent Linda Douglass'.

Within the reporter's frame the number of participants are few. Other than the vague reference to 'critics', references are strictly limited to Hillary Clinton and, by implication in the pronoun 'we', her husband, Bill Clinton. There we find the following referenced participants:

The First Lady	her
Hillary Clinton	we (6)
Mrs Clinton	I (5)
she (3)	critics

This study does not provide sufficient data to make much of the use of the pronouns 'we' (6 times). This use of the personal pronoun of inclusion does correspond to Tannen's (1990) assessment of the modal stance taken in the discourse of women. Further, it does contrast with the use of the government source in the *South China Morning Post* White Paper story who covered his or her identity behind generalizing statements: 'It's not sensible to bombard . . .', not 'we didn't want to bombard'.

What is probably more important here is the rather close focus upon a single participant and her partner in contrast to the rather diffused set of participants found in the newspapers' stories. As we will see in the story below, it appears that in television news stories, in contrast to newspaper stories, where there are multiple participants, they are isolated to some extent and placed within different story frames.

In following up Bell's (1991) observation that news is authoritative people speaking to journalists, this story provides two interesting wrinkles. The focus in this story is not so much on what Hillary Clinton does say as upon what she does not say. She is said to have 'resisted discussing' the Whitewater affair and the lead-in or 'segue' indicates that what will follow will be evidence that she is avoiding talking about the main issue.

VOICING IN TELEVISION NEWS

What can be seen from the transcript is that voicing in this story is considerably more clearly delineated than in the two newspaper stories we considered above. From the presenter's opening frame through to 'The First Lady suggested', the voices are first that of the presenter and then that of the formally delegated reporter. This reporter's narration remains clear of ambiguities, holding both authorship and principalship through to her introduction of Hillary Clinton. There the reporter shifts to indirect quotation and in doing so delegates principalship to Hillary Clinton for the statement that it is hard to stay focused in the White House. This transitional state of delegated principalship leads directly into the actuality in which Clinton is given and takes up both authorship and principalship.

On taking over authorship and principalship Clinton then is shown actually to break through the customary frame placed around news discourse by talking directly to the audience of listeners, college students, and very explicitly not speaking to the journalists gathered thereabout. In doing so she uses the pronoun 'you' along with strong hand gestures towards the students and away from the cameras, and furthermore directs her gaze towards them, clearly signalling that her intent is to avoid engagement with the journalistic discourse regarding the Whitewater affair and to set the discourse upon her own footing. This move by the First Lady is no less than a move to wrest the floor along with the right to topical precedence away from the journalists.

Noble attempt that this is, it is immediately seen to be futile; it is clear who controls this particular discourse when the next scenes shown are not those of the student gathering which she has just addressed and their responses but, rather, a military review clearly staged elsewhere on the First Lady's visit to Colorado. Her attempt to steal the floor is indirectly commented upon by the reporter when she says that Clinton has been resisting responding to the journalists' topic for weeks.

Victory for the journalists is announced when it is said that 'finally' Clinton has responded to a few questions from 'local reporters in

Denver'. In the actuality which follows, the 'you' has now shifted to ratify the journalists' victory over this recalcitrant newsmaker. The 'you' in this case is not actually 'you' but the Southern American 'you all'; that is, she is showing here some degree of capitulation to the entire horde of journalists which 'for weeks' have been trying to get her to respond.

The subject matter of this news story, then, bears out Bell's (1991) claim that news is what authorities tell journalists. It is still news in this case when the authorities refuse to speak to journalists. This story displays rather clearly the framing of news stories as being a journalists' game in which newsmakers may provide materials for the reporters' stories, or they may refuse to respond and thereby intensify the interest of the story. What newsmakers may not do apparently is to take the floor and introduce their own topics to which the journalists are obliged to respond.

ANOTHER WOMAN REFUSES TO TALK

It is not my motive to provide commentary on the Whitewater affair as such. Nor is it my interest to become involved in contrastive studies of the framing of women in news discourse.[5] Nevertheless, of the stories I have studied, just two of them have had a woman as the principal newsmaker and just two of them, the same two, have had contestation of the journalists' control of the floor surface as a central issue. Not surprisingly the two women are former business partners, both of them are involved in the Whitewater affair, and the two stories were run in tandem in the same CBS Evening News report.

The second of these stories involves Susan McDougal, a former partner of the Clintons. The full text marked for voicing follows:

CBS News, 15 March 1994, 7:30 am, Evening news.

[PRESENTER] In Arkansas today one of the Clintons' original partners in the Whitewater real estate deal, made her first public statement in months. But Susan McDougal (Photo: Susan McDougal) ended up shedding more tears than light. Correspondent Scott Pelley reports from Little Rock.

[REPORTER] She's called *the mystery woman of the Whitewater affair,* and Susan McDougal's first public appearance today was awaited with great anticipation from Little Rock to the White House.

[ACTUALITY] **Sorry, I'm a little nervous**.

[REPORTER] She is a key player; with her former husband she controlled the Madison Guarantee Savings and Loan and was an equal partner with the Clintons in Whitewater Development, but today she refused to answer the many questions.

[ACTUALITY: On-screen identification; Susan McDougal, Whitewater Partner] **We have suffered enough. This can only be judged persecution after eight years. I want it to stop**.

[REPORTER] McDougal is involved in two key questions from the nineteen eighties: Did Madison make an improper seventy-five hundred dollar payment on a personal loan held by the Clintons, and did Bill Clinton use his influence as Governor to secure a three-hundred thousand dollar loan for her? Today McDougal wouldn't say. Her lawyer insisted that *if it did happen, she doesn't know it*.

[ACTUALITY: On-screen identification; Bobby McDaniel, McDougal Attorney] **There's no knowledge of any inappropriate or illegal transfer of funds** {interrupted}

[REPORTER] But lawyer McDaniel added that *she can't check her records because they were delivered to the Arkansas Governor's mansion just before the Presidential campaign*.

[ACTUALITY] **The Clintons asked for the records and they were delivered to the Governor's mansion at the request of the Clintons**.

[REPORTER: On-screen identification; Scott Pelley] Madison Guarantee was investigated in the nineteen eighties. Susan McDougal was never indicted. Her husband James was acquitted of charges of misusing Madison funds. But now with her old friends in the White House, the questions are being asked again, and next time it's likely to be before a grand jury. Scott Pelley, CBS News, Little Rock.

[PRESENTER] A new development in another long-running dispute (new topical frame)

Again, in this story the topical frame is the resistance of the newsmaker to respond to the journalists' queries. She is said to have 'refused to answer' or it is said that she 'wouldn't say'. The whole story is framed by the presenter as 'shedding more tears than light'.

The resistance shown by McDougal to the journalists' topical framing is countered by them in presenting her as somewhat less than fully competent. The lead builds her up saying that the appearance has been anxiously awaited. Following the first actuality she is referenced as a 'key player'. Nevertheless, the shot placed before us shows a woman behaving nervously and the actuality we are given in line, 'We have suffered enough', hardly displays a powerful legal and financial figure.

The second actuality again shows McDougal, while not trying to wrest the floor away from the journalists, asking, almost begging them to relent. She terms their topical insistence 'persecution'.

In both of these cases, the contents of the stories aside, what we see is newsmakers putting up rather valiant resistance to the framing of their discourse by journalists. In the case of Clinton, she takes active measures to take control of the floor herself. Ultimately she fails. In the case of McDougal, after eight years (she claims) of such resistance, she is weary of it, makes no attempt to take the floor, but simply begs for relief.

THE CONSTRUCTION OF THE NEWSMAKER

The newsmaker, far from being the powerful agent of world events about whom the journalist writes, is in journalistic discourse a figure crafted out of the words and characterizations of the journalist. The newsmaker is rarely given voice and where that does happen it is most often done as a way of delegating principalship or responsibility to the newsmaker to leave the journalist in the clear. The point I believe we can draw from this analysis is that in the discourse of journalist with journalist, the role of the newsmaker is not to create events, but to provide statements as the raw material of the journalists' stories. Not only do journalists present these newsmakers in a woven texture of heavily evaluated story, they strongly resist letting the floor be taken from them by the challenging newsmaker. Where they win in this battle, as they apparently have in these two contested cases, the story goes on the broadcast. Where they lose, the tape is erased and no one is the wiser.

NOTES

1. Quotation marks are used in English, that is. Yung (1995) has shown that this is often not the case in Chinese journalism where the attribution is much more variable than in English.
2. S. Scollon and Yung (1997) have shown how much editing liberty is taken with such 'actualities'.
3. Interesting in this respect is that since this portion of the study was completed a new paper, *Apple Daily*, was introduced on to the Hong Kong market. The owner claimed that he would use a very high level of direct quotation to give the reader a great sense of involvement. *Apple Daily* has in a very short time come to challenge the supremacy of *Oriental Daily News*'s circulation figures.
4. The paper is entitled 'Representative Government in Hong Kong' and was published by the Hong Kong Government dated February 1994. Inside is the following statement:
   This White Paper reproduces the text of the White Paper presented to Parliament by the Secretary of State for Foreign and Commonwealth Affairs by Command of Her Majesty on 24 February 1994.
   The White Paper was published in parallel English and Chinese editions.
5. For further discussion of the framing of women in news discourse see Caldas-Coulthard (1993).

PART IV:

MEDIA STUDIES AND SOCIAL INTERACTION

EIGHT

Interdiscursivity and identity

TEXTS, MEDIATED ACTION, AND COMMUNITIES OF PRACTICE

I began in Chapter 1 by outlining three foci of research: (1) the texts which form the crucial centre of critical discourse analysis (Fairclough 1992, 1995a, 1995b); (2) the mediated actions which are the primary unit of analysis for which Wertsch (1991) argues as the centre of sociocultural psychological analysis; and (3) the communities of practice (Lave and Wenger 1991) at the centre of theories of situated learning. To this I added the notion of sites of engagement – those windows constructed of social practice through which the texts become available for appropriation (R. Scollon 1997a). I argued that four crucial concepts, *mediated action, sites of engagement, communities of practice* and *mediational means* or texts form a useful framework for understanding mediated discourse as social interaction.

In the preceding several chapters I have developed the idea that the sender–receiver model of communication is largely inappropriate for the analysis of the discourse of the media because journalists and their readers/viewers function within rather separate communities of practice, with newsmakers on the whole forming yet another and separate community of practice. The people who make the news – political figures, accident victims, corporations and the like – stand very much apart from the journalists who use their activities and statements as the raw material in the production of their own mediated actions. As journalists produce the texts of news stories for print or broadcast, they position themselves in relationship to others within their own community of practice and in doing so construct for themselves the crucial journalistic identities of editors, reporters, presenters, owners and the rest. The newsmakers are, on the whole, positioned as being outside the community of practice of journalists through practices of discourse representation (Fairclough 1992, 1995a, 1995b) such as citation and attribution.

In a similar way, the readers and viewers of these mediated actions of the journalistic community of practice are positioned as being outside this primary discourse. As I have argued above, readers and viewers are positioned not as participants in the community of practice or players in the game, but as spectators of a spectacle. This spectacle is ostensibly staged on their behalf, to be sure, but that is a far cry from an invitation to come down on to the field and play ball. Only in the very rare cases where a hotline is set up in an emergency or in letters to the editor do we see a direct invitation to a very limited mode of participation. And, of course, that participation is discursively marked as *not* being an interaction *within* the community of practice. It is cast in the nature of side-play (Goffman 1981) to the main social interaction which remains interaction among the community of practice of journalists.

The communities of practice of the readers and viewers of this news discourse, the spectators, are themselves set off by a set of social practices for observation which preclude mistaking spectatorship for participation. These social practices privilege a range of actions from backgrounding or ignoring the productions of the news media to open, critical, or even abusive commentary. As I have suggested above, the viewers of television can play the news broadcast as background ambience for a dinner conversation, they can comment on either the content or presentation of the news, they can switch channels, or they can turn it off. The readers of the daily newspaper can skip the news entirely and get on to reading the entertainment sections or they can use the newspaper to wrap fish. The social practices by which the communities of practice of readers and viewers appropriate the texts of news discourse into their ongoing mediated actions show very little entrainment with the social practices of the journalists who produce those same texts.

The sites of engagement within which the texts of news discourse are open for appropriation are constructed through social practices which are largely out of the control of the community of practice of journalists. Once the deadline is met, the newspaper printed and distributed to news-stands or delivered to subscribers, the readers and viewers may pick it up from their doorstep and read it immediately or put it off until they are on the train or even until they return home in the evening. While the news broadcast is scheduled for a particular time slot in the broadcast day, the use of video recorders now makes it possible, even if perhaps not likely, that the viewer can watch it at his or her convenience, not so unlike the reader of the daily newspaper. The journalistic community of practice has no say over who sits around the morning tea table using their stories as the discursive means by which they position themselves as knowledgeable or ignorant, as aloof from the world of politics or engaged in it, as engaged in the current conversation or as keeping out of it.

In earlier chapters I have developed the argument that these 'productive' and 'receptive' communities of practice are largely separated from each other as a way of arguing against the use of any direct sender–receiver transmission model of communication. I have wanted to argue that if we use the same criteria for the analysis of social interaction – the Maxims of Stance – that we use in other cases, there is little basis for considering writers and readers/viewers of news discourse to be in social interaction with each other. Nevertheless, that theoretical separation cannot be rigorously maintained if we take into consideration the rather extensive interdiscursivities of practice we find in our contemporary world. While it can be argued, as I have done earlier, that journalists *as journalists* are not in social interaction with readers and viewers *as readers and viewers*, in day-to-day practice journalists are themselves readers of news discourse as they sit and converse with families and friends. Readers and viewers emerge from their communities of practice from time to time to become, if not journalists, newsmakers as they become the victims of accidents, as they are interviewed for human interest by journalists, or as journalists and readers or viewers go about other mediated actions not directly connected to news discourse. Journalists and readers alike shop in the same stores, go to the same movies and sporting events, and attend family events together.

In this chapter, then, I want to take up two aspects of this interdiscursivity which must be kept in mind as we come to analyse the social practices of news discourse. In the first case I will report on a series of studies undertaken to answer the question of what are the actual receptive practices of young adults. My purpose is to demonstrate through ethnographic analysis at least some of the social practices by which the sites of engagement of news discourse are actually constructed. These social practices produce a complex level of interdiscursivity within the communities of practice of viewers and readers of news discourse. Then I will turn to look at several of the ways in which interactions among print, television and computer media are producing significant interdiscursivities as well. While my goal in the preceding chapters has been to argue that the sender–receiver model is inadequate for treating news discourse as social interaction, my goal in this chapter is to put brackets around setting up any polarized two-communities analysis of news discourse. I will argue that as all communities of practice are, in fact, in various forms of interaction with each other, the concept of the clear separation of journalistic and reader communities of practice is equally problematical. My goal is to argue that the analysis of news discourse, when taken from an social-interactional point of view, must continually problematize any categorical separation of entities whether those are individual senders and receivers or productive communities of practice and receptive communities of practice. I will end by suggesting that the social construction of identity which takes place in and through news discourse is a highly interdiscursive process in which identities are claimed and disputed, ratified and repudiated, displayed and masked depending on the ongoing social-interactive processes of the production of identity in discourse.

INTERDISCURSIVITY

Texts incorporate other texts; texts speak in reponse to and anticipation of other texts. In Chapter 1 I commented on the use of the terms *intertextuality* and *polyvocality* to refer to the ways in which texts incorporate the voices of other texts. I returned to this notion in some detail in Chapter 7 to show how the voices of newsmakers are marginalized within the texts of news discourse. A related concept, that of *dialogicality*, attends to the ways in which texts speak to other texts. Today's news broadcast is seen as a follow-up to yesterday's story. In Chapter 5 the radio story of the New Year's accident in Hong Kong's Lan Kwai Fong district included the question from the studio: 'Can you give us the latest figures?' It is implied that earlier figures have been given and that later figures will follow in later broadcasts. The feature of newsworthiness (Bell 1991) which values a continuation story highly depends on this dialogicality or intertextuality of texts speaking to other texts.

Interdiscursivity operates on a different level or dimension from intertextuality in that it is genres, situations, registers, social practices or communities of practice which are appropriated as significant aspects of the mediated action. Fairclough (1992, 1995a, 1995b), for example, elucidates an example in which the discourse of advertising has been appropriated interdiscursively as part of academic discourse. A university produces a brochure which not only uses the genre of advertising to promote the university and its courses, but takes on the language of advertising to position the university as a commodity within the discourses of a consumer society. Conversely, he shows how advertisements can also take on the discourses of academics or medical practice as a strategy to lend scholarly credence to advertising claims.

Musson and Cohen (1996), in a study of medical practice in Great Britain over the past decade, have observed a progressive colonization of the discourse of medicine by the discourse of enterprise. For example, where doctors might have talked at one point of the effectiveness of treatment, they have shifted in some cases to speaking of the cost effectiveness of treatment. This invasion or colonization by the discourse of enterprise has produced a significant interdiscursivity between enterprise and medicine which goes considerably beyond just the moments of medical treatment in playing out society-wide shifts from state-supported medical practice to privately organized medicine.

In what follows I will argue that a significant interdiscursivity has now developed between what at one time might have been two somewhat independent discourses, news discourse and entertainment discourse. We have both news programmes in the format of entertainment programmes or features and entertainment features which appropriate the style and language of news reporting. What is significant for our purposes here is that I will argue that while it is a convenient analytical fiction that news discourse forms a separable order of discourse, in practice there is such a high level of interdiscursivity between the discourses of the news and other discourses in our contemporary society that this interdiscursivity must be taken as the fundamental social matrix in which the social practices of news discourse are played out. In the discussion which follows I will focus first on various aspects of interdiscursivity within the community of readers and viewers of news discourse. I will follow that with a discussion of journalistic interdiscursivity.

RECEPTIVE COMMUNITY INTERDISCURSIVITY

The basis for this discussion of interdiscursivity within the receptive community is a series of research projects which we have conducted at the City University of Hong Kong during the past several years (R. Scollon, Bhatia, Li and Yung 1996; R. Scollon and Yung 1996; R. Scollon, Tsang, Li, Yung and Jones 1996). Our general goal in this research has been to come to understand the ways in which the language, especially the English, of students at the university level can be said to be appropriated from sources of public discourse such as print and broadcast news, entertainment and advertising.

These studies have included participant-observation ethnographic research into the positioning of news discourse within the speech community, ethnographic interviewing and surveys of the young adult population including focus group analysis, and quantitative analysis of broader based questionnaire surveys of reading and other media practices. The broader ethnographic studies have ranged across the entire speech community from young children to retired adults. Our more focused interviews have narrowed that range primarily to students at City University of Hong Kong as our goal was in part to relate this research to language and communication teaching and learning practices. Our quantitative surveys have included students in several different disciplines and have compared City University students with students in other Hong Kong universities on the one hand and university students with older young adults now in the workplace.

The methodologies we have used, which have been designed to produce a methodological interdiscursivity to parallel the interdiscursivity found within the communities of practice we have studied, will be taken up in more detail in Chapter 9. Here I will turn our attention to the main findings of this research which have relevance to my argument that news discourse cannot be easily isolated from other major discourses from the point of view of the receptive communities.

Our main findings can be summarized by saying that 'news discourse' is virtually never received as 'news discourse' by the young adult, university population we studied. That is to say, while they do read the papers and watch television news programmes and while they do evidence knowledge of key 'news stories', this 'news discourse' interpenetrates the more fundamental discourse of entertainment. Conversely, entertainment as a discursive framing category for our students does not exclude what journalists might want to call the news. In surveys, in day-to-day viewing/reading practice, and under direct questioning, the discursive separation between hard news stories and entertainment features is not to be found. Instead one finds that items from either of these broad discourses are appropriated into conversations, responses to questions, and other speaking and writing to produce a register in which neither the contents nor linguistic styles are clearly differentiated.

A corollary of this finding is that we argue that the concept of the implied, single, rational, cognitive-processing reader cannot be maintained in respect to this news/entertainment order of discourse. The stories of the news or of entertainment discourses are appropriated, not as self-contained logico-narrative structures, but as information bits to be integrated into ongoing talk. For example, a tragic event in which over 20 young people were trampled to death in a popular nightclub area, Lan Kwai Fong (Li et al. 1993) becomes the source of the term 'a Lan Kwai Fong' as in 'Let's not let this become a Lan Kwai Fong', with the meaning that the situation should not be allowed to get out of hand in one case but that the place is too crowded in another case.

These findings are summarized from seven main characteristics of the receptive public discourse of the community of practice we studied, as I will develop below.

Four scenes

City University students spend the vast majority of their time in just four 'locations' or 'activities': (1) at the university doing class-related activities; (2) at home; (3) in transit between the university and home – for many students this can involve a commute of an hour or more each way on public transportation; (4) and in small fast-food restaurants. In spite of the very high enthusiasm for shopping and for visiting the many Hong Kong shopping malls, we found that even on weekends and holidays our students spend a very small amount of their time actually going to those places. In other words, the places where our students are open to engagement with the media of news or entertainment discourse are largely at home, on busses or mass transit trains, or in small fast-food restaurants.

Polyfocal attention

One consequence of the places our students inhabit in a very populated urban environment is that the normal attention pattern is simultaneously to keep open several competing sites of engagement. By that I mean simply that we found that in virtually all cases our students were reading while listening to CDs or tape recordings. Along with these the television is playing and often a computer with an MTV CD as well. It is particularly important to note that this condition of multiple and competing media discourses is considered by them to be a good or desirable condition, not something to be avoided. For example, student research assistants who were given the task of transcribing the audio text of a news broadcast turned on the television set in the research laboratory saying that it was, 'so that we can concentrate'. Students working in a communication laboratory on video editing put CDs on the computer so that there will not be a silent environment. Students in a social gathering put on both a CD of music and a television broadcast to set the background for their conversations.

To check the way in which these background materials are appropriated into ongoing activities, focus groups were given a task to accomplish which could be done without any reference to materials beyond the table at which they were seated. Video clips were played on television sets in the room behind them as background noise. From time to time members of the group would bring items from the background video into the accomplishment of the focus tasks.

Never alone

A second consequence of the populated urban environment is that these students are virtually never alone except when sleeping. Their homes are very small, busses and trains are crowded, the university spaces are crowded, and fast-food restaurants in Hong Kong regularly record the highest turnover customer rates in the world. Nevertheless, whether or not it is by necessity, students find it uncomfortable to be isolated and if they are alone seek out other people to accompany them in their activities.

Multiparticipant social life

A consequence of never being alone is that this population organizes virtually all social life as multiparticipant social life. This is particularly crucial to the question of focused attention to the texts of news discourse. As one is never alone and there is never a single medium present from which to appropriate text, there is a constant interweaving of themes, topics, information bits, and images from all of the present media into the ongoing social interaction. As the topical floor moves from participant to participant, so does the attention move not just from text to text but from discourse to discourse. Thus the community of practice weaves a nearly seamless interdiscursivity among texts and discourses.

Group reception

We would distinguish group reception from multiparticipant social life by saying that not only are there multiple participants in virtually all communicative events, each of whom calls attention to items and brings them to the floor, there is also a strategy of holding reception in abeyance until there has been a communal negotiation over its meaning. Goffman's (1981) three production formats – animator, author and principal – which have been mentioned above, can be paralleled as the receptive roles, *receptor*, *interpreter* and *judge* (R. Scollon 1996c). That is, the receptor, like the animator, is a mechanical role of simply receiving the communication without interpretation or judgement. A person can repeat the message but may have no idea of its meaning. The interpreter, like the author, is the role in which rhetorical interpretation is made. The interpreter takes responsibility for deriving a meaning from the communication. The judge takes on the communicative role corresponding to the principal. That is, this role takes responsibility for action.

It could be argued that the community of practice we have studied closely distributes these three roles to the individual, the group, and the society respectively. That is to say, in polyfocal, multiple participant groups, individuals hear or see the texts of the media but, we believe, tend only to pass quite literally what they have seen or heard to others in the group. Once the items are on the floor for group discussion a group interpretation is achieved which becomes the interpretation for everyone in the group. In many cases, however, we believe that responsibility for action is further delegated outside the group. This delegation may be to the government, to teachers or the university, to parents, or to others who, in keeping with somewhat traditional Confucian practice, have the authority to direct the lives of young people.

This latter point goes considerably beyond the scope of my argument here and I would not want to place too fine a point on it. My main consideration here is that we have evidence that within the community of practice we have studied the three receptive roles are not normally taken up by single individuals but, on the contrary, there is a considerable amount of group consensus work in interpreting the meanings of appropriated texts.[1]

Short, light, entertainment pieces

A significant outcome of these complex, multiple participant and multi-media sites of engagement is that there are very few places in their lives where it would even be possible to develop a mono-discursive, focal attention on any one text from any single discourse. Within this environment there is what is probably an inevitable preference for short, light, entertaining texts whether in print or broadcast media. The alternative is very difficult to achieve. Mono-discursive focal attention, which some have argued remains the dominant metaphor underlying concepts of media reception (Keller-Cohen 1993a), is almost impossible to construct within the social practices of this speech community.

News from television

In keeping with the preference for, or necessity for, short items, we found that virtually all news within this community of practice was received first from television. Second to this was word-of-mouth. On the whole the practice is either to see a news item on television and then follow it up in a newspaper or weekly news/entertainment magazine or to hear of the item from a close friend, family member or acquaintance and then to watch for it during the next news broadcast. It should be reiterated, however, that these 'news items' are not much talked about as news. That is, they are not discussed at any length in terms of their news values or social or political significance. They are appropriated largely as items to display one's ability to 'not be left behind'. This latter is a concern which is often expressed whether in respect to news items, current music, gossip items concerning entertainers, fashions, especially in clothing or grooming, or even ways of thinking.

These seven features of the community of practice we have studied, university students in Hong Kong, may be argued to be rather particularistic to this community of practice. Our broader ethnographic studies across the speech community, however, have ranged from young children through to retired adults. Even the rather extended periods of time they spend at the university, which might be argued to be exceptional, are paralleled in the equally long periods of time spent at offices by non-university young adults in a community dominated by service industries. Our students comment after graduation, for example, that in their new jobs they have less time, not more, to give over to leisure activities, at least in the young adult years.

Without parallel studies in other communities I cannot argue here that the high levels of interdiscursivity we have observed in these young adults is matched by corresponding populations in other places. Rather informal surveys in Australia, North America and Britain, however, suggest that what we have observed in Hong Kong is not so very different from normal practice throughout the world where mass media communications are widely available in the form of cable television, multi-media home entertainment installations, internet access and the rest. One colleague in an American research laboratory has commented that his research assistants have adopted the practice of playing background video CD music while doing their research much as our assistants have done. A recent *Doonesbury* cartoon[2] centres on a new employee who has been hired to produce a small company Web site. He gives as a requirement that he has to have very loud music in order to think. This further suggests both that polyfocal attention is growing as a receptive norm and that there is a generation which finds this lamentable.

My concern here has been to argue that within the receptive discourse community there is a high level of interdiscursivity of reception that makes it difficult to argue for any unitary, focused 'audience' of the texts of mediated discourse. News texts are appropriated in a site of engagement which includes MTV or karaoke video background music, computer games or internet information, and multiple printed items as a kaleidoscopic mixture for momentary attention by a multiple-participant group within which the news item in question stands in varying positions of attention for different members. While the case I have described here may be extreme, I believe it can be argued that it is not so extreme as to invalidate my argument that single focus and single discourse reception is the rarity, not the norm.

JOURNALISTIC INTERDISCURSIVITY

It would be impossible to sort out to what extent it is the interdiscursivity of reception which is pushing journalistic production towards its own interdiscursivity and to what extent it is journalistic production which is leading the way. The direction of causation is beyond the scope of my argument here. My purpose is just to argue that there is now an increasing amount of penetration of news discourse by the discourses of entertainment or even ordinary conversation. Perhaps it is now commonplace and needs no argument that there has been a rapid increase in 'infotainment' programmes.

In Hong Kong and elsewhere there are programmes which present themselves as dealing with news issues but which use high-profile entertainers as the 'reporters'. One of the clearest forms of interdiscursivity here is the camera focus. In the news broadcast the reporter largely remains off-camera and speaks a narration as the camera shows shots of key figures in the story or at least related file footage. In the infotainment programmes, at least in Hong Kong, the camera is normally on the 'reporter', that is, the entertainment figure who is conducting the interview. We see her – women are dominant in this form of entertainment – reactions to the story being told by the 'newsmaker'. The newsmaker, whether accident victim or eyewitness, is shown from the back or in shadow. Thus the camera makes clear what is not otherwise stated: this programme is about the emotional reactions of people to events, not about the events themselves. In taking this perspective the infotainment shows have appropriated the human-interest aspects of the hard news as the core focus in this discursively re-distributed participant structure.

On the other side of the coin, the ordinary 'person on the street' is being interdiscursively transformed into a news-knowledgeable commentator. Perhaps at one time the role of the person-on-the-street interview was largely as eyewitness of some event which was the focus of the news story. As I have argued in Chapter 7, news stories are often not about events so much as about narrations of events. A bill has been introduced to the Legislative Council. It has been introduced about 4:30 in the afternoon. The first news story about the text of this bill is to appear on the evening news at 7:30. The newspaper stories will appear the next morning. The public has no knowledge of this bill. As I enter the train station a television crew approaches me, bright lights are turned on, the camera comes on and a reporter steps up to me and asks whether I am in support of a bill to do X, Y and Z. I answer that I have not heard of this bill and would need to have more information about it before I could give a fair answer. The lights switch off about half way through my answer, the reporter mumbles 'Thank you', even as she is already searching the crowd for another possible person on the street. I return home and a bit later watch the evening news broadcast. The presenter introduces the story with one sentence and delegates the floor and topic to the reporter as I have detailed in Chapter 5. It is the same reporter I had met in the station. The reporter gives a two-sentence introduction to the bill while there are shots of the Legislative Council. The camera then switches to a person who is standing on the spot I had stood on earlier. He is authoritatively giving an opinion of the merits of the bill and its effects on the ordinary people of Hong Kong. This has proved to be a much more acceptable man on the street. He is a person with no doubts or any requirement for further information. He carries his opinions well-formed and prepared and is pleased to express them as part of the co-construction of the evening news broadcast. The viewer is given no clue that this man on the street had first heard mention of this bill just moments before he spoke. He is presented as a thoughtful respondent to the public discourse which, in fact, is created through this conversational co-construction between man on the street and reporter.

Journalists, entertainers and people on the street have begun engaging in the interdiscursive co-construction of the news story. I would argue that as the journalist and entertainer come to expose more and more of their own lives, feelings and reactions to the viewer, and thus become less the objective reporter of someone else's events and more the subject of their own reports, at the same time the non-journalist is coming to take on more and more of the style of the authoritative, knowledgeable and objective reporter of events. In this way journalistic text and ordinary conversation are coming to approximate each other.

This has occurred not just between journalists and non-journalists such as entertainers and the person on the street. More and more the conversational metaphor has come to overtake the reporting metaphor in news practice. News stories are made to seem as if they are conversations among newsmakers. This was widely observed during the Gulf War when George Bush and Saddam Hussein in person and through spokespersons carried on 'conversations' with each other as conversations with CNN and other news reporters. More recently, in March 1996, when China tested missiles in the Taiwan Straits, 'conversations' between China's Qian Qichen and the United States's Warren Christopher took place regarding the role of US warships in the vicinity of Taiwan (S. Scollon and Yung 1997). By editing actualities of Qian's answers to reporters' questions at a press conference in Beijing in juxtaposition with actualities of Warren Christopher speaking in Washington, the discursive format of a conversation, albeit a somewhat hostile one, was produced. When the American First Lady, Hillary Clinton, spoke against China's policy on birth control before the International Women's Conference in Beijing she was edited together with Li Peng's conversation a day or so later with former US President George Bush and another 'conversation' was produced (Scollon and Scollon 1997).

Meyrowitz (1985) has discussed the progressive interpenetration of frontstage and backstage (Goffman 1974, 1981) actions in news and media discourse. Until relatively recently very little was known by the public about their leaders. He points out, for example, that Dwight D. Eisenhower was the first US President to allow his press conferences to be filmed. Before him everything said was considered off the record until the stories were submitted to the White House for clearing. When Eisenhower allowed filming, it was nevertheless only a cleared, scripted set of questions and practised answers which were filmed. J. F. Kennedy was the first to allow a live television press conference in which he answered questions without knowing beforehand what those questions would be. Thus it is only since the early 1960s that Americans have had even that slight window on potential emotional responses or other cracks in the formal public face of a president. Of course, as Meyrowitz points out, it was not long before L. B. Johnson was showing a surgery scar on national television and now, of course, there is very little of the backstage lives of public figures we do not hear about and see in media broadcasts.

As I have suggested above, there is a progressive interdiscursive, one might say Habermasian blurring of the distinction between public life and private life, between governmental action and private action, between the genres of formal discourse and the gossip genres of the backdoor. As Fairclough (1995b) has analysed, this blurring of genres is reflected in the increasingly common 'living-room' interviews of public figures. Where once the public figure appeared either in the television studio or the interview took place in formal governmental offices, now we see extended conversational interviews taking place in studio 'living-room' suites. These sofas and coffee tables are, of course, interdiscursively appropriated from the presenters of such morning mixed-genre programmes as 'Good Morning, America' where we see a newspaper-like mix of news bits, weather, fashion features and celebrity chatting.[3]

While news discourse appropriates more and more of the genres of intimate, conversational discourse, the ordinary citizen is taking on a kind of journalistic stance, especially in the use of the media which were once the prerogative of news journalists. As handicams have increased in quality, while dropping in both size and price, one sees people everywhere become the documenters of their own lives. As they do this they take on the roles and stances once reserved for journalists. In our ethnographic observations we have seen tourists directing others into capturable scenes, they conduct interviews, and they engage in extended discussions about how to plan and accomplish a shoot much as if they were working on the preparation of a broadcast documentary.

Of course there are a number of cases where amateur handicam videos have come to play a significant role in news broadcasts and in the judicial process. Goodwin's (1994) study of the use of the handicam video of the beating of Rodney King is just one example of the non-journalistic community taking on journalistic practices. A very popular television programme in the US is based on 'funny' home videos now and it seems not unlikely that we will come to see citizen video as a growing aspect of 'news' discourse in the future as the quality of these videos approaches broadcast quality.

Finally, journalists, when they are not doing their journalistic work, do the things the rest of us do, including taking handicam pictures of their families at birthdays. Ordinary people go on television and radio to become entertainment celebrities, if not journalists, through the medium of the talk shows. It would go considerably beyond the scope of this book to try to do more than sketch out these extended amounts of interdiscursivity between professional activity and private and personal activity. Zhang (1988) notes, for example, that newspaper journalists in Hong Kong normally start the day with television and radio news to find out 'what's going on'. He argues that they are keyed into the day's central stories much in the same way any ordinary person is and that what journalists do when they get to their offices is not a great deal more than using his or her professional contacts and training to put a sharp edge on the commonsense of the day.

IDENTITY IN AN INTERDISCURSIVE WORLD

In closing perhaps it is useful to return to a focus on the discursive construction of identity. Where communities of practice are clearly distinguishable, membership and identity are also likely to be more clearly differentiated. In Chapter 5 I gave an example of a radio journalist who momentarily misinterpreted the situation as a telephone call rather than as a news broadcast. This misinterpretation led him to take on rather different identities which produced a different vocal style and presentational stance. Here I would like to recall Goffman's (1981) argument that smooth professional role and identity maintenance are never more than a slip of the tongue away from collapse. The nearly flawless identity positionings we find in news discourse on the whole are carefully staged and scripted discursive performances, not essential or inherent person identities.

In this chapter I have argued that it is difficult to maintain that there are very clear and separable communities of practice. I have argued that there is much interdiscursivity among contemporary journalistic, entertainment and other discourses on the one hand and on the other that it is impossible to maintain that there is a clear, separable and identifiable receptive community of practice. In such a view, the concept of identity is problematical in the extreme. It is from this point of view that I have put forward the concept of the Maxims of Stance in Chapter 2. It is because of the inevitable interdiscursivity of all communities of practice, indeed all communicative events, that in any particular situation the first issue is: what kind of event is this? It would be more accurate to say that the first question is: what sort of event are we constructing this to be? That can simply never be taken for granted. In each instance it must be constructed among the participants.

With some sense of what sort of event is being constructed there are then implied various necessary identities and it is to those identities that the event must turn. I say this sequentially but I only mean to suggest a logical sequence. It is equally reasonable to say that if a group of people are constructing for themselves the identities of presenters, producers, reporters and the like, that the event constructed will be a news report. The point is that in the view I am taking here the ongoing discursive co-construction of identity is inseparable from the ongoing negotiation of what sort of event is being constructed. From the point of view of the production of news discourse, the events and identities which are constructed around news reports appear to be under seige from discourses of entertainment on the one hand and private life on the other. It goes beyond the scope of this book to gaze into a crystal ball and guess whether we are seeing the very last historical stages of what may after all be a phenomenon of no more than a few hundred years since the start of the first newspapers (R. Scollon 1997b).

From the point of view of receptive communities of practice I would argue that identity is an equally problematical concept. As in any social interaction, I would argue that the first question is: what sort of event is being constructed? My research leads me to believe that this question is virtually never answered in favour of news-watching. Further from that is the notion that news-watching identities are being constructed. In virtually all cases the events being socially constructed are 'family gathering', 'a gathering of a group of friends', 'a lunch among friends', 'passing the time', 'doing homework'. Even more broadly taken, it would be hard to argue that the identity being constructed is 'TV watcher' or 'reader'. These mediated actions, in our data, take place within identities which are not so narrowly constructed, within identities which are based on polyfocal attention and more complex group memberships. Thus it is very difficult to argue that, except in rare cases perhaps in an older generation, the answer to the question 'What's going on here?' would be 'We're watching the evening news'.

NOTES

1. One consequence of group reception shows up in retail marketing where customer across-the-counter services tend to be very minimal. The newsstand I have discussed in Chapter 4 is of a kind with many retail encounters in Hong Kong. The customer arrives at the point of sale with his or her decision about what to buy already formed through the group process. Individual decision-making at the point of sale is rather minimal and thus negotiations between the customer and the sales person are minimal and may concern only the price.

2. *Sunday Morning Post*, 1 June 1997, *Money*, p. 10.

3. The variety of these features staggers at least my imagination. In Chicago in March 1996 on a station, which I unfortunately neglected to identify, there was a 30-minute segment on the morning television show in which a photograph of a dog was shown on the screen for the benefit of dogs and other pets who would be viewing the programme.

NINE

A social-interactional perspective on ethnographic studies of media

WHAT IS A SOCIAL INTERACTIONAL PERSPECTIVE ON ETHNOGRAPHIC STUDIES OF THE MEDIA?

Since the seminal studies of the 'Birmingham School' (Hall 1980; Morley 1980) there has been a growing awareness in media studies and cultural studies of the need for ethnographic analysis of media audiences. At the same time, and participating in that growing awareness is a general questioning of content analyses in news and mass communication studies, though to no great extent have there been calls for ethnographic studies of the production of news discourse. Van Dijk's (1988) and Bell's (1991) keystone work signalled the entry of discourse analysis into the study of news discourse. As I have argued in Chapter 1, my purpose here is to bring a social interactional perspective to bear on media studies, especially through the use of ethnographic methodologies.

In the preceding chapters I have argued that mediated discourse may be usefully analysed as social interaction – social interactions among the producers as one community of practice and among receivers as other communities of practice. I have argued that the relationship between producers and receivers is not that of senders and receivers of messages but as producers of a spectacle and as observers of that spectacle. My reasons for this are based on the argument that in any communication, the primary players or participants are those who are in such a relationship with each other that they mutually co-construct both the events in which they participate and the identities of themselves in those events. I argued that these co-constructions of event and identity are logically prior to introducing topics and the production of texts though, of course, not necessarily produced in a temporal sequence. This logical hierarchy I phrased as the Maxims of Stance in Chapter 2.

Those maxims then set the stage for the study of photo-taking in which I developed the basis for the spectacle–observer model I used thereafter in my analysis of news or media producers, the spectacle makers, and the receivers or observers of those spectacles – the media 'audience'. It was then important to show that the concept of the 'audience' is a misleading cover term for a complex set of social practices by which the texts of the media become available for reception in the sites of engagement. Because of the complexity of those social practices for the appropriation of media texts, added to the fact that there is no mutual co-construction of events and identities between receivers of the media and news producers, I argued that it is very difficult to maintain any direct sender–receiver relationship.

Three separate chapters on the discursive construction of television journalists, newspapers journalists and newsmakers argued that the same processes by which events and identities are constructed in face-to-face and telephone conversations are at work in the production of the texts of news stories whether printed or broadcasted. That is, the social interactions which produce events, identities and texts as news stories display the same social-discursive practices I have described as the Maxims of Stance.

In the preceding chapter my purpose was to problematize my own spectator–observer model by showing that there is massive interdiscursivity both among the discourses of production – news and entertainment primarily – and the communities of practice of reception. I am particularly concerned that the spectator–observer model does not simply become a somewhat more complex version of the sender–receiver model.

An equally central issue is methodological. How does the analyst develop an approach to the news media or other forms of mediated discourse which is founded in ethnography on the one hand and which can link social practice and discourse theory to the social-interactionist literature on the other? I have tried to exemplify my approach in the preceding chapters by bringing to bear studies which have been based on quite different methodological strategies. The material in Chapter 2, for example, relies heavily on methodology developed within conversational analysis and interactional sociolinguistics. Chapters 3 and 4 are more dependent on participant–observation ethnographic analysis. Chapters 5 through 7 make use of discourse analysis in the close attention to the texts of news discourse. In Chapter 8 I presented the results of a set of studies which made use of these three methodologies but added to them interviewing, survey and focus groups. My purpose in this chapter, then, is to draw together these various methodological strategies into one place and to put forward practical suggestions for approaching studies of mediated action using ethnographic and social-interactional methodologies.

RESEARCH PARADOXES

Centrifugal–centripetal

In research of the kind I have relied upon in this book there are two, counterveiling pulls. One is a centrifugal pull inwards towards the textual focus of study. Linguists and discourse analysts can be pulled down into the vortex of linguistic analysis and can sometimes lose sight of the ways in which texts are the tools of mediated action in social situations. At the same time there is what might be called a centripetal or outward pull towards the situational context or the social practices of the society within which the text is contextualized. Ethnographers, sociologists or cultural studies theorists tend to be pulled away from the concreteness of the texts and the mediated actions in which the texts are used towards an analysis of the broader social forces at play. If one is interested in how texts are appropriated, there is a tendency to excessively play down the place of the text itself in the situation. On the other hand, as attention to the text arises, one is pulled rapidly into a study of the sites of engagement in which the text is produced.

It is obvious that one researcher, one research project or one book cannot cover the whole range, but what I have proposed in the research reported here is that the methodological trick is not to be thrown off balance in either direction. The trick is to maintain an interdiscursive tension between the fine-grained analysis of specific mediated actions and a socioculturally contextualized analysis of the historical and social production of the sites of engagement.

In conducting the research I report here, when my colleagues and I have spoken casually, or even where we were engaged in the not so casual presentation of academic conference papers, we found we were constantly being pulled in these opposing directions, often against our will. For example, we wanted to talk about how students, sitting with their families together at home, partially appropriate texts through polyfocal attention using the news, a music CD and a computer game. To make our analysis concrete, we have spoken of the news text as being a story of the Taiwan Straits missile crisis. We have found that shortly we are in a discussion of the role of the US in sending aircraft carriers into the Taiwan Straits or of how that particular story shows whether or not the US and China are seeking (or sliding into) Cold War II. It is difficult to talk of 'the news' as a research project without the discussion itself slipping interdiscursively into a common chat about current events.

In other cases we speak of the positioning of the journalist *in the text* in a position subordinate to the presenter. It is not long before we find somebody speculating on the power relations within the television studio and so forth. Of course power struggles in the studio are directly related to textual positioning, but those behind-the-scenes power relations are not available to the viewers of the television programming and so not directly relevant to the issue of whether or not a viewer, while appropriating the text of the news, is also appropriating the discursive means of positioning.

From the point of view of this paradox, the problem is to keep the research centred on the tension between text and social practice and not to drift into either a text-free analysis of social situations or a decontextualized analysis of text.

Observer's paradox

While it is commonplace to note that one cannot observe a situation without in some way intervening in that situation, this observer's paradox is particularly crucial in ethnographic research. The students we have studied in Hong Kong live in very small flats normally with four to six or seven inhabitants. These people live in each other's presence in tightly synchronized social arrangements which preclude any but very intimate visitors. It is the Hong Kong practice, for example, to entertain non-family intimates outside the home, normally in restaurants and other public places. The non-family, non-intimate ethnographer has no place. There are no social practices into which he or she can gear participant observation. If the ethnographer is in the flat, it is impossible for day-to-day routine social practices to be carried out. If the ethnographer is not in the flat, there is limited opportunity for observation.

As I will discuss below, we have found various means of constructing reasonably useful data about behaviour in such places, but we have had to do this by taking the opposite strategy of training legitimate members of these family units to be the observers. Obviously, these student assistant/normal family members are then required to perform in double and paradoxical roles and in a sense we have only relocated the paradox on a different site – the student researcher. As I will argue below, however, this has proved to be a useful strategy.

Deconstruction of object of study

The third paradox is in some ways the most serious from the point of view of the relationship between theory and method. As I have suggested in the chapters preceding this one, over the course of this research I have decomposed or deconstructed the original object of study. My original goal was to analyse the process of communication between the producers of the news media and the reception of those products by a specific audience – university students. As the study progressed it became clear that I could not argue for any direct-line communication between journalists and any audience. Instead, I found different and separable communities of practice, albeit ones in which considerable interdiscursivity is taking place. On the one hand I could not argue for a clear, distinct community of practice of journalism but rather several communities of media production including both journalism and entertainment. On the other hand I could not locate either individual viewers/readers or a community of practice for whom the primary focus was the reception of media texts.

If the methodology one adopts has the net result of decomposing the object of study, one is left with little theoretical ground to stand upon other than a regression of deconstructive methodological actions. It becomes clear that any object of study apparently 'discovered' by the research will, in turn, be subjected to the same deconstructive spotlight and show itself to be interdiscursively continuous with the universe.

Perhaps research methodologies could be classed as deductive, inductive and deconstructive. By deductive we would mean that one begins with a theoretical point of view, some set of givens, or some largely accepted hypothesis and the goal of the research would be to develop empirical proofs in support of those givens or that hypothesis. By inductive we would mean that one is considerably less certain of the theoretical point of view or of the nature of the givens and through some set of methodological procedures one would begin to amass data which themselves would point to a conclusion. By deconstructive we would mean that one would begin with an object of analysis – a text, a social practice, a concept which is taken as unassailably true – and then begin to argue that this object is, in fact, not what it appears. One argues that the 'object' would be seen as a very different phenomenon if one only shifted the point of view. Further, one argues that the 'object' has been seen as an object precisely because of a particular point of view. This is normally argued to be an ideology, that is, a point of view constructed upon particular historical, social and cultural antecedents.

Seen in this way, the research I report here would need to be classifed as deconstructive. The 'object' with which I began was the sender–receiver model of mediated communication as well as the implied theories and language of journalists as writers and produ-cers of texts and the implied theories of 'readers' and 'viewers' of the texts of journalism. I have then set about arguing that these objects are, in fact, false objects. I have worked at decomposing the con-struction of journalistic texts from an action which is driven by the production of texts *for readers/viewers and for the transmission of informa-tion* into an action which is driven by the social practices within the community of practice for the positioning among themselves of the members of that community of practice. At the same time I have argued for the decomposition of the 'audience' as a concept and put in its place the concept of multiple and complexly inter-discursive communities of practice within which the texts of news discourse are the raw materials (along with many other media products) for taking mediated actions which are rarely keyed to receiving information.

What is paradoxical here is that this method and approach are, in fact, rather deductive in nature. One could argue with consider-able justice that the object with which I began was not, in fact, the sender–receiver model of communication and its related theories and discourses. What I began with was the socially constructed nature of identity/discourse. This is the theoretical position I set out in Chapter 1 in making reference to Fairclough, Lave and Wenger,

Wertsch and others. From this point of view, this 'apparent' decon-
struction of mediated discourse could be argued to be an explication,
argument for, or testing of how well a social-constructive view of
discourse could be made to fit with a particular case of discourse –
the discourse of the news media. It could be argued that at least in
this case deconstructive methodologies are a deductive method for
the explication of the fundamental premise which is that social
reality, including identity, is discursively constructed.

ETHNOGRAPHIC METHOD

Much has been written about ethnographic method from Malinowski's early anthropological work down to the new enthusiasm in
cultural studies for ethnography. A number of good, introductory
texts are also available (Agar 1980, 1986; Spradley 1980; Hammersley
and Atkinson 1983; Fetterman 1989; Jorgenson 1989; Moores 1993).
Perhaps the most thoughtful contemporary discussion of the problems of ethnography is Rosaldo (1993). Here my purpose is not to
review that literature but simply to reiterate a few of the key points
of the methodology as a way of introducing some of the innova-
tions we have made in our own work. I will address four questions
regarding ethnography:

1. What is ethnography?
2. Is ethnography a methodology?
3. What are the key elements of ethnography?
4. What are the main tools or methods used by ethnographers?

WHAT IS ETHNOGRAPHY?

The main schools of ethnography are anthropological ethnography,
sociological ethnography, educational ethnography and the ethnography of communication. Recently there has developed a kind of
media-studies ethnography (Moores 1993) which is largely derived
from sociological ethnography and I will not treat it separately. All
derive from Malinowski's anthropology originally, though more
recently many ethnographers have begun to object to the 'we-study-
you' power implications of traditional anthropological ethnography
(Rosaldo 1993). The first ethnographies were not much different

from rather elaborate travelogues of powerful or socially well-placed researchers (often from aristocratic families) from powerful societies (Euro-American) who often consulted relatively little with 'their people' about the validity of their analyses.

Anthropological ethnography

The focus is usually on non-western or tribal societies. The goal is often to rescue the knowledge and life of an entire people from oblivion before civilization has swept them away. The main theoretical concern is usually to try to capture a holistic view of a people's way of life and particularly modes of thought and social organization. Often this work is divided between anthropologists and linguists; the latter tend to focus on just the language of a people while the former focus on everything but language. For example, in 1925 the Linguistic Society of America was founded largely by this split in interests. In the present, much ethnography is done by what have come to be called *linguistic anthropologists*. Gregory Bateson's *Naven* (1936) is sometimes considered the best example of a traditional ethnography in the anthropological school, though many would quarrel with that as well.

Sociological ethnography

The focus is mostly on urban societies or sub-cultures. Sociologists from the 'Chicago School' are often thought to be among the main forerunners of urban ethnography or sociological ethnography. This work differs from anthropological ethnography not only because of the different populations, but also because different research questions are usually asked. Often questions of political life and political reality lie at the heart of the work of sociological ethnographers. Many are Marxist in their theoretical orientation and have therefore found social relations within urban populations of more direct theoretical concern than the last few people of an aboriginal society who in Marxist terms are only in the earliest stages of social development. Anthropologists would argue strongly that there are *no people* more highly developed than others, only differently developed. Sociologists often counter that this is simply a dodge of the fact that anthropologists behave in most ways as if their own theoretical constructs are of greater value than those of the people they study. Whyte's *Street Corner Society* (1981) is considered by many the classic urban or sociological ethnography.

Educational ethnography

There are two sub-schools of educational ethnography. In one school the concern is to construct an anthropologically valid picture of the whole society, but with a special focus on education or schools within that society. The other school treats the school itself as a kind of micro-society amenable to ethnographic study. As sociologists have focused on sub-cultures, educational ethnographers have focused on the sub-sub-culture of the school. George and Louise Spindler's (Spindler 1982) various studies are considered foundational works.

Ethnography of communication

After linguists in America split off from anthropologists and founded the Linguistic Society of America, their work became increasingly removed from ethnography. By the 1970s a group of scholars with a broad interest in the relationships between language and culture developed a new approach in which they were concerned to re-unite anthropological concerns with the whole society or, as they call it 'speech community', on the one hand with meticulous attention to the actual language used by people in the society on the other. There are as yet no ethnographies of communication, though there have been many partial studies of particular aspects of the ethnography of communication. John Gumperz and Dell Hymes's *Directions in Sociolinguistics* (1972) is the foundational collection of papers.

IS ETHNOGRAPHY A METHODOLOGY?

Nearly every book on ethnography one picks up begins by saying that nobody who practises ethnography can or will define a specific methodology. They will often say that ethnography cannot be taught, but only learned within the community of practice. In fact, in most graduate programmes where people ultimately learn to do ethnography, no specific courses in ethnography are given. People seem to learn it through reading the research of others, through working together with other ethnographers, and through their own fieldwork. I would agree that ethnography is not in itself a methodology, but a point of view or a stance. An ethnography (the concrete noun meaning the report which is written) is the result of looking in particular ways at particular phenomena and reporting on them in particular ways. There is nothing in ethnography (the abstract noun meaning the field of study) which will tell a researcher just how to do this observation and reporting though I hope below to provide some useful suggestions.

WHAT ARE THE KEY ELEMENTS OF ETHNOGRAPHY?

To say that ethnography is a stance rather than a methodology does not mean that there is nothing systematic about what ethnographers do. I would think that four elements define the essence of ethnography:

1. Fieldwork.
2. Participant observation.
3. 'Strange making'.
4. Contrastive observation.

Fieldwork

With the rare exception of Ruth Benedict's *Chrysanthemum and the Sword* (1946) in which, during wartime, she developed a full-blown ethnography of the Japanese without setting foot in Japan, most ethnographies are based upon fieldwork. Ethnographers relish their fieldwork, many of them finding going to live with a completely different group of people the richest aspect of their work. Some of them scorn libraries and university offices and would much rather be doing an ethnography of the community of tipplers at the neighbourhood local. Ethnographers have often suffered some fieldwork-incurred disease from malaria and leeches to alcoholism and drug addiction, though no specific examples will be given here.

Participant observation

The essence of fieldwork is participant observation by which is meant somewhat paradoxically learning to become a member of the group under study while at the same time keeping observational distance. The danger is always 'going native', a state in which the ethnographer completely forgets why he or she began the study or simply fails to return home from the field. In subtler ways, the ethnographer begins by studying the 'other' and ends by becoming the 'other' in the attitude he or she takes up against the research or academic establishment. In this sense ethnographers may often become advocates for the ideas and causes of the groups they study. In spite of these dangers, ethnographers feel that their participation gives them a certain measure of the 'inside view' of members and that this is essential to understanding the overall picture of the groups they study.

'Strange making'

This is the opposite of participant observation. This term has arisen largely in urban ethnography or other forms of ethnography where the ethnographer is himself or herself a member of the general culture of study. When an ethnographer studies a school very much like the ones he or she attended as a child, it is essential to see this school as if it were in a foreign culture. Thus the ethnographer treats everything familiar as strange and looks for explanations for the obvious as a way of getting at the underlying structure. This aspect of ethnography is, perhaps, best written by Erving Goffman who would never call himself an ethnographer. His studies of the common social situations of everyday life highlight the constitutive social practices while making highly entertaining reading.

Contrastive observation

While it may take many forms, virtually no ethnographic research is without a major component of cultural or group contrast. In earlier research this contrast was implicit; the anthropologist described the 'other' in contrast to his or her own cultural expectations. The 'home' culture of the anthropologist was taken as life as usual and the 'other' was described as departing from this normal life in interesting ways. Even where the goal of the anthropologist was 'strange making' – to describe how others live so that we could see our own oddities – the implicit comparison was between the ethnographer's cultural group and the 'other'. More recently, as the research literature has grown, studies have included comparisons across three or sometimes many groups in an effort to seek genuinely universal principles.

One of the major aspects of contrastive observation displayed by most ethnographers is to use multiple sources of data or observation. Recently, researchers have come to call this triangulation, but it has always been the foundation of ethnographic work. Ruesch and Bateson's (1968 [1951]) *Communication: The Social Matrix of Psychiatry* outlined four general types of observation which are generally present in any ethnographic research:

1. Members' generalizations.
2. Neutral (objective) observation.
3. Individual member's experience.
4. Observer's interactions with members.

A community of practice, a social group or a culture is peopled by members who in many cases, but certainly not all cases, have clearly articulated views about themselves and their own social practices. The ethnographic search to elicit members' generalization has the goal of discovering the view members take of their own practices. Some analysts have called this the *insider's view* or the *emic view*, though I would take issue with using *emic* simply to mean consciously articulated views of members. As Bond and his colleagues (Bond 1996) have demonstrated so clearly in relationship to Hong Kongers, often members of a group can and do articulate clear views about the social practices *as these might apply to other members* but completely fail to recognize or at least to claim those practices as their own.

Members' generalizations may be found in many ways, most easily by simple interviewing. They are also available abundantly in the products of popular culture. Carbaugh (1989) has used the statements made by participants on the 'Donahue' television talk show as a particular rich source of members' generalizations about the nature of American communicative practice.

Because members' generalizations are always partial and because members of a particular community of practice are always patently unaware of very significant aspects of their own social practices, it is essential to play such members' generalizations off against neutral outsiders or, if you like, objective observation. Each of these terms is problematical, of course. The goal of making observations from a standpoint completely outside a community of practice can never be realized because of the observer's paradox noted above. More important than seeking a spurious 'outsider's' stance is for the researcher to develop an acute and trained sense of 'strange making'. Indeed, much of the fieldwork training of an ethnographer consists of learning to see the obvious as strange and unaccountable. In this the ethnographer relies more and more on the technologies of recording. First phonetic or other written coding systems were developed. More recently photography and film, audio and video recording, and many other instrumental devices for producing, if not ever totally objective recordings, at least relatively fixed and invariant recordings to which the ethnographer and others may return to look for factors which might have been missed in the first instance of human perception.

These neutral observations are sometimes called *etic* observations in parallel with the term *emic* on analogy with phonological research. Again, while this analogy is really only partial – in phonological study phonetic observations are not non-human instrumental observations – if used with caution, the terms *emic* and *etic* may be used to capture the distinction between recording what members think is obvious (*emic*) and what the trained observer notes that is largely out of the awareness or consciousness of the member (*etic*).

A third type of data is significant in ethnographic study in order to capture the richness of lived, individual experience in contrast with generalized social practice and this is what Ruesch and Bateson call the individual member's experience. For this, case studies, oral histories and longitudinal studies are the most characteristic type of data collected. As Bond's (1996) research has so amply demonstrated, while generalizations may be drawn about whole populations, the lived experience as well as the claims made by individuals may be at considerable variance from the researcher's generalized picture. The analytical point which has to be resolved is whether the divergence of the individual experience from the generalized experience is the result of false or excessive generalization on the part of the researcher on the one hand or, on the other hand, if it is part of the social practices of individuals within the community of practice or culture being studied. For example, it is commonplace since Alexis de Tocqueville (1969), a century and a half ago, that Americans are highly collectivistic. It is also commonly articulated by Americans that each person is a highly individualized self (Bellah 1986; Carbaugh 1989; Scollon and Scollon 1992). The issue is not to decide whether Americans are individualistic or collectivistic but to understand that within American self-reflection there is a strong tendency to take exception to any generalization made regarding cultural or social practice (Gitlin 1995).

The fourth type of data of major significance to ethnographers is particularly useful in resolving the divergence between generalized analysis and individual experience and that is achieved through the observer's interactions with members. Naturally, there will be many interactions between the observer and members in the course of ethnographic fieldwork. In this case, however, reference is being made to bringing the observer's records and analysis to members of the community of practice. In earlier ethnographies this was rarely practised as the anthropologists and sociologists would normally retreat from 'the field' and in most cases never return. They remained the sole interpreters of their field data. More recently, as Rosaldo (1993) has so cogently and poignantly argued, it is crucial to re-engage the researcher in the community of practice so that the analysis can be subjected to critique by the community of practice itself.

Obviously, these four categories of data are not necessarily collected separately through different methodologies. They often can arise in a single extended face-to-face interview. For example, a member could say, 'We normally do X, but, of course, I don't do that at all', from which one could extract the member's generalization as well as a statement about personal experience. Naturally an ethnographer would add to this his or her own observation of that person's behaviour to check against both the normative statement and the personal narrative. Furthermore, most would then return to this person with the results of this check to test it against interaction with the member. That is, the ethnographer might come back and say, 'You said your group normally does Y, and you don't, but I saw you do it and I haven't actually seen many others do it at all'. The response to this challenge then provides a richer view than the generalization, the personal narrative, or even the objective observation. It is this richer, contested view of reality which the ethnographer seeks.

WHAT ARE THE MAIN TOOLS USED BY ETHNOGRAPHERS?

Having suggested that ethnography is more a stance or a point of view than a methodology, what are the methodologies which are used by ethnographers? There is actually a very large number of these, with individual ethnographers having their preference for a few of them. We have used a large number of tools in constituting the data for this study which might be placed in six categories:

1. Field notes.
2. Artifacts.
3. Records.
4. Constructed data.
5. Coded data.
6. Processed data.

Perhaps the most basic tool and certainly the most antiquated, but still crucial, is the field notebook. Notes are kept as close to the moment of observation as possible, but also summary notes are made at frequent intervals. In periods of field study this is at least once a day. Now, of course, we normally transfer summary field notes to a word processor for further analysis.

Artifacts are manifold. For this study we have collected thousands of newspapers, magazines and other periodicals. We have handbills, tissues, and even condoms which are handed out on the streets. We have restaurant menus and placemats as well as packaging materials. The main characteristic of these artifacts is that they are items which are not produced by the researcher but simply collected in the sites of engagement being studied.

Records differ from artifacts in that they are produced by the researcher or the researcher's team. These include photographs, videotapes, audiotapes, maps and diagrams. These records are extremely important as they provide the 'objective' records to which we have been able to return again and again to check our analysis against what actually occurred in the situation being studied. The concern in making these records as well as in collecting artifacts is to prepare a much larger range of objective materials than one is likely to need as a way of reconstructing the original sites of engagement after time has passed and memory has faded. Like the evidence which appears in courtrooms, one major use of these artifacts and records is to jog the memories or challenge the interpretations of members of the community of practice who are often more likely to remember a member's generalization than their actually lived experience.

Constructed data goes a step beyond the record and the artifact. This category includes the transcripts, charts, catalogues and data bases which are made to provide better access to the raw data. While it might be simply called 'the data', I prefer to call it constructed data because I want to remain aware of the significant and pre-theoretical actions of the research in producing this level of data (R. Scollon 1976; Ochs 1979). We know that significant selection occurs when the original video or audio tape recording is made. We have focused on one participant rather than another by the placement of the microphone. We have had the tape recorder running during one period judged to be important and turned off at another time when we thought nothing of significance was happening. Now in making a transcription we have decided to make a rough, sentence-level transcription that leaves out pauses and mistakes because we were after the general idea. But perhaps later we discover that we have missed significant detail because our transcription is not fine-grained enough to tell us that the person was extremely nervous which could be heard in his or her stuttering or tone of voice. Data at this level is always constructed and so we have marked it carefully to indicate what level of transcription we have made. Normally constructed data should record the time, place, occasion on which it was recorded and by whom it was recorded as well as the same details regarding how and when the transcription was made.

Coded data goes another step beyond constructed data in that the transcriptions (photographs, etc.) are studied and coded for analytically significant features. By this stage the researchers are looking for particular points and coding the constructed data for those points so that they may be assembled, counted, contrasted or otherwise processed.

Finally, the data is processed. This processing can include a wide range of strategies from corpus software programmes which will search for significant words or terms used in a large body of transcription to statistical procedures to count the occurrence and significance of various factors under analysis. What is important to remember in ethnographic research at this stage is that what one is counting and analysing is not the concrete world of one's original observations. One is processing an inferential chain of analytical processes by which data were found, recorded, constructed and coded. What makes ethnography differ significantly from at least some other research methodologies is that the ethnographer generally maintains a thoroughgoing scepticism about the objectivity of his or her 'data' throughout these processes of collection, processing and analysis. This is why the fourth category – interactions with members – is so crucial in the stance towards research called ethnography. When the work is 'done' from the point of view of processing the data and deriving an analysis, the ethnographer wants to return to the field to see if the analysis works. The ethnographer wants to know if the story thus constructed is one which members are willing to interpret and, more importantly, accept as offering insight into the substance of their lives.

INTERDISCURSIVITY OF METHOD

A crucial issue in all research into social practice is that of power. E. N. Goody (1978) pointed out that questions govern two social practices, one of information gathering and one of social control. A literal question such as 'What did you have for dinner?', while posing as a request for information, more implicitly demands a response from the interlocutor. By extension of this concept Rosaldo (1993) has argued that any research agenda, while posing as the researcher's need to gather information, is, in fact, a demand to accept the categories as given by the researcher and to respond not only to the content of the probing but to the implicit demand to produce answers.

The methodology we have used in this research has sought to mitigate this control function by developing a methodological interdiscursivity within which the communities of practice of the researched and of the researcher interpenetrated each other. A specific example might help to clarify this. As I have noted above, the home settings of Hong Kong university students are virtually impossible to observe for university-based and especially senior researchers. We needed crucial ethnographic observations of social practices within the home setting. Prior to that we had had to determine that the home setting was, in fact, a crucial setting.

As we found it difficult to cut this Gordian knot on our own, we enlisted the thinking of our student research assistants. These research assistants were themselves members of the community of practice we wanted to learn about. Thus the question was reformulated. While at first the question was 'What are social practices of media appropriation in students' homes?', now the question put to the students was 'How can we together (researchers and assistants) discover what is going on in your homes?'

The students suggested two strategies which proved to be highly insightful and useful. The first was to do a 'pager survey' and the second was to do a 'scene survey'. As our students virtually all have pagers (if not mobile telephones), they suggested we could randomly sample a population of students by paging them over the course of a week. When the random page was received they were to note where they were, who was with them, what they were doing at the moment and, within that context, what media were being appropriated for what purposes. Over the course of a week we were able to dip into students' lives at moments which were unpredictable to them and therefore somewhat difficult to 'prepare' for. We were able to sample a wide range of times and places where they were spending their time, with whom, and how the media figured into those actions. It was the pager survey which allowed us to identify the four crucial scenes I noted in Chapter 8 – the university, the home, small fast-food restaurants, and public transportation.

Once we had identified the home as a crucial site we nevertheless had the problem of penetrating that site for observations. Our students, of course, were frequently in their homes, but as students they could not be expected to make fully developed or very accurate ethnographic observations. Again, it was the students who suggested the solution which was to give them specific training in what we wanted to observe and to do it in a site which would provide a certain degree of reciprocal power equalization. They suggested that they begin with a scene survey of the home(s) of the primary researchers in the project. In this scene survey they were expected to make observations, take photographs, and produce maps of media use which would provide the basis for an analysis of media use in the researcher's home. This scene survey was then paralleled in their own homes and those of their friends to produce relatively accurate and *etic* descriptions of media use even within homes which had otherwise been impenetrable. This training of members of the community of practice as our research assistants had the further practical value that from those specific observations onwards, they became collaborators in the overall research project as researchers and not just as subjects.

To offset the potential for confounding *emic* and *etic* views of this community of practice we came at the question from an orthogonal direction. If our concern in the first instance was with a community of practice, that is, with understanding the ways in which social practices produced sites of engagement such as the home for the appropriation of news media texts, our second concern was with the texts of news discourse. We wanted to track a specific story and to see how it entered and was diffused throughout that community. For that triangulation we conducted what we termed an 'event survey'.

For the event survey we first collected the texts of all the major news sources available in Hong Kong for a period of two weeks (R. Scollon and Yung 1996). This included Hong Kong and over-seas television and radio main news broadcasts, infotainment broadcasts, and key newspapers and periodicals. We then conducted a daily survey of four categories of people: (1) City University students; (2) non-City University students; (3) City University staff; and (4) other non-student adults. In the survey we asked questions such as, 'What is the main story in the news today?', 'How did you first hear about this story?', 'When you heard about it, what did you do?'. Our purpose with these questions was to identify what each of these populations considered to the most important news stories in the first place and then to map the pathway through the community. Thus we discovered, as I noted in Chapter 8, that tele-vision was the first source of news stories, followed by word of mouth. Newspapers were used to follow-up stories which had already been identified within the community as of salient interest.

METHOD OR MECHANICAL PROCEDURES?

The word 'methodology' has come to mean for many a set of fairly mechanical or even technological procedures for turning raw observations into analysis. This, of course, is a trivialization of the concept of research method and a far cry from the idea as it was first developed by Peter Ramus (Ong 1974; J. Goody 1977) in the sixteenth century. I am not suggesting a return to sixteenth-century methodology, of course, but I would like to suggest that as Ramus introduced the concept, his concern was with having sys-tematic and logical ways of setting out a subject matter, largely so that gaps could be identified in the reasoning process. I would argue that ethnographic method does not depart so radically from the original methodism of Peter Ramus. By this what I mean to say is not that ethnography should be consigned to historical oblivion but that ethnography at its best is a way of recursively thinking through both the theoretical and the field problem, looking for gaps to be investigated and looking for alternative perspectives which can be taken to achieve triangulation. Rather than a fixed set of procedures for arriving at an analysis, it is a frame of mind in which the researcher is constantly seeking to uncover his or her own systematic misconceptions.

It follows that I would not be able either to suggest that the reader make any attempt to replicate the study undertaken here or to suggest that the reader use this method to undertake the analysis of a different research problem. What can be done, however, is to suggest a set of heuristic questions which we have used in this research and which can be used in any ethnographic research to guide the search for relevant perspectives and to call up for analysis significant gaps in fieldwork strategies. It is to these questions I turn now to close this study.

Five questions can be used to orientate the research project overall. They are:

1. What is the initial problem?
2. Why is this research project necessary or useful?
3. How can an overall research project be designed?
4. What is the most effective starting point?
5. How can the four crucial types of observation be made?

What is the initial problem?

Any research begins with a problem to be solved. This problem might come from social life in the community (What is the most effective language of instruction in the classrooms of a bilingual speech community? How can we improve the English of Hong Kong tertiary students? What is personal identity in a unified Europe?). More often, perhaps, the problem of the research derives from the research literature as an extension of prior research. The researcher may identify gaps, faulty interpretations or misapplied theoretical frameworks.

A surprising number of research projects in my experience are unclear on this issue. I believe the lack of clarity comes from confusing research problems which arise from the research literature with problems which arise from the speech community or community of practice under study. Most often the 'problem', as understood within the community of practice, is analysed by researchers as having been stated incorrectly. With 'correct' statement that problem disappears and another one is seen as more salient. Thus researcher and community go off in different directions and while research gets done, connecting the research back to the community of practice, an essential aspect of ethnographic research, as I argue it should be practised, is forever made impossible.

The solution here is to work out from the start if possible a statement of the research problem which fully acknowledges both community and theoretical statements of the problem. By building in this research–community interdiscursivity from the outset, the research project positions itself for useful engagement with the community throughout the life of the research project.

Why is this research project necessary or useful?

This question arises as part of the thinking about what is the initial problem. Most commonly, to get research support the research project must be stated as significant and useful for the research or theoretical community. Unfortunately, in most research environments whether governmental or academic, the underlying necessity for the project is that the researchers must do research for job security and advancement, the institutions must do research for institutional security and development. A social practice perspective would be blind indeed not to take into account these ubiquitous personal and institutional requirements. At the same time, it must be acknowledged that social practice requires that any research be stated as *not being about* such personal and institutional practices.

In this environment, as in the case of the statement of the problem itself, the research must build into the project from the outset an interdiscursivity of motive. A research project, in order to be supported and to succeed, must be predicated on the personal and institutional needs of the researcher. At the same time it must also be predicated on the needs of the community of practice which lies outside the corridors of research institutes and academic departments. There is nothing to be gained either by blindly ignoring the institutional social practices through which research gets supported on the one hand or by cynically posing non-existent problems for the sake of advancement. I am suggesting neither of these approaches. I am arguing that the fundamental interdiscursivity of practice which runs through all institutional–community engagements must be understood by the effective ethnographer and as much as possible designed into the research project from the beginning.

To make this a bit more specific, most research funding cycles are too short for serious ethnographic work. The research I have written about here was conducted over a period of almost five years. No single research grant lasted more than two of those years. Furthermore, the time between proposal writing and approval is normally between six months and one year. The solution is that the research project needed to be thought through overall and then broken into separate stages. At any one time the research team is working at three stages of sub-projects. Proposals for later stages of the project are being written and submitted to funding agencies. At the same time current research is being carried out on current projects. Finally, completed stages of the project are being written up in final reports, conference papers and journal articles.

Because of the long-term nature of ethnographic research, and because of the necessity to gear into institutional processes of support, there is a fairly large element of project management involved in any major ethnographic research project. I would argue that a researcher interested in ethnographic research would do well to begin very early to form research teams among colleagues and to formulate umbrella projects as the most effective way to achieve the methodological interdiscursivity needed for successful completion.

How can an overall research project be designed?

As I have argued above, there are four major elements of an ethnographic research project:

1. Fieldwork.
2. Participant observation.
3. 'Strange making'.
4. Contrastive observation.

In keeping with what I have just said about the need to design a long-term strategy, preferably with a research team of colleagues, these four elements of the project can be built in either across the board in each sub-project or, to some extent, longitudinally across the duration of the research project. Fieldwork is a long-term commitment to the extent it is participant observation. That is, it normally takes a year or more to achieve significant entry into any community of practice. Many researchers plan multiple field visits, arguing that two visits of three months are worth more in terms of rapport and involvement than one visit of six months where the relationship can become rather 'stale'. What is most important, of course, is that 'participation' is in most cases at considerable odds with the researcher's participation in his or her home academic environment. This is not just simply in terms of the time it takes to perform in multiple communities of practice, but because of the socialization practices of two different communities that pull towards the development of different and often conflicting identities. Thus 'strange making' works in part by the researcher finding it is the research project and his or her own institutional goals which have been made strange in the process of developing entry into the community of practice being studied.

The design of an ethnographic research project needs to make quite specific plans for both entry and departure, and for re-socialization. It is particularly important to achieve contrastive observation by having more than a single researcher making these transitions on the one hand, and wherever possible, designing contrastive analyses across more than just two communities of practice. A major weakness of much ethnographic research is that the only contrastive dimension is between the 'self' of the researcher and the 'other' of the studied population (Said 1979). Such problems can be mitigated through team design, through collaborative procedures by which the 'studied' population are actively involved in the research, and through multiple and contrastive research sites.

What is the most effective starting point?

I have used four concepts in organizing the research presented in this book:

1. Mediated action.
2. Sites of engagement.
3. Communities of practice.
4. Mediational means.

While I would argue that all of these should be integrated into any general research project, in keeping with my argument above that a general ethnographic research project needs to be managed as a series of linked sub-projects, each of these four concepts is a useful focus for sub-projects. For example, in Chapter 2 just one type of mediated action was the focus of that sub-project – the business telephone call. In the study I cited as part of Chapter 4 (R. Scollon 1997a), the central focus was the site of engagement in which hand-bills are distributed in pedestrian walkways. Perhaps most discourse analysis of news discourse has focused on the mediational means, that is, it has focused on the texts of news discourse, while the community of practice, sites of engagement, and an analysis of the actions as mediated actions has been set aside.

In many cases the most effective entry point is an analysis of the mediational means. A few texts can be collected and analysed as a way of opening a window on the overall research project. The danger, from an ethnographic point of view, is in becoming fixed to the texts and not moving outwards into the communities of practice to see how those texts are used in social practice. A successful research project would probably design separate sub-studies of each of these four elements in a way that they can be brought together, perhaps with different colleagues focusing on one or another aspect of the study.

How can the four crucial types of observation be made?

Like the four elements just mentioned, it is important to seek out four distinct types of observation, as I have argued above:

1. Members' generalizations.
2. Neutral (objective) observation.
3. Individual member's experience.
4. Observer's interactions with members.

As I have said, often these types of observation come mixed into a single discursive format. An interview might provide both members' generalizations and individual member's experiences. At the same time an audio or video recording might supplement this content with more objective observations which can be made after the fact. There is some time-sequencing involved, however. Observer's interactions with members as a kind of testing of analyses against the perceptions and interpretations of the community of practice inevitably come later rather than earlier. In the same way, the easier material with which to start is likely to be members' generalizations. It is often the case that this is how the research is originally started. Members' generalizations are often the problem which is phrased by the community as needing solution. I argued above that there is often a considerable divergence between the research problem as stated by the research community and as understood by the community of practice. One might argue the tension between these two stances is, in fact, the dialectic which drives the research engine. In any event, the researcher should work to uncover observations which go beyond this simple dialectic of researchers' views and community views.

SOCIAL INTERACTION AND IDENTITY

I will close with what is often cited as the central problem of ethnographic research – 'going native'. In the research outlined here the focus is on collaborative study of social interaction. As I have argued throughout this book, social interaction is inherently constructive of discursive identity. In a real sense we are who we speak ourselves to be. But this sentence must not be read: 'One is who one speaks himself/herself to be'. That is, it must not be given a singular, individualist or essentialist reading. The reading I intend is more like the very awkward: 'We co-construct our identities in social interactions with the others with whom we speak'.

Research which is inherently collaborative and inherently social-interactionist is inherently transforming of identity – the identity of the researcher as well as of the participants in the study. To be sure one can to some extent dash into a situation, collect artifacts, recordings and texts and then retire to the quiet contemplation of this data without further interaction within the source community of practice, but this is not ethnography. I would not even want to adjectivize it to 'ethnographic' research which seems a contemporary dodge of the issue of involvement in the community of practice. To do ethnographic research is to take on a commitment to identity negotiation. No researcher should blindly enter into this process. Those who do become ethnographers, however, find the involvement with a wider range of communities of practice the most rewarding single aspect of their academic research.

Bibliography

A Handbook of Chinese Journal Terminology (Chinese–English–French) (1987). Compiled by the Beijing Foreign Languages Institute. Hong Kong: Joint Publishing Company.

Agar, M. H. (1980) *The Professional Stranger: An Informal Introduction to Ethnography.* Orlando, FL: Academic Press.

Agar, M. H. (1986) *Speaking of Ethnography.* Newbury Park, CA: Sage.

Amis, K. (1991) *Memoirs.* Harmondsworth: Penguin Books.

Ang, I. (1996) *Living Room Wars: Rethinking Media Audiences for a Postmodern World.* London: Routledge.

Atkinson, P. (1990) *The Ethnographic Imagination: Textual Constructions of Reality.* London: Routledge.

Bakhtin, M. M. (1981a) *The Dialogic Imagination.* Austin, TX: University of Texas Press.

Bakhtin, M. M. (1981b) Discourse in the novel. In *The Dialogic Imagination.* Austin, TX: University of Texas Press.

Bakhtin, M. M. (1986) *Speech Genres and Other Late Essays.* Austin, TX: University of Texas Press.

Bakhtin, M. M. (1990) *Art and Answerability: Early Philosophical Essays by M. M. Bakhtin.* M. Holquist and V. Liapunov (eds). Austin, TX: University of Texas Press.

Bakhtin, M. M. (1993) *Toward a Philosophy of the Act.* M. Holquist and V. Liapunov (eds). Austin, TX: University of Texas Press.

Bateman, D. N. and Sigband, N. B. (1989) *Communicating in Business.* Glenview, IL: Scott, Foresman and Company.

Bateson, G. (1936) *Naven: A Survey of the Problems Suggested by a Composite Picture of the Culture of a New Guinea Tribe Drawn from Three Points of View.* Cambridge: Cambridge University Press.

Bateson, G. (1972) *Steps to an Ecology of Mind.* New York: Ballantine.

Bell, A. (1991) *The Language of the News Media.* Oxford: Basil Blackwell.

Bellah, R. (1986) *Habits of the Heart: Individualism and Commitment in American Life.* New York: Harper & Row.

Benedict, R. (1946) *Chrysanthemum and the Sword*. Boston, MA: Houghton Mifflin.

Berger, J. (1972) *Ways of Seeing*. Harmondsworth: Penguin.

Besnier, N. (1988) The linguistic relationships of spoken and written Nukulaelae registers. *Language* 64(4): 707–36.

Besnier, N. (1989) Literacy and feelings: the encoding of affect in Nukulaelae letters. *Text* 9(1): 69–92.

Besnier, N. (1991) Literacy and the notion of person on Nukulaelae Atoll. *American Anthropologist* 93: 570–87.

Bond, M. H. (1996) Chinese values. In M. H. Bond (ed.), *The Handbook of Chinese Psychology*. Hong Kong: Oxford University Press.

Booth, W. C. (1975) The rhetorical stance. In W. R. Winterowd (ed.), *Contemporary Rhetoric: A Conceptual Background with Readings*. New York: Harcourt Brace Jovanovich.

Bourdieu, P. (1977) *Outline of a Theory of Practice*. R. Nice (trans). Cambridge: Cambridge University Press.

Bourdieu, P. (1990) *Photography: A Middle-brow Art*. Cambridge: Polity Press.

Boyarin, J. (1993) *The Ethnography of Reading*. Berkeley, CA: University of California Press.

Brown, G. and Yule, G. (1983) *Discourse Analysis*. New York: Cambridge University Press.

Brown, M. (1994) Estimating newspaper and magazine readership. In R. Kent (ed.), *Measuring Media Audiences*. London: Routledge.

Brown, P. and Levinson, S. (1978) Universals in language usage: politeness phenomena. In E. Goody (ed.), *Questions and Politeness: Strategies in Social Interaction*. New York: Cambridge University Press. Revised and separately published in 1987 as *Politeness*. Cambridge: Cambridge University Press.

Burke, K. (1945) *A Grammar of Motives*. Englewood Cliffs, NJ: Prentice-Hall.

Burke, K. (1950) *A Rhetoric of Motives*. Englewood Cliffs, NJ: Prentice-Hall.

Burke, K. (1989) *On Symbols and Society*. Chicago: University of Chicago Press.

Caldas-Coulthard, C. R. (1993) From discourse analysis to critical discourse analysis: the differential re-presentation of women and men speaking in written news. In J. M. Sinclair, M. Hoey and G. Fox (eds), *Techniques of Description: Spoken and Written Discourse*. London: Routledge.

Caldas-Coulthard, C. R. (1994) On reporting reporting: the representation of speech in factual and factional narratives. In M. Coulthard (ed.), *Advances in Written Text Analysis*. London: Routledge.

Caldas-Coulthard, C. R. and Coulthard, M. (1996) *Texts and Practices: Readings in Critical Discourse*. London: Routledge.

Candlin, C. (1987) Explaining moments of conflict in discourse. In Ross Steele and Terry Treadgold (eds), *Language Topics: Essays in Honour of Michael Halliday*. Amsterdam: John Benjamins Publishing Co.

Candlin, C. (1996) Competing discourses: plenary address to Sociolinguistics Symposium 11 at Cardiff, 5–7 September 1996.

Carbaugh, D. (1989) *Talking American: Cultural Discourses on DONAHUE.* Norwood, NJ: Ablex.

Carrell, P. L. (1983) Some issues in studying the role of schemata, or background knowledge, in second language comprehension. *Reading in a Foreign Language* 1(2): 81–92.

Carrell, P. L. (1984a) Evidence of a formal schema in second language comprehension. *Language Learning* 34(2): 87–112.

Carrell, P. L. (1984b) The effects of rhetorical organization on ESL readers. *TESOL Quarterly* 18(3): 441–69.

Carrell, P. L. (1989) Metacognitive awareness and second language reading. *Modern Language Journal* 73: 121–34.

Chai, C. and Chai, W. (1966) *Li Chi: Book of Rites.* Secaucus, NJ: University Books.

Chaiklin, S. and Lave, J. (1993) *Understanding Practice: Perspectives on Activity and Context.* Cambridge: Cambridge University Press.

Chang, F. C. (1992) *Far East Chinese–English Dictionary.* Taipei: The Far East Book Co.

Chatman, S. (1978) *Story and Discourse.* Ithaca, NY: Cornell University Press.

Chun, A. (1996) Discourses of identity in the changing spaces of public culture in Taiwan, Hong Kong and Singapore. *Theory, Culture and Society* 13(1): 51–75.

Collins, R. (1981a) On the microfoundations of macrosociology. *American Journal of Sociology* 86(5): 984–1014.

Collins, R. (1981b) Micro-translation as a theory-building strategy. In K. Knorr-Cetina and A. V. Cicourel (eds), *Advances in Social Theory and Methodology: Toward an Integration of Micro- and Macro-Sociologies.* Boston, MA: Routledge and Kegan Paul.

Cook-Gumperz, J. (1986) *The Social Construction of Literacy.* New York: Cambridge University Press.

Cook-Gumperz, J. and Keller-Cohen, D. (1993) Alternative literacies in school and beyond: multiple literacies of speaking and writing. *Anthropology and Education Quarterly* 24(4): 283–7.

Coulthard, M. (1994) *Advances in Written Text Analysis.* London: Routledge.

Dennerline, J. (1988) *Qian Mu and the World of Seven Mansions.* New Haven, CT: Yale University Press.

Doyle, R. (1993) *Paddy Clarke Ha Ha Ha.* New York: Viking.

Duncan, S. Jr (1972) Some signals and rules for taking speaking turns in conversations. *Journal of Personality and Social Psychology* 23: 283–92.

Duranti, A. and Goodwin, C. (1992) Editor's introduction to 'Assessments and the construction of context'. In A. Duranti and C. Goodwin (eds), *Rethinking Context.* Cambridge: Cambridge University Press.

Eco, U. (1995) Phenomena of this sort must also be included in any panorama of Italian design. In R. Lumley (ed.), *Apocalypse Postponed (Essays by Umberto Eco)*. London: Flamingo.

Engeström, Y. (1997) Talk, text and instrumentality in collaborative work: an activity-theoretical perspective. Paper presented at the Annual Conference on College Composition and Communication, Phoenix, 12–15 March 1997.

Erickson, F. and Shultz, J. (1982) *The Counselor as Gatekeeper: Social Interaction in Interviews*. New York: Academic Press.

Evans, H. (1976) *Editing and Design: A Five-volume Manual of English, Typography and Layout: Book Five: Newspaper Design*. London: Heinemann.

Fairclough, N. (1989) *Language and Power*. London: Longman.

Fairclough, N. (1992) *Discourse and Social Change*. Cambridge: Polity Press.

Fairclough, N. (1995a) *Critical Discourse Analysis: The Critical Study of Language*. London and New York: Longman.

Fairclough, N. (1995b) *Media Discourse*. London: Edward Arnold.

Ferguson, C. A. (1994) Dialect, register, and genre: working assumptions about conventionalization. In D. Biber and E. Finegan (eds), *Sociolinguistic Perspectives on Register*. Oxford: Oxford University Press.

Fetterman, D. M. (1989) *Ethnography Step by Step*. Newbury Park, CA: Sage.

Fiske, J. (1991) Writing ethnographies: contribution to a dialogue. *Quarterly Journal of Speech* 77: 330–5.

Fong, B. (1992) *Postscript: Inside the 'South China Morning Post'*. Burnaby, British Columbia: Grapevine Press.

Foucault, M. (1973a) *The Order of Things*. New York: Random House.

Foucault, M. (1973b) *The Birth of the Clinic*. London: Tavistock.

Foucault, M. (1977) *Discipline and Punish*. New York: Pantheon Books.

Fromson, M. (1994) The role of the international reporter. Department of Journalism, Hong Kong Baptist College, Distinguished Visitor Lecture, 23 February 1994.

Garfinkel, H. (1967) *Studies in Ethnomethodology*. Englewood Cliffs, NJ: Prentice-Hall.

Gee, J. P. (1986) Orality and literacy: from 'The Savage Mind' to 'Ways with Words'. *TESOL Quarterly* 20: 719–46.

Gee, J. P. (1990) *Social Linguistics and Literacies: Ideology in Discourses*. Bristol, PA: Falmer Press.

Geertz, C. (1986) Making experiences, authoring selves. In V. W. Turner and E. M. Bruner (eds), *The Anthropology of Experience*. Urbana, IL: University of Illinois Press.

Giroux, H. A. (1994) Consuming social change: the 'United Colors of Benetton'. *Cultural Critique* (Winter): 5–32.

Gitlin, T. (1995) *The Twilight of Common Dreams: Why America is Wracked by Culture Wars*. New York: Henry Holt and Company.

Goffman, E. (1959) *The Presentation of Self in Everyday Life*. New York: Doubleday.

Goffman, E. (1961) *Asylums*. Garden City, NY: Anchor Books.

Goffman, E. (1963) *Behavior in Public Places: Notes on the Social Organization of Gatherings*. New York: The Free Press.

Goffman, E. (1967) *Interaction Ritual*. Garden City, NY: Anchor Books.

Goffman, E. (1971) *Relations in Public*. New York: Harper & Row.

Goffman, E. (1974) *Frame Analysis*. New York: Harper & Row.

Goffman, E. (1979) *Gender Advertisements*. London: Macmillan.

Goffman, E. (1981) *Forms of Talk*. Philadelphia, PA: University of Pennsylvania Press.

Goodwin, C. (1981) *Conversational Organization: Interaction between Speakers and Hearers*. New York: Academic Press.

Goodwin, C. (1986a) Gestures as a resource for the organization of mutual orientation. *Semiotica* 62(1/2): 29–49.

Goodwin, C. (1986b) Audience diversity, participation and interpretation. *Text* 6(3): 283–316.

Goodwin, C. (1994) Professional vision. *American Anthropologist* 96(3): 606–33.

Goodwin, C. and Duranti, A. (1992) Rethinking context: an introduction. In A. Duranti and C. Goodwin (eds), *Rethinking Context*. Cambridge: Cambridge University Press.

Goody, E. N. (1978) Towards a theory of questions. In E. Goody (ed.), *Questions and Politeness: Strategies in Social Interaction*. New York: Cambridge University Press.

Goody, J. (1977) *The Domestication of the Savage Mind*. New York: Cambridge University Press.

Goody, J. and Watt, I. (1963) The consequences of literacy. *Comparative Studies in Society and History* 5: 304–45.

Gordon, C. (1980) *Power/Knowledge: Selected Interviews and Other Writings, 1972–1977, by Michel Foucault*. New York: Pantheon Books.

Grimshaw, A. D. (1994) What we have learned: some research conclusions and some conclusions about research. In A. D. Grimshaw (ed.), *What's Going On Here? Complementary Studies of Professional Talk (Volume 2 of the Multiple Analysis Project)*. Norwood, NJ: Ablex.

Gumperz, J. J. (1977) Sociocultural knowledge in conversational inference. In M. Saville-Troike (ed.), *28th Annual Round Table Monograph Series on Language and Linguistics*. Washington, DC: Georgetown University Press.

Gumperz, J. J. (1982) *Discourse Strategies*. New York: Cambridge University Press.

Gumperz, J. J. (1992) Contextualization and understanding. In A. Duranti and C. Goodwin (eds), *Rethinking Context*. Cambridge: Cambridge University Press.

Gumperz, J. J. and Hymes, D. (1972) *Directions in Sociolinguistics: The Ethnography of Communication*. New York: Holt, Rinehart & Winston.

Gusfield, J. R. (1989) Introduction. In K. Burke, *On Symbols and Society*. Chicago: University of Chicago Press.

Hall, S. (1980) Encoding/decoding. In S. Hall, D. Hobson, A. Lowe and P. Willis (eds), *Culture, Media, Language: Working Papers in Cultural Studies, 1972–1979*. London: Hutchinson.

Halliday, M. A. K. (1978) *Language as Social Semiotic*. London: Edward Arnold.

Halliday, M. A. K. (1985) *An Introduction to Functional Grammar*. London: Edward Arnold.

Halliday, M. A. K. (1989) *Spoken and Written Language*. Oxford: Oxford University Press.

Hammersley, M. and Atkinson, P. (1983) *Ethnography: Principles in Practice*. London: Tavistock.

Heath, S. B. (1983) *Ways with Words*. New York: Cambridge University Press.

Houtkoop-Steenstra, H. (1991) Opening sequences in Dutch telephone conversations. In D. Boden and D. H. Zimmerman (eds), *Talk and Social Structure: Studies in Ethnomethodology and Conversation Analysis*. Cambridge: Polity Press.

Howe, N. (1993) The cultural construction of reading in Anglo-Saxon England. In J. Boyarin (ed.), *The Ethnography of Reading*. Berkeley, CA: University of California Press.

Howlett, B. (1997) *Hong Kong 1997*. Hong Kong: Hong Kong Government Printer.

Hu, H. C. (1944) The Chinese concept of 'face'. *American Anthropologist* 46: 45–64.

Hutcheon, R. (1983) *SCMP: The First Eighty Years*. Hong Kong: *South China Morning Post*.

Hymes, D. (1966) Two types of linguistic relativity. In W. Bright (ed.), *Sociolinguistics*. The Hague: Mouton.

Hymes, D. (1972) Models of the interaction of language and social life. In J. J. Gumperz and D. Hymes (eds), *Directions in Sociolinguistics: The Ethnography of Communication*. New York: Holt, Rinehart & Winston.

Hymes, D. (1974) *Foundations in Sociolinguistics: An Ethnographic Approach*. Philadelphia, PA: University of Pennsylvania Press.

Jones, L. and Alexander, R. (1989a) *International Business English: Teacher's Book*. Cambridge: Cambridge University Press.

Jones, L. and Alexander, R. (1989b) *International Business English: Student's Book*. Cambridge: Cambridge University Press.

Jones, L. and Alexander, R. (1989c) *International Business English: Workbook*. Cambridge: Cambridge University Press.

Jones, R. H. (1995) Talking about AIDS in Hong Kong: cultural models in public health discourse. Paper presented at the Regional Language Center Conference, Singapore, April 1995.

Jorgensen, D. L. (1989) *Participant Observation: A Methodology for Human Studies*. Newbury Park, CA: Sage.

Keenan, E. O. and Schieffelin, B. (1976) Topic as a discourse notion. In C. N. Li (ed.), *Subject and Topic*. New York: Academic Press.

Keller-Cohen, D. (1993a) Rethinking literacy: comparing colonial and contemporary America. *Anthropology and Education Quarterly* 24(4): 288–307.

Keller-Cohen, D. (1993b) Colonial literacy. *Encyclopedia of the North American Colonies*, Vol. 3. New York: Scribners, pp. 3–12.

Keller-Cohen, D. (1993c) The web of literacy: speaking, reading and writing in seventeenth- and eighteenth-century America. In D. Keller-Cohen (ed.), *Literacy: Interdisciplinary Conversations*. Cresskill, NJ: Hampton Press.

Keller-Cohen, D. (1993d) *Literacy: Interdisciplinary Conversations*. Cresskill, NJ: Hampton Press.

Kendon, A. (1994) Do gestures communicate?: A review. *Research on Language and Social Interaction* 27(3): 175–200.

Kent, R. (1994) *Measuring Media Audiences*. London: Routledge.

Kertész, A. (1971) *On Reading*. New York: Penguin Books.

Kintsch, W. (1977) On comprehending stories. In M. Just and P. Carpenter (eds), *Cognitive Processes in Comprehension*. Hillsdale, NJ: Lawrence Erlbaum Associates.

Kintsch, W. and Greene, E. (1978) The role of culture-specific schemata in the comprehension and recall of stories. *Discourse Processes* 1(1): 1–13.

Kress, G. (1993) Cultural considerations in linguistic description. In D. Graddol, L. Thompson and M. Byram (eds), *Language and Culture*. Clevedon: BAAL and Multilingual Matters.

Kristeva, J. (1986a) Word, dialogue and novel. In T. Moi (ed.), *The Kristeva Reader*. Oxford: Basil Blackwell.

Kristeva, J. (1986b) The system and the speaking subject. In T. Moi (ed.), *The Kristeva Reader*. Oxford: Basil Blackwell.

Lakoff, G. (1987) *Women, Fire, and Dangerous Things: What Categories Reveal about the Mind*. Chicago and London: University of Chicago Press.

Lakoff, G. and Johnson, M. (1980) *Metaphors We Live By*. Chicago: University of Chicago Press.

Lakoff, R. (1973) The logic of politeness; or, minding your p's and q's. *Papers from the Ninth Regional Meeting of the Chicago Linguistic Society*. Chicago: Chicago Linguistic Society.

Lakoff, R. (1974) What you can do with words: politeness, pragmatics and performatives. *Berkeley Studies in Syntax and Semantics*, Vol. XVI: 1–55. Institute of Human Learning, University of California, Berkeley, CA.

Lave, J. (1988) *Cognition in Practice*. Cambridge: Cambridge University Press.

Lave, J. and Wenger, E. (1991) *Situated Learning: Legitimate Peripheral Participation*. Cambridge: Cambridge University Press.

Li, D., Poon, W., Rogerson-Revell, P., Scollon, R., Scollon, S., Yu, B. and Yung, V. (1993) Contrastive discourse in English and Cantonese news stories: a preliminary analysis of newspaper, radio, and television versions of the Lan Kwai Fong news story. Research Report No. 29, Department of English, City Polytechnic of Hong Kong.

Li, J. (1989) *Xianggang Baoye Zatan*. Hong Kong: Joint Publishing Company.

Li, T. S. (1993) *The World Outside when the War Broke Out*. Hong Kong: Hong Kong Institute of Asia-Pacific Studies, The Chinese University of Hong Kong.

Littlejohn, S. W. (1992) *Theories of Human Communication*. Belmont, CA: Wadsworth Publishing Company.

Livingstone, S. M. (1992) The resourceful reader: interpreting television characters and narratives. *Communication Yearbook* 15: 58–90.

Malinowski, B. (1923) The problem of meaning in primitive languages. In C. K. Ogden and I. A. Richards (eds), *The Meaning of Meaning*. New York: Harcourt, Brace.

Mey, J. (1993) *Pragmatics: An introduction*. Oxford: Basil Blackwell.

Meyrowitz, J. (1985) *No Sense of Place: The Impact of Electronic Media on Social Behavior*. New York: Oxford University Press.

Moores, S. (1993) *Interpreting Audiences: The Ethnography of Media Consumption*. Newbury Park, CA: Sage.

Morley, D. (1980) *The 'Nationwide' Audience: Structure and Decoding*. London: British Film Institute.

Morley, D. (1990) The construction of everyday life: political communication and domestic media. In D. L. Swanson and D. D. Nimmo (eds), *New Directions in Political Communication*. London: Sage.

Morley, D. and Silverstone, R. (1991) Communication and context: ethnographic perspectives on the media audience. In K. B. Jensen and N. W. Jankowski (eds), *A Handbook of Qualitative Methodologies for Mass Communication Research*. London: Routledge.

Musson, G. and Cohen, L. (1996) The enterprise discourse: an empirical analysis of its effects. Paper presented at the conference 'Communication and Culture: China and the World Entering the 21st Century', Beijing University, 13–16 August 1996.

Ochs, E. (1979) Translation as theory. In E. Ochs and B. B. Schieffelin (eds), *Developmental Pragmatics*. New York: Academic Press.

Ong, W. J. (1974) *Ramus, Method and the Decay of the Dialogue*. Ithaca, NY: Cornell University Press.

Ong, W. J. (1982) *Orality and Literacy*. New York: Methuen.

O'Sullivan, T., Hartley, J., Saunders, D., Montgomery, M. and Fiske, J. (1994) *Key Concepts in Communication and Cultural Studies*. London: Routledge.

Owen, M. L. (1981) Conversational units and the use of 'well'. In P. Werth (ed.), *Conversation and Discourse*. London: Croom Helm.

Pan, Y. (1996) Facework in Chinese service encounters. Paper presented at the Annual Meeting of American Association for Applied Linguistics, Chicago, Illinois, 26 March 1996.

Pennycook, A. (1996) Borrowing others' words: text, ownership, memory, and plagiarism. *TESOL Quarterly* 30(2): 201–30.

Reddy, M. J. (1979) The conduit metaphor: a case of frame conflict in our language about language. In A. Ortony (ed.), *Metaphor and Thought*. Cambridge: Cambridge University Press.

Rosaldo, R. (1993) *Culture and Truth: The Remaking of Social Analysis*. London: Routledge.

Roseanne (English, US). Monday, 5 December 1994, Hong Kong: TVB Pearl, 6:50–7:15 pm.

Ruesch, J. and Bateson, G. (1968[1951]) *Communication: The Social Matrix of Psychiatry*. New York: W.W. Norton & Company.

Sachs, H. (1984) On doing 'being ordinary'. In J. M. Atkinson and J. Heritage (eds), *Structure of Social Action: Studies in Conversational Analysis*. Cambridge: Cambridge University Press.

Said, E. W. (1979) *Orientalism*. New York: Vintage.

Sapir, E. (1921) *Language*. New York: Harcourt, Brace.

Sapir, E. (1929) The status of linguistics as a science. *Language* 5: 207–14.

Sartre, J. P. (1969[1943]) *Being and Nothingness: An Essay on Phenomenological Ontology*. London: Methuen.

Saville-Troike, M. (1989) *The Ethnography of Communication*. Oxford: Basil Blackwell.

Schank, R. C. and Abelson, R. P. (1977) *Scripts, Plans, Goals and Understanding*. Hillsdale, NJ: Lawrence Erlbaum Associates.

Schegloff, E. (1972) Sequencing in conversational openings. In J. J. Gumperz and D. Hymes (eds), *Directions in Sociolinguistics*. New York: Holt, Rinehart & Winston.

Schegloff, E. (1986) The routine as achievement. *Human Studies* 9(2/3): 111–51.

Schegloff, E. (1992) In another context. In A. Duranti and C. Goodwin (eds), *Rethinking Context*. Cambridge: Cambridge University Press.

Schegloff, E. and Sachs, H. (1974) Opening up closings. In R. Turner (ed.), *Ethnomethodology*. Harmondsworth: Penguin.

Schuesser, A. (1989) *The Dictionary of Early Zhou Chinese*. Honolulu: University Press of Hawaii.

Scollon, R. (1976) *Conversations with a One Year Old: A Case Study of the Developmental Foundation of Syntax*. Honolulu: University Press of Hawaii.

Scollon, R. (1985) The machine stops. In D. Tannen and M. Saville-Troike (eds), *Perspectives on Silence*. Norwood, NJ: Ablex.

Scollon, R. (1991) In defense of writing: the contemporary merger of ethnography and fiction. *Redneck Review of Literature* 20(Spring): 35–7.

Scollon, R. (1993) Cultural aspects in constructing the author. In D. Keller-Cohen (ed.), *Literacy: Interdisciplinary Conversations*. Cresskill, NJ: Hampton Press.

Scollon, R. (1994) As a matter of fact: the changing ideology of authorship and responsibility in discourse. *World Englishes* 13(1): 33–46.

Scollon, R. (1995) Plagiarism and ideology: identity in intercultural discourse. *Language in Society* 24(1): 1–28.

Scollon, R. (1996a) Indexing the implied reader of the Hong Kong newspaper. Paper presented at the Annual Meetings of the American Association for Applied Linguistics, Chicago, 25 March 1996.

Scollon, R. (1996b) The depicted watch: cross-cultural variation in media pictures of people watching others in Hong Kong and China. Paper presented at the conference on 'Communication and Culture: China and the World Entering the 21st Century', Beijing University, 13–16 August 1996.

Scollon, R. (1996c) Discourse identity, social identity, and confusion in intercultural communication. *Intercultural Communication Studies* VI(1): 1–18.

Scollon, R. (1997a) Handbills, tissues, and condoms: a site of engagement for the construction of identity in public discourse. *Journal of Sociolinguistics* 1(1): 39–61.

Scollon, R. (1997b) Hong Kong newspapers on the pre-transitional stage. *AsiaPacific MediaEducator* (2): 48–59.

Scollon, R. (in press) Attribution and power in Hong Kong news discourse: framers, players, and observers. *World Englishes*.

Scollon, R., Bhatia, V., Li, D. and Yung, V. (1996) Blurred genres and fuzzy identities in Hong Kong public discourse: foundational ethnographic issues. Unpublished manuscript, Department of English, City University of Hong Kong.

Scollon, R. and Scollon, S. (1981) *Narrative, Literacy and Face in Interethnic Communication*. Norwood, NJ: Ablex.

Scollon, R. and Scollon, S. (1991) Topic confusion in English–Asian discourse. *World Englishes* 10(2): 113–25.

Scollon, R. and Scollon, S. (1992) Individualism and binarism: a critique of American intercultural communication analysis. Research Report No. 22, Department of English, City Polytechnic of Hong Kong.

Scollon, R. and Scollon, S. (1994) Face parameters in East–West discourse. In S. Ting-Toomey (ed.), *The Challenge of Facework*. Albany, NY: State University of New York Press.

Scollon, R. and Scollon, S. (1995a) *Intercultural Communication: A Discourse Approach*. Oxford: Basil Blackwell.

Scollon, R. and Scollon, S. (1995b) Somatic communication: how useful is 'orality' for the characterization of speech events and cultures? In U. M. Quasthoff (ed.), *Aspects of Oral Communication*. Berlin: DeGruyter.

Scollon, R. and Scollon, S. (1997) Point of view and citation: fourteen Chinese and English versions of the 'same' news story. *Text* 17(1): 83–125.

Scollon, R., Tsang, W. K., Li, D., Yung, V. and Jones, R. H. (1996) Voice, appropriation, and discourse representation in a student writing task. Unpublished manuscript.

Scollon, R. and Yung, V. (1996) The social location of reading: methodological issues in the study of reading as social practice. Paper presented at the Centre for Language in Social Life, Macquarie University, Sydney, Australia, 8 October 1996.

Scollon, S. (1997) Metaphors of self and communication. *Multilingua* 16(1): 1–38.

Scollon, S. and Yung, V. (1997) Framing, contextualization cues, and intertextuality in print and broadcast media: discourse representation of one statement by Qian Qichen. Paper presented at the 6th International Conference on Cross-cultural Communication: East and West, Tempe, Arizona, March 1997.

Scribner, S. and Cole, M. (1981) *The Psychology of Literacy*. Cambridge, MA: Harvard University Press.

Shannon, C. and Weaver, W. (1949) *Mathematical Theory of Communication*. Urbana, IL: University of Illinois Press.

Sherman, B. and Strowel, A. (1994) *Of Authors and Origins*. Oxford: Clarendon Press.

Sontag, S. (1979) *On Photography*. Harmondsworth: Penguin.

Spence, J. (1992) *Chinese Roundabout: Essays in History and Culture*. New York: W.W. Norton & Company.

Spindler, G. (1982) *Doing the Ethnography of Schooling: Educational Anthropology in Action*. New York: Holt, Rinehart & Winston.

Spradley, J. P. (1980) *Participant Observation*. New York: Holt, Rinehart & Winston.

Street, B. (1984) *Literacy in Theory and Practice*. New York: Cambridge University Press.

Swales, J. M. (1990) *Genre Analysis: English in Academic and Research Settings*. Cambridge: Cambridge University Press.

Tannen, D. (1986) *That's Not What I Meant!* New York: Ballantine Books.

Tannen, D. (1989a) *Talking Voices: Repetition, Dialogue and Imagery in Conversational Discourse*. Cambridge: Cambridge University Press.

Tannen, D. (1989b) The pragmatics of cross-cultural communication. *Applied Linguistics* 5(3): 189–95.

Tannen, D. (1990) *You Just Don't Understand: Women and Men in Conversation*. New York: William Morrow and Company.

de Tocqueville, A. (1969) *Democracy in America*. San Bernardino, CA: Borgo Press.

Uspensky, B. (1973) *A Poetics of Composition*. Berkeley, CA: University of California Press.

Van Dijk, T. A. (1988) *News Analysis: Case Study of International and National News in the Press*. Hillsdale, NJ: Lawrence Erlbaum Associates.

Verhoeven, J. C. (1993a) Backstage with Erving Goffman: the context of the interview. *Research on Language and Social Interaction* 26(3): 307–15.

Verhoeven, J. C. (1993b) An interview with Erving Goffman: 1980. *Research on Language and Social Interaction* 26(3): 317–48.

Vološinov, V. N. (1986) *Marxism and the Philosophy of Language*. Cambridge, MA: Harvard University Press.

Vygotsky, L. S. (1978) *Mind in Society: The Development of Higher Psychological Processes*. Cambridge, MA: Harvard University Press.

Wang, J. (1987) *Zhongguo Chengyu Dacidian*. Shanghai: Shanghai Cishu Chubanshe.

Wells, L. (1997) *Photography: A Critical Introduction*. London and New York: Routledge.

Wertsch, J. V. (1991) *Voices of the Mind: A Sociocultural Approach to Mediated Action*. Cambridge, MA: Harvard University Press.

Wertsch, J. V. (1994a) The primacy of mediated action in sociocultural studies. *Mind, Culture and Activity* 1(4): 202–8.

Wertsch, J. V. (1994b) The role of abstract rationality in Vygotsky's image of mind. In A. Tryphon and J. Voneche (eds) (in press), *Piaget–Vygotsky: The Social Genesis of Thought*. Hillsdale, NJ: Lawrence Erlbaum Associates. Manuscript in press.

Wertsch, J. V. (1995a) Mediated action and the study of communication: the lessons of L. S. Vygotsky and M. M. Bakhtin. *The Communication Review* 1(2): 133–54.

Wertsch, J. V. (1995b) Sociocultural research in the copyright age. *Culture and Psychology* 1: 81–102.

Whyte, W. F. (1981) *Street Corner Society: The Social Structure of an Italian Slum*. Chicago: University of Chicago Press.

Wu, J. (1981) *The Pinyin Chinese–English Dictionary*. Hong Kong: The Commercial Press.

Yngve, V. H. (1970) On getting a word in edgewise. In M. A. Campbell et al. (eds), *Papers from the Sixth Regional Meeting of the Chicago Linguistic Society*. Chicago: Chicago Linguistic Society, pp. 507–78.

Young, L. (1982) Inscrutability revisited. In J. J. Gumperz (ed.), *Language and Social Identity*. New York: Cambridge University Press.

Young, L. (1994) *Crosstalk and Culture in Sino-American Communication*. Cambridge: Cambridge University Press.

Yung, V. (1995) The presentation of voice in Chinese and English newspapers in Hong Kong. *Perspectives, Working Papers of the Department of English* 8(1): 64–96. City University of Hong Kong.

Yung, V. (1996) A readership study of tertiary students in Hong Kong. Paper presented at the conference on 'Communication and Culture: China and the World Entering the 21st Century', Beijing University, 13–16 August 1996.

Zhang, G. (1988) *Understanding the Hong Kong Chinese Newspapers*. Hong Kong: Wide Angle Press.

Zhu, J., Weaver, D., Lo, V., Chen, C. and Wu, W. (in press) Individual, organizational, and societal influences on media role perceptions: a comparative study of journalists in China, Taiwan and the United States. *Journalism and Mass Communication Quarterly* 74(1).

Index

308 INDEX

Fong, B., 215
football games, 150, 154
footing, 35, 36, 52, 64
formula of address, 180
Foucault, M., 9, 87, 89
frame departure, 187
framed observations, 102–4
framing practices, 21, 156, 243, 244, 246
Frankfurter Allgemeine, 208
Fromson, Murray, 188, 216
frozen smile pose, 106

game model, 152
Garfinkel, H., 33
Gee, J. P., 7, 119, 122, 136
Geertz, C., 85
gender stratification, 29
gestures, 27, 173
Giroux, H. A., 153
Gitlin, T., 280
Goffman, E., 9, 13, 15–17, 27, 33–8, 56, 61, 64, 67, 76, 80, 83–90, 98, 113, 119–21, 159, 162, 174, 183, 189–91, 199, 216, 217, 231, 232, 250, 257, 262, 264, 277
  Frame Analysis, 9, 85, 120
  Gender Advertisements, 16
  The Presentation of Self in Everyday Life, 84
Goodwin, C., 81, 82, 87, 89, 90, 119, 263
Goody, J., 119, 283, 285
Gordon, C., 87
Greene, E., 120
group reception, 257–8, 266
Guardian, The, 29, 200, 209
Gumperz, J. J., 28, 33, 78, 82, 275
Gusfield, J. R., 84

Hall, S., 116, 146, 267
Halliday, M. A. K., 8, 80
Hammersley, M., 273

handbills, 12, 20, 77, 136–40, 143, 281
  as site of engagement, 138–9, 146, 290
handicams, 263
headlines, 194, 196, 210, 226
heroic pose, 106
hesitations, 71
heteroglossia, 9, 124, 219
Hong Kong, ix, 29, 31, 39, 59, 95, 105–7, 115, 121, 162, 190, 218, 270
  City University students, 254–9, 270, 283
  infotainment shows, 215
  newspaper purchases, x, 124–36, 145, 206
  transfer to Chinese sovereignty, 22, 220–2, 224–8, 233
Hong Kong Standard, 126, 129, 130
hostility, 73
hotline, 186, 187, 250
Houtkoop-Steenstra, H., 37, 81, 179
Howe, N., 109, 110
Howlett, B., x, xi
Hu, H. C., 119
Hutcheon, R., 214, 215
Hymes, D., 28, 78, 79, 84, 86, 120, 275
  Directions in Sociolinguistics, 275

identification sequence
  telephone calls, 36, 38, 48–50, 55, 57, 61, 69–70, 159, 161
  television news, 163, 165, 172, 176, 179–85
identity, 9, 19, 21, 174, 252, 291
  change of, 13
  co-construction of, 267–8
  discursive construction of, 264–5
identity frame, 184